Criminal

TOM GASH

Criminal

The Truth about
Why People Do Bad Things

ALLEN LANE
an imprint of
PENGUIN BOOKS

ALLEN LANE

UK | USA | Canada | Ireland | Australia
India | New Zealand | South Africa

Allen Lane is part of the Penguin Random House group of companies
whose addresses can be found at global.penguinrandomhouse.com.

First published 2016
001

Copyright © Tom Gash, 2016

The moral right of the author has been asserted

Set in 10.5/14 pt Sabon LT Std
Typeset by Jouve (UK), Milton Keynes
Printed in Great Britain by Clays Ltd, St Ives plc

A CIP catalogue record for this book is available from the British Library

ISBN: 978-1-846-14593-3

For my family

Contents

List of Figures

Sources and acknowledgements are given in the notes. Every effort has been made to contact copyright-holders, and the author and publishers will be happy to make good in future printings any errors or ommissions brought to their attention.

Introduction: A world of fictions

'Tis strange – but true; for truth is always strange; Stranger than fiction.

Lord Byron, Don Juan, Canto XVI (1824)

The moment we want to believe something, we suddenly see all the arguments for it, and become blind to the arguments against it.

George Bernard Shaw[1]

A TRUE STORY

For West Germany in the 1980s, the mystery was motorcycle theft. When West Germany won the UEFA European Football Championship in 1980, such thefts were close to a record high. Over 150,000 motorcycles were stolen each year and vehicle crime in general was becoming a top priority for police and politicians. West Germany was struggling with other problems: violence had also increased throughout the 1970s. But motorcycle theft was a particularly pressing concern. It cost German citizens hundreds of millions of euros in today's money and left victims increasingly concerned for their safety.

Then something changed. From 1980 to 1983, motorcycle thefts fell by a quarter. And the decline accelerated, as they fell by another 50 per cent over the next three years. In 1986, just 54,000 motorcycles were stolen – one third of the number only six years earlier.[2]

Such seismic shifts are not easy to explain at first glance. The number of motorcycles in West Germany was broadly the same in 1986 as in 1980.[3] Motorcycles were still fun to joyride and could be resold on the black market.[4] And they were still simple to hot-wire and steal. Yet something happened that within six years slashed motorcycle insurance costs and meant that each year 100,000 German motorcycle owners were saved from being victims of theft.

The secret behind this surprising drop in crime is profoundly important. It begins to unlock many of the hidden truths about crime and its causes. It indicates the ways in which crime can be decreased, illustrating how some countries have succeeded in spending taxpayers' money wisely and have reduced crime, while others have wasted billions and allowed their populations to suffer countless avoidable murders, assaults and thefts. And it exposes as myths many of our most deep-rooted beliefs about crime, human nature and society.

In 2005 I had no idea that Germany had experienced this drop in crime, let alone the reasons for it. I was a young graduate employed by a consulting firm to find ways of making companies more profitable. But that year I was appointed as an adviser on 'home affairs' in the Prime Minister's Strategy Unit – not because of any outstanding qualifications I had but because it was a time when both the Civil Service and politicians looked kindly on those with private-sector experience. I enjoyed writing a leaving note saying that I was 'off to do drugs, crime and alcohol with the Prime Minister'. The minor hardship of saying goodbye to generous expense accounts was more than offset by my excitement at the prospect of playing even a small part in helping the country to reduce crime.

On my first day, I was struck by the contrast between the grand façade of our office in Admiralty Arch and the building's run-down interior. The shabby room where I sat with two computer screens on the go was where I started to discover facts such as that of German motorcycle theft. But it was also where I began to realize that my work would take place against a turbulent backdrop: there was a passionate battle of ideas about the nature of crime and its causes, one that shaped many of government's decisions about how to tackle crime. In meetings with the Prime Minister's closest advisers – for I met Tony Blair very rarely – two competing but compelling theories of crime always emerged in some form. And when I spoke to friends about my job and they volunteered their own views about 'what really causes crime' or 'what the government should really do', they spoke in phrases that betrayed their adherence to one of the two opposing camps.

Much of my work at the Strategy Unit and subsequently has involved questioning the truth of these conflicting views and the strength of their foundations. Both are highly persuasive and both are repeated frequently in various forms, but they represent fundamentally contradictory attitudes to human nature, government and society.

TWO ETERNAL VIEWPOINTS

Our two views of crime are seen so frequently that it is possible to find them in the aftermath of most criminal cases. Take the debate that followed the riots that spread from London to other major English cities in 2011.

The Prime Minister, David Cameron, blamed the riots on 'Irresponsibility. Selfishness. Behaving as if your choices have no consequences. Children without fathers. Schools without discipline. Reward without effort . . . Crime without punishment. Rights without responsibilities. Communities without control. Some of the worst aspects of human nature tolerated, indulged.'[5] For Cameron this was a moral issue and it was essential that he and the criminal justice system condemned the rioters who had shown themselves so willing to flout society's moral codes. Actions should have consequences, partly to satisfy justice but also to prevent future wrongdoing. He therefore announced an immediate crackdown by ensuring that judges would hand out 'exemplary sentences'.[6] He also pointed towards longer-term solutions by making it known that he would increase funding for a new national citizen service to instil in society the moral values he saw as lacking.[7]

Some on the political left called for a different response, however. While condemning the rioters, they were more sceptical of the benefits and fairness of tough sentences, pointing out that the (mostly) poor rioters, who came disproportionately from ethnic minority backgrounds, had in some sense been pushed into rioting by their circumstances.

They argued that the best way to prevent future riots – and indeed deal with criminal behaviour generally – was to tackle the root causes of crime by addressing poverty and lack of government support for the poor. As the Labour Party MP and media commentator Diane Abbott put it, 'Just as with the original riots [in the 1980s], parts of the community seem to have been a tinderbox waiting to explode. Haringey Council [which oversees Tottenham, the area at the centre of the riots] has lost £41m from its budget and has cut youth services by 75 per cent. The abolition of the education maintenance allowance hit Haringey hard, and thousands of young people at college depended on it . . . with these and other cuts in jobs and services, it is difficult to see how areas like Tottenham can become less flammable soon.'[8]

Those like Diane Abbott who emphasized that social factors had contributed to the rioting also pointed to the behaviour of the police as an aggravating factor. The riots were, after all, triggered by the police shooting of a black man and, though it was later ruled that his killing was lawful, people in Tottenham had long argued that the black community was over-policed and under-protected. Black men in London were by many calculations at least six times more likely than whites to be stopped and searched without any 'reasonable suspicion'.[9] Whereas Cameron and many others focused on the individual choices leading to the riots, this group emphasized collective responsibility for creating the conditions for rioting. Whereas Cameron and those like him focused on the need for tough policing and sanctions, this group emphasized the need for social support. Whereas Cameron's account saw the justice system as part of the solution, this group generally perceived the justice system as part of the problem.

I have developed a shorthand for these two paradigms of crime. The first I call the 'Heroes and Villains' view, because of its moral emphasis and its central premise that those who commit crime must be confronted by the full force of the justice system to avoid society becoming corrupted. The second I call the 'Victims and Survivors' view, reflecting the argument that crime is not simply a selfish choice but often one forced by adverse circumstances.

When I was at the Prime Minister's Strategy Unit I was working in a climate in which assumptions pushed policies towards the Heroes and Villains viewpoint, which has been in the ascendancy for several decades in the UK – and indeed in many developed countries. Since the 1980s, all major English-speaking nations have moved to condemn those who flout the law, to keep (presumed irredeemable) criminals incapacitated for longer periods and to ensure that 'crime doesn't pay'. 'Prison works,' claimed Michael Howard, the Conservative British Home Secretary from 1993 to 1997, prior to a doubling of England's prison population over the next twenty years.[10] We must wage a 'war on drugs', explained the US President, Ronald Reagan, shortly before upping penalties for drug offences and signing a drug enforcement bill that budgeted $1.7bn to combat the threat.[11]

These policies have often been accompanied by reductions in benefits for jobseekers and a steady rise in income inequality. After all, the Heroes and Villains view reflects and influences wider beliefs about the proper role of the state and the rights and responsibilities of the individual. As Reagan put it in 1983, 'what we're trying to do to the bloated Federal Government today [is to] remove it from interfering in areas where it doesn't belong, but at the same time strengthen its ability to perform its constitutional and legitimate functions . . . In the area of public order and law enforcement, for example.'

There was a time, however, when our approach to crime was influenced far more by those espousing the Victims and Survivors view – and indeed there were people I worked with in government who naturally inclined to it. In the 1960s the solution to crime was partly perceived as being state expenditure to guarantee full employment, and there have been some signs in recent years that we are increasingly seeing crime as a response to economic need. 'We can assume that with lawful work available . . . crime in any community would drop,' asserted Barack Obama, shortly before taking office and pushing through a range of job-creation measures.[12] The dramatic growth in the number of people in prison has recently slowed or stopped in many developed countries, though this is partly because governments have been forced to cut expenditure in all areas following the banking crisis and the global economic downturn.

The two views of crime that dominate political debate also dominate the content of our televisions, newspapers and magazines.

Documentaries recording the daily exploits of the police, prison officers and other protectors of social order have become wildly popular in recent decades, partly due to the low cost of producing them. The events that unfold in these 'true-crime' dramas lend strong support to the Heroes and Villains view, as they allow us access to the brave men and women who protect us from selfish and determined criminals. Each episode of the series *Brit Cops* opens with scenes of criminal activity and police action, with an explanatory voice-over. 'Twenty-first-century policing,' its presenter, Richard Bacon, says, 'is a relentless battle against violence, drugs, robbery and organized crime. And it is our inner-city cops who are in the firing line.'[13] The documentary *COPS* is the longest-running American television series and paints the same picture in still more vivid colours. For example, in one episode we ride along with clean-cut Kansas City police officer Caleb Lenz.[14] After arresting a man who tried to shoot his colleague who was in the line of duty, we hear from him first-hand the importance of policing in keeping us safe: 'You know, you do this job every day,' he explains, 'and, you know, you get in car chases and we chase people with guns and, you know, sometimes they shoot at you . . . It's an eerie feeling when you hear the call come out, "Officer shot, officer shot." You know. But luckily I think he's gonna be all right and we got the suspect in custody and you know he'll never do this again.'[15]

Somewhat fewer documentaries project the world of Victims and Survivors, perhaps because it is difficult to gain the trust of those who commit crime. One book that does is *Gang Leader for a Day*. This fantastically entertaining story records the journey of its author, Sudhir Venkatesh, into Chicago's most deprived neighbourhoods. In its first chapter, 'How it feels to be black and poor', Sudhir – then a student but now a Harvard sociologist – meets J. T., a gang leader who controls his area's drug trade. In the opening exchange J. T. sums up his reality as a black man living in the US and immediately makes it clear that his occupation has been forced on him by unfavourable circumstances. 'I'm a nigger,' J. T. says. '*African Americans* live in the suburbs. African Americans wear ties to work. Niggers can't find no work.'[16] In a similarly brilliant British documentary novel, the journalist Nick Davies writes of the country's *Dark Heart*. In his opening chapter Davies depicts children forced into street prostitution, before going on to show readers other cases of forced criminality and the wider hardships he sees as the consequence of decades of neglect of the country's poor.

I noticed, too, how easy it is to fit fictional accounts of crime into one of our two dominant paradigms of crime. We seek out the Heroes and Villains view voraciously and find it in perhaps its purest form in detective novels and television series. We follow great detectives – Sherlock Holmes, Poirot and Miss Marple – as they thwart determined foes. The forensic scientists of one of the world's most watched television series *CSI : Crime Scene Investigation* use the powers of modern science rather than phenomenal intellect, but their plots are essentially the same.[17] Almost always we face a determined villain who will kill again unless caught, and we are encouraged to empathize with a selfless hero who will need all his or her resourcefulness to ensure that moral order is restored. James Bond shifts the action away from country houses and onto the international scene, but is essentially defending his nation – and indeed the Western world – against seemingly unstoppable malign forces. And Superman and Spiderman fight the same battles – though in fancy costumes.

The Victims and Survivors view is also found in its most unalloyed form in fiction. The HBO drama series *The Wire* is highly persuasive of this take on crime and society, with many people I speak to referring to it as the justification for their own beliefs. Unlike the largely shadowy perpetrators in shows like *Inspector Morse* or *Crime Scene Investigation*, we get to know the criminals in *The Wire* well and are encouraged to sympathize with them. Serious crimes – including murder – are sometimes committed by these characters. But we grow to understand the reasons for their actions and realize that they are essentially trapped in an unfair system that gives them few choices. As one young drug dealer, Preston, puts it, 'This game is rigged, man. We be like them little bitches on the chess board.' The police play their part, but they are not always centre-stage. We are shown that for every young black man who is arrested, another will take his place unless the fundamental causes of crime are addressed.

This view has deep roots in literary fiction too. It's found in tales where the oppressed do the wrong things for the right – or at least understandable – reasons. The story is one told by Émile Zola, as he describes the hardships that provoke a French mining community to violent rioting in *Germinal*. It appears in American novels set against the backdrop of the Great Depression, such as Steinbeck's *Of Mice and Men*. And it is found in narratives of criminal subcultures, including Mafia films like *The Godfather*. Here we are shown the social factors behind criminality – in this case the economic and social isolation of immigrant communities in pre-war America. And again we see that criminals too have moral codes that we can relate to, such as the desire to protect one's family. In this world, crime can be noble – as when Robin Hood robbed the rich to feed the poor – defiantly challenging the injustice of our social structures.

That attitudes to crime – and the entire genre of crime fiction – could be broken down into just two types might be surprising. But pick your favourite show and try to categorize it using the table below. Which approach informs the show you like so much? And, thinking about your own experiences of crime, which of these views do you most sympathize with?

	Heroes and Villains	*Victims and Survivors*
Examples	(*Inspector Morse, CSI, Sherlock Holmes, Superman*)	(*The Wire, The Godfather, Germinal, Robin Hood*)
Views of human nature	Essential and rarely changing	Heavily influenced by social structures and experiences
Views of society	Essentially good – to be protected	Essentially unjust – to be reformed
Views of crime	Usually a free choice	Usually a forced choice
Views of criminals	Motivated by greed and selfish drives; 'not like us'	Motivated by need and circumstance; 'much like us'
Views of the criminal justice system	A necessary – if occasionally inadequate – tool for social order	A sticking plaster for social problems which serves the powerful
Views of morality	Black and white	Grey

CRIME FACTION

Even though these narratives of crime are so dominant in fiction, documentaries and political debates, it is far from clear that we have been correct to use them to determine government policy. Indeed, in one sense it is obvious that these two competing accounts of crime cannot both be true: crime is either influenced heavily by economic and social circumstances, for example, or it is not. Criminals either more commonly commit crime due to a lack of other options – or they do so largely through greed.

There are also good reasons to doubt the impartiality even of factual accounts of crime – and indeed to question whether they are purely factual at all. The US series *COPS*, for example, certainly depicts events that happen but the documentary's editors select their stories from hundreds of alternatives, cutting over 400 hours of possible footage to produce each twenty-two-minute episode. As John Langley, the show's creator, explains, there is a clear formula: 'You know the action pieces are always interesting to viewers but we try to balance it out. We'll have an action piece and then we'll have what I call an emotional piece or a lyrical moment in which you see, you know, real people and real stories.'[18] There is a degree of censorship. The police forces involved know they are being recorded and have the right to view and veto the screening of the final footage. And police forces have their own agendas in supporting the show. *COPS*, they believe, is a practical tool for recruiting officers and emphasizes the importance and excitement of police work.[19]

Venkatesh's *Gang Leader for a Day* is likewise edited to achieve a particular effect. It is noticeable that Venkatesh emphasizes that J. T.'s most violent behaviour is forced by circumstances and that he accepts J. T.'s own justifications for his behaviour unquestioningly. After one attack, Venkatesh explains: 'J. T. personally helped beat them up; the BKs [J. T.'s gang] also took their guns and money. Because these young rivals had "no business sense," as J. T. told me later, there was no hope of a compromise. Physical retaliation was the only measure to consider.'[20]

The media similarly select their stories, to draw in wider audiences or to appeal to existing readers' preferences. Some papers clearly espouse the Heroes and Villains view – or at least feel it serves them well. Stories of determined evil attract readers, so extreme violence and sexual crimes occupy many more column inches.[21] Coverage soars too when victims can be presented as perfectly innocent and perpetrators as irredeemable.[22] Young, white, female and middle-class victims all attract disproportionate attention. In 2002, two ten-year-old girls, Holly Wells and Jessica Chapman, went missing after going to the local shops. Their case had vast international coverage even before it was discovered that they had indeed been murdered.[23] On Boxing Day 1996, two boys of similar age, Patrick Warren, eleven, and David Spencer, thirteen, went missing: they were last seen at just before 1 a.m., begging biscuits at the petrol station forecourt where Patrick's Christmas present, a new bike, was also found abandoned. But their case barely drew attention outside the local press.[24] Examples of selective reporting abound. Half of all missing children in the US are white, for example, but white children attract three quarters of the missing person's coverage on CNN.[25] Gang-related murders are vastly under-reported; and when such murders are covered, stories are on average much less likely to focus on the victims than on what the case tells us about the general threat of gang violence in the inner city. The front page of the *Daily Mirror* below is a clear example of the type of victims the media like best. The battered faces it shows are predominantly female or older. Yet, in reality, the most likely victim of violence in the UK is a male teenager or a young man. And while the media chooses to present victims and villains as mutually exclusive categories, perpetrators of crime are in fact particularly likely to be victims.[26]

While the Heroes and Villains view appears to dominate media and fictional accounts of crime, not all newspapers like it. It is noticeable that the liberal left-wing press is generally more reluctant to dwell on individual cases and keener to ask questions about crime overall. In what could be seen as a nod to the Victims and Survivors view, the *Guardian*, for example, dedicated vast resources to a project called 'reading the riots' that explored whether and how social factors and policing practices could have contributed to the London riots in 2011. Similar newspapers are more likely to question state

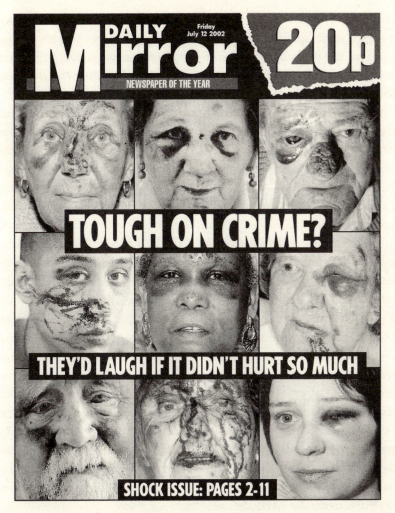

Fig. 1: Victimhood according to the *Daily Mirror*[27]

authority and morality: for example, by exposing police malpractice and miscarriages of justice.

These clear signs of bias are worrying, not least because of the pervasiveness of media accounts of crime: one 1990s study found that around a third of British newspaper content was dedicated to crime, while a Canadian analysis showed that somewhere between half and three quarters of news and radio coverage was about some form of deviance.[28] Many rarely question the accounts they see, hear and read, let alone the fundamental views of crime and society that might lurk within these accounts. Nine out of ten people surveyed in a UK poll in 2003 said they 'trusted newspapers to tell them the truth about how crime is being dealt with'.[29]

We obviously face a problem. The stories we hear so frequently about crime are selective, partial and biased in fundamental ways. How can we find the truth when fact and fiction are so frequently blurred? And what other, more reliable, sources of information are there?

STRANGE TRUTHS

Since I joined the Strategy Unit I have found that one of the most valuable uses of my time has been to immerse myself in (sometimes) dry academic studies – which are seldom accessed by politicians, journalists or documentary makers, let alone the general public.

Pat Mayhew and her long-time associate Ron Clarke have dedicated most of their lives to researching crime. In 2015, they won the Stockholm Prize in Criminology for their contribution to understanding patterns of crime. Sitting across the table from Pat Mayhew, I ask her about how she and Ron Clarke came to discover the German drop in motorcycle thefts. It was partly a matter of attention. 'In the late 1980s,' she says, 'the two crimes that were really talked about were burglary and vehicle crime . . . We would have kept an eye on anything to do with vehicle crime because it was high-profile.'[30]

But the discovery was also a product of a persistent belief in the power of statistics over impressions. Mayhew dedicated much of her three-decade career at the Home Office to improving and monitoring patterns of crime, so that policymakers in the UK and worldwide could better understand it. In 1981, she launched the British Crime Survey with Mike Hough, now a Professor of Criminology at Birkbeck College, University of London, which introduced a new way of measuring UK crime trends that relied not on figures collected by the police (which vary hugely depending on people's willingness to report crimes) but on the confidential feedback of a large, carefully selected sample of the UK population. Before and after then she also collated and regularly reviewed crime data, not just from the UK but from across the world. In the case of German motorcycle thefts, the work compiling data was done.

'We had got into contact with a man called Edwin Kube at the Bundeskriminalamt,' she explains, 'and the Germans, being Germans, had terribly, terribly good crime figures.' This was important to Mayhew and her collaborators because in many countries it was difficult to split out thefts of motorcycles from those of cars and bicycles. And this more detailed information showed that the German fall in motorcycle theft was certainly not part of a wider crime trend in Germany. While motorcycle thefts fell by two thirds in the six years from 1980, car thefts remained broadly the same, rising slightly from 64,000 in 1980 to 82,000 in 1983 before falling back to around 70,000 in 1986.[31] Bicycle thefts were also roughly stable, following a similar pattern. The German population had not suddenly become more law-abiding in general – but something had changed.

'It's sort of obvious, isn't it?' Mayhew says.

'For you perhaps,' I think.

Mayhew, after all, knew that in 1973 motorcycle thefts had fallen suddenly in the UK. And she knew that there had been a similar decrease in Holland in 1975. Yet when I stumbled across this study at the Strategy Unit, the explanation for the phenomenon was far from obvious – and indeed it profoundly challenged some of my own prejudices about crime's causes and its remedies.

What had changed was that European countries had woken up to the dangers of road travel. Vehicle accidents were responsible for an unacceptable number of road deaths and there was a growing consensus that the public would have to take precautions to protect their own safety but also manage the spiralling costs of accident-related healthcare. In 1973, the use of motorcycle helmets was made compulsory in the UK; motorcycle thefts in London fell by a quarter the following year. In 1975, helmets were made compulsory in the Netherlands; the percentage of people who said they had experienced a motorcycle theft in the past year suddenly fell from 10 per cent to around 6 per cent. The German case was perhaps still more dramatic. There, various laws were introduced in stages which led to the two-thirds reduction. Almost immediately after helmets were made compulsory for all motorcycle riders in July 1978, thefts started falling slightly and the drop accelerated in 1980 when the authorities introduced on-the-spot fines for those caught driving without helmets and started to enforce the law.[32]

Behind these statistics, there were thousands of individuals making different moral choices as a result of changes that were not intended to have any impact on crime whatsoever. People who used to steal motorcycles stopped doing so because they realized they were much more likely to be caught if they were riding without headgear. Intriguingly, these same people did not – as the more thorough German data shows – then decide to steal other vehicles to get their thrills or to make a quick buck.

The reason why this case is so important and captured my imagination is because it markedly conflicts with the two views of crime that dominate crime fiction, journalism and politics. The Heroes and Villains view seems to match up poorly. Where, after all, is the determination of these real-world criminals? It doesn't take much organization to carry a helmet with you when hunting for unattended motorcycles, yet it appears to have been a step too far for many would-be thieves. Where is the evidence that we need to pull out all the stops to condemn and punish wrongdoers in order to reduce crime? Sentences for motorcycle theft didn't change and the fall was not due to criminals having been locked up for ever-longer periods. And where is the need for the all-action hero to fight determined criminality? The police played an important role in the drop in crime, but it is intriguing that they did so less through dramatic pursuit of criminals than through what some officers would consider 'grunt work' that distracts from 'real' police work – the enforcement of everyday traffic violations.

What of the Victims and Survivors view? The idea that crime won't fall without social conditions changing dramatically appears to have been disproved. A two-thirds reduction in motorcycle theft is hardly inconsequential, yet German benefits systems or wealth distribution did not change significantly in these years. Other types of crime did not rise to compensate for the lost criminal earnings of those 'forced into crime to make ends meet'.

GLOBAL LABORATORY

I discovered more little-known data in the 2000s which led me to question and change my own views of crime. Yet as my time at the Strategy Unit wore on and my opinions became more informed, I became increasingly frustrated as I saw that political decisions were often based more on myths about crime than on facts.

This was the time when the idea of this book first came to me. I wanted to share what I was discovering in order to help others question their own preconceptions about crime – and through this to improve our collective understanding of human nature and society more generally. Allowing people to see what is so often hidden from view might enable them to recognize which government policies had a good chance of working and which didn't – and to nudge politicians into better decisions. I wanted people to understand the limitations of our two dominant narratives of crime and regard as fiction much of what we are told about crime on a daily basis.

The information that we can now access should, after all, have dramatically reduced our reliance on unquestioned beliefs about crime. Prior to 1989, observers had very little to go on to compare crime rates in different countries, but now international victim surveys allow us to determine more objectively which countries are experiencing higher or lower crime rates. At a national level, police are gathering more data than ever on crime rates and victims. And data on wider social trends is also improving, providing us with a global data laboratory in which to investigate crime's causes and possible solutions.

This new information can also be processed far more effectively. New statistical techniques can be used to gain a better understanding of the characteristics of high- and low-crime locations. Even in the developed West, countries have vastly different economic, social and cultural features, so we can now use mathematical models to isolate which variables appear to be most closely related to high or low crime. As we'll see, statistical tools must be used with caution, but these methods do very quickly allow us to challenge our accepted views on crime.

*

More importantly, perhaps, we can today access much better information about the people who commit crime. A number of major studies have carefully tracked large groups of offenders (and non-offenders) over their lifetimes, examining patterns of offending but also looking at the factors that appear to increase or decrease criminality. These studies mean that we can now make reasonable predictions about which people are most likely to go on to commit crime and also anticipate when they might stop offending.

Academic research is complemented by previously unparalleled access to those who commit crime and those trying to tackle criminality. High-profile accusations of corruption and malpractice have led politicians to push for a far more transparent justice system, which has in turn eased the path of researchers seeking to understand the realities that the police, lawyers and prison officers face on a daily basis. My role in the Strategy Unit and the relationships I formed during my time there and subsequently mean that I am lucky enough to have enjoyed even greater contact with those working and living in the justice system.

It is thanks to this openness that I've been able to access prisons of all types and sizes; police forces focusing on issues ranging from anti-social behaviour to gang crime; and local authorities, social services and youth organizations struggling to cope with seemingly endless troublemaking in their communities. The stories provided by those on the front line can be over-interpreted, but they do have their own power. It's these real-world encounters and connections that often provide the best 'sniff tests' for apparently alluring theories. I'm greatly indebted to those who've spoken to me openly (be they jailers or jailed) and allowed me to stay in touch with reality. And I am grateful too that some journalists and broadcasters have also taken advantage of this openness and used the insights they gain to combat lazy stereotypes.

One of the most useful tools for those seeking to understand crime is also one of the least used. Randomized control trials (RCTs) assign groups of people or places to a specific 'treatment' and look at what happens to them compared to individuals and areas that are left alone. In crime research, RCTs are most common in seeing what works to reduce reoffending. Do, for example, boot camps deter would-be criminals? Should we pay for offenders to have anger-management classes? So-called 'natural experiments' are also useful. We will learn a lot about policing, for instance, by examining the period during the Second World War when Denmark had to make do without a police force, and even more from the period following the terrorist attacks in London on 7 July 2005.

We cannot use evidence unquestioningly, of course. A few studies have been grossly oversold, both by their authors and by the media and politicians who use data selectively to justify their own positions and actions. And this is why, throughout this book, I will show the ways in which evidence has been misrepresented and how to separate fact and fiction. Evidence can also suffer from a narrow perspective. Crime has been studied by psychologists, biologists, economists and sociologists, but too often those working within one discipline are blind to insights from others. Economists are more likely to look at economic factors and rational incentives; sociologists will favour social and cultural accounts; psychologists will look for psychological explanations. I approach research from a highly pragmatic starting point – that we need answers to questions about crime so that we can better prevent and respond to it. And I believe that the best way to find those answers is to borrow liberally from all fields. Examining the broadest and best evidence will allow us to question what has been presented to us as *obvious truths*.

Each chapter of this book tackles a different myth about crime. And by the end of the book, it is my hope that you will recognize that both of our stereotypical attitudes to crime and its causes are dangerously misleading. The Heroes and Villains view will face profound challenges. It is likely that after reading this book you will no longer have much faith in the idea of the determined criminal out to get you (Myth 3), and you will probably not trust those who tell you that tougher sentences are the best route to safer societies (Myth 9). And you will see that – contrary to what true-crime documentaries would have us believe – policing is much safer than building work or bin collection and that the macho image of policing is one of the major obstacles in efforts to reduce crime (Myth 8).

The Victims and Survivors view will also crack under examination. I hope that you will come to wonder whether crime is really caused by poverty at all (Myth 6). And you will also realize that we can become much safer than we are now without fundamental social change (Myth 11). You will also, I hope, see that our criminal justice system is essential to our safety even if it is partially flawed (Myths 8 and 9).

You will have a chance to explore some of life's biggest questions. For example, we will see how far our willingness to break the law might be biologically determined (Myth 5). We will question our assumptions about childhood innocence (Myth 2). And we will examine the basic building blocks of social order (Myth 8). Your individual decisions relating to crime might change too. This is not a self-help book, but we look at how we should protect ourselves and our families from crime, how to bring up our children, and which types of charity – or political party – deserve our support.

One of the conclusions of this book is that universal truths are hard to come by. Surprisingly, perhaps, fraud and murder can have some common causes, but there are important differences even between different crimes of the same type. Two murders can be similar but are rarely the same – which is why our best responses to crime are likely to be highly tailored to the immediate contexts in which it takes place (Myth 11). I argue that our obsession with 'big arguments' about crime's causes can lead us to ignore this – and to implement bold and popular but ultimately damaging policies. What's more, policymakers can too readily take individual cases as *proof* of universal rules. California introduced its 1994 'three strikes' law partly in response to the violent murder of twelve-year-old Polly Klaas by a repeat offender – but the law has affected thousands of men and women very unlike Polly's murderer, Richard Allen Davis, as we find when we examine the limited impact of tough sentencing in Myth 9.

There is something we find uncomfortable about a world without obvious answers, which is one reason, of course, why we cling stubbornly to our dominant views of crime. Our thirst for certainty may also explain why a number of theories about crime have, when stated boldly, gained alarming and unjustified popularity. In Myth 1 we will see just how much we have been misled by some sweeping claims – including the argument that abortion rates have a major impact on crime (as argued in Dubner and Levitt's popular book

Freakonomics) and the idea that gun ownership actually *reduces* crime (popularized by the US commentator and academic John Lott). We crave simplicity, a stand-alone reason for things.

Consider for a moment your own experience of crime. You will soon realize that this notion of a single cause of crime is entirely unsustainable. Think of the last time you committed a crime (contrary to our Heroes and Villains view, most of us have) – or, if you are in the minority, think of a recent case you know of. Then consider the forces at work affecting your behaviour. I am certain that you will most likely uncover layer upon layer of possible influences, many considerations interacting in complex ways to facilitate the crime in question.

This does not mean that there are not certain factors that are particularly important in understanding criminal behaviour, nor does it mean that it is impossible to find patterns that we can learn from and exploit to reduce crime. For, despite the complexity of the real world, we can and indeed must develop new ways of thinking that help us better to understand the worst aspects of human behaviour. And it is for this reason that throughout this book I will try to persuade you of three important truths.

1. The power of opportunity

First, that you cannot understand crime simply by thinking about human motivations. As you may have noticed, our two dominant crime narratives attempt just this. Crudely, the Heroes and Villains view aims to deter and incapacitate would-be law-breakers by punishing crimes ever more severely. The Victims and Survivors approach, meanwhile, seeks to remove the need for lawlessness by improving the economic and social conditions of the most disadvantaged: for example, by providing jobs or more generous benefits.

Of course, it's important – and fascinating – to understand what makes us tick. But in the real world we are often greatly influenced by our immediate circumstances. At the time of the 2011 London riots, I was living near Shadwell in East London. Shadwell is among the most deprived areas of the city, where quiet urban sprawl is interspersed with collections of mid-rise buildings dominated by exactly the kinds of young men that were at the heart of London's 2011 riots.

But there was no rioting. The riots did not, after all, simply require poor, angry young men. Almost every area that was badly hit was also home to a reasonable supply of attractive commercial premises – something, much to my annoyance until the night of the riots, that Shadwell almost entirely lacks. Perhaps a few people from Shadwell travelled to cause trouble elsewhere, but for most the extra effort involved was off-putting, or it didn't even occur to them to join in.

This is an example of what I call the *power of opportunity*. We all have tipping points at which usually unacceptable behaviour becomes irresistible to us. So the temptations and provocations we face are often as important as our innate desire to be law-abiding. Almost all of us are corruptible – as we see from those cases in the London riots where normally law-abiding citizens were looting alongside gang members or, still more worryingly, during those ugly moments in history where entire populations colluded in genocide. But, on a more positive note, even the most antisocial can be radically constrained by the circumstances they encounter. The homicidal maniac who lives alone in the desert is no serial killer, just as the car-less burglar living in a village is less prolific than his urban counterpart. Making criminal opportunities even marginally less obvious or appealing can therefore have a major impact, as in the motorcycle helmet example.

Considering the power of opportunity reveals a world of possibilities that we too rarely take into account. We realize that poverty, rather than causing crime by increasing people's motivation to steal, might contribute to lower crime rates by limiting the number of high-value items to be stolen. And we start to wonder whether the fact that children who stay in school have fewer run-ins with the law could be due not just to their improved job prospects but also to the fact that they have less unsupervised time in which to get into trouble.

I will suggest that the most plausible explanation for shifts in crime rates across the twentieth and twenty-first centuries involves specific economic, social and technological changes that have radically altered the number and types of criminal opportunities we encounter in the course of daily life. I will argue that the emancipation of women was bad news for burglary rates, that technological change lies behind rises in muggings, and that computer games, far from turning our children into violent maniacs, probably reduce youth violence. And I will point out too that our actions as individuals – in securing our-selves and our possessions – have had as great an impact on crime rates as any set of government policies.

2. The limits of reason

Second, I will try to persuade you that the forces of logic must not be overestimated when it comes to crime. There is a common assumption that underpins both of our dominant attitudes to crime: that people calculate and respond swiftly to incentives. The Heroes and Villains view assumes that if we ensure crime doesn't pay, no one will do it. The Victims and Survivors view holds that if we make mainstream jobs attainable and attractive, then few will want or need to commit crime. Both sides borrow from the alluring logic of economics.

Professor Gary Becker won the 1992 Nobel Prize in Economic Sci-ences 'for having extended the domain of microeconomic analysis to a wide range of human behaviour and interaction'. Accepting his prize, he described one of the moments that led him to study crime: 'I began to think about crime in the 1960s after driving to Columbia University for an oral examination of a student in economic theory. I was late and had to decide quickly whether to put the car in a parking lot or risk getting a ticket for parking illegally on the street. I calcu-lated the likelihood of getting a ticket, the size of the penalty, and the cost of putting the car in a lot. I decided it paid to take the risk and park on the street. (I did not get a ticket.)'[33] 'I figured this is a really good problem to work on, so I started thinking more systematically about it.'[34]

The conclusion Becker reached and first published in 1968 was essentially that criminals were much like him. Or, as he later put it, 'The economic approach means that people are acting rationally, driven in their behaviour by the benefits and costs, taking account of all the ethical and psychic and other aspects that go into determining their behaviour.'[35] There is an implicit assumption in Becker's writing and many other portrayals that crime is a straightforward alternative to other forms of work. As Becker puts it, many 'become criminals because of the financial rewards from crime compared to legal work, taking account of the likelihood of apprehension and conviction, and the severity of punishment'. In an elegant step, he adopts both the Heroes and Villains and the Victims and Survivors views, for 'Clearly, the type of legal jobs available as well as law, order and punishment are an integral part of the economic approach to crime.' And he adopts both left- and right-wing political solutions, though with an emphasis on the latter. For example, he writes that teenagers are 'encouraged' to commit crime by lenient sentences for first offences.

There is much to be said for understanding the costs and benefits of crime, particularly certain types of criminality, but I will argue that this focus on incentives overstates our ability to make good choices. The economists' rule of thumb is that people make 'efficient' decisions, but I will point out that one of the defining characteristics of much crime is that a lot of it is *not* rational in any recognizable sense of the word.

If we take a selection of cases from the London riots, we can see rational decisions to loot alongside much more limited rationality. There was the teenager who posted a photograph of himself on a social networking site to celebrate his theft of a large bag of basmati rice from Tesco's supermarket. There were countless rioters who assaulted police when vastly outnumbered or who risked prison for the theft of items of exceptionally low value. Nicholas Robinson, twenty-three, shot to a strange kind of fame when he stole six bottles of mineral water from a ransacked Lidl store. As his solicitor told Camberwell Magistrates' Court before his six-month prison sentence was handed down, he had 'got caught up in the moment' and was 'incredibly ashamed'.[36]

The limits of reason are not only exposed when we consider the many crimes that are destructive and self-destructive mistakes. They are highlighted too when we bear in mind the countless occasions where it 'makes sense' to commit crime but people choose not to. Think of the number of times when you could break the law undetected. Is it simply rational factors that prevent you from taking such opportunities? Or could it be both that you rarely consider the option of law-breaking and then, when you do, regard it as morally wrong to harm others for your own benefit?

Neglecting the irrational aspects of crime – and of remaining law-abiding – leads us to an excessive focus on our economic self-interest and obscures the reality that criminal choices are heavily shaped by the immediate contexts people encounter and by the ideas they develop about what constitutes acceptable and unacceptable behaviour. Rather than assuming self-interest and rationality, we need to work far harder to understand the extent of rational calculation in crimes of all kinds. For, as we'll see, there are in fact rational ways of preventing irrational acts. And we will see that improving the ability of certain groups to resist irrational temptations may in fact be a highly effective way of reducing crime (Myth 3).

3. The beauty of small things

Third, I will encourage you to realize that small things matter. There are two senses in which this is true. First, that small changes can have dramatic effects. We have already seen how reshaping the moment when someone considers stealing a motorcycle had a drastic impact on crime in West Germany. But there are a million such moments that can be influenced. Details matter – and this includes understanding the times when people are most likely to change. We know that drug addicts can best be persuaded to seek treatment after a friend overdoses, for example, and that the first week after a prisoner's release from prison carries special dangers.

Some crimes have epidemic properties, spreading exponentially before decreasing in patterns that are not dissimilar to those seen in the study of virus outbreaks. This is most apparent in cases such as gang-related violence, where one unplanned incident can spark a series of escalating tit-for-tat reprisals. But what this means is that preventing one such crime can prevent many more. This is even arguably the case when we look at serial murders. Contrary to the myth that they are 'born to kill', it appears that serial killers can be created almost by accident. Serial killers like Henry Lee Lucas, Jeffrey Dahmer and Edmund Kemper committed their first murders at times when they were experiencing extreme stress of various kinds – but then the satisfaction either of the kill or of evading detection provided a psychological thrill they then sought again, with tragic consequences.[37]

Richard Kuklinski, the American hitman and serial killer who was convicted of five murders but claims to have killed over 100, describes his first murder in a measured voice, speaking with scarcely a trace of sentiment. 'I got into an argument, a fight, in a bar . . . and I hit him with a cue stick. A few too many times. And he died . . . But, surprising[ly], I felt sadness and after a while I felt something else. I didn't feel sad. I was sad [but] with some sort of a rush that I had killed someone . . .'. Actions provoked by small circumstances can affect the range of possibilities we consider and lead us to remake our own identities in ways that increase or decrease our chances of committing crime in future.

Another sense in which small is beautiful is that big changes can have unpredictable and variable effects. We must be extremely careful about applying broad-brush solutions to problems which are highly specific. We will see countless examples of bold policies that prove unworkable: the US attempt to check all cars crossing the Mexican border in 1969 (which did little to disrupt drug trafficking but much to undermine legitimate business); mandatory sentencing policies (which filled prisons with low-risk prisoners); and huge urban regeneration schemes (which failed to recognize that shiny buildings are not always safer ones).

We will discover that most governments are remarkably poorly equipped to deal with a world where small things matter and big policy shifts rarely achieve what we hope for. For the past seven years I have worked at the Institute for Government, leading research projects which examine how government operates – and I have perceived that at its best government can achieve great things. But my work has also persuaded me that current methods of policymaking and public-sector management need to change if we are to be truly effective in addressing crime and other complex social problems.

This book gets part of its energy from my personal frustration at those times when I have seen governments rush to hasty, myth-based decisions in response to high-profile incidents. It is charged by my annoyance at the implementation of grand plans without properly testing how they will work – or even proper dialogue with those who will have to put them into practice or be on the receiving end of them. And it is fuelled by a disappointment at governments' repeated fixation on restructuring government institutions for no discernible benefit. In the final chapter we explore what needs to change in order to consign myth-based policy to history and to build institutions capable of experimenting and learning still more about how to reduce crime.

TABULA RASA

These three ideas draw on the work of dozens of people who have dedicated their lives to carefully examining the realities of crime, many of whom we will meet as the book progresses. Yet their work rarely cuts through into popular discourse and remains largely beyond our reach. We've heard our dominant, fictionalized and politicized narratives of crime so often that they are deeply ingrained in our consciousness – and it's these that will still spark our first reactions when we hear the latest crime report on the radio or read it in a newspaper. We need to wash away these fictional accounts one by one and create a new library of mental references – true stories, intriguing facts and new ways of thinking – which rest on firmer, factual foundations. We must suspend our outrage to understand crime as a risk that can be managed as well as a wrong to be condemned.

So each chapter of this book takes on a different myth about crime and builds towards a different way of seeing the world. In the first chapters we begin by exposing some fundamental misconceptions about crime and the people who commit it. We then go on to test the most popular explanations for crime and see where they are helpful and where they are grossly misleading. And in the final chapters we look at remedies for crime.

My primary focus throughout is crime in developed countries. This is partly forced by circumstances. Developed countries produce much useful and reliable evidence about their crime problems, with North America, Scandinavia, Germany, the Netherlands and Britain generating most. But the choice is also deliberate. Crime in developed countries often has a different look and feel from crime in the developing world, where social safety nets do not exist and state apparatus has not always evolved to the same extent. Likewise, I do not cover terrorism, which has commonalities with crime but also important differences. You will notice that I use US examples quite heavily. This again is partly because of that country's exemplary investment in top-quality research. But it also owes something to America's sheer scale and the global influence of its approaches and media representations. The US provides examples for policymakers to emulate, including its use of 'predictive policing' methods (Myth 8). But in promoting a Heroes and Villains view of crime as if it were fact, the US has also led the world towards some great follies: for example, wasting vast sums building the largest global per capita prison population (Myth 9).

There is no one right way of reading this book. Each chapter can, if you wish, be read in isolation. But you may also like to see these myths dissolve in the sequence laid out. After all, each chapter builds on the previous one and it's naturally easier to understand crime's cures once we have understood its causes. However you read this book, I hope you enjoy these arguments and use them well. For I do have a slightly ambitious dream – that by asking the right questions and challenging dominant assumptions, we might be able to elevate the public and political debate about crime, and in so doing create a platform for saner thinking and action.

If you choose to read and reject any arguments here, I particularly commend you. After all, my main aim is to let the questioning begin . . .

Myth 1: Crime is rising

... there is always a well-known solution to every human problem [that is] neat, plausible, and wrong.

Henry Mencken, writer and satirist[1]

STORMY WATERS

Six policemen jog purposefully towards the junction, neatly spaced at two-metre intervals. Batons are raised; round, transparent shields protect their bodies. They are determined, disciplined, unstoppable.

Faced by the surge, a group of ten or more young men in hoods and hats and bandanas scatter, turning their backs and running. A teenager on a bike wheels around swiftly. 'Oh no!' one shouts.

The policemen slow as they reach the crossroads, then stand in a fixed, staggered line blocking off the street, chests lifting and falling after their efforts.

But just for one second. Almost before they settle, glass smashes by the foot of one officer and the step he takes backwards to avoid it acts as an immediate cue. All the officers do the same, then they are in full retreat, reversing as a crowd of twenty or more jog towards them. Some of the young men have grabbed metal newspaper stands and are carrying them; one holds what looks like a shop clothes rail, others throw still more bottles.

'Oh!' It's now the crowd of onlookers who are shocked – amazed by the decisiveness of the fightback and the complete inability of the police to resist it.

At least, some are. Other onlookers are exhilarated. Before long, they are joining the young men who now walk calmly through the broken glass of Debenhams department store. Men, women and children flow in empty-handed and, having shopped around, leave – arms overflowing with goods. But for the glass, onlookers might think it was simply a late-night shopping evening. Most people have found branded shopping bags to carry their loot, though one young man staggers under the weight of a flat-screen television so wide that he can barely stretch his arms to carry it. As dusk falls the looting continues, the police nowhere to be seen.

This is Clapham, England, a usually genteel suburb on the third day of the London riots, 8 August 2011. The scenes were captured by onlookers on videophones and spread across social and mainstream media. The violence extended beyond London that day too, looting breaking out briefly in many UK cities. Birmingham, Liverpool and Manchester all suffered before order was fully restored two days later. For a few days the world was turned upside down. 'Normally the police control us,' said one rioter. 'But [during the riots] the law was obeying us.'[2]

It was an extraordinary episode. Hundreds of shops were looted and around 4,000 arrests eventually made.[3] Lives, few but important, were lost. The cost to the country through criminal damage, stolen goods, lost shop revenues and extra policing was estimated to be hundreds of millions of pounds.[4]

It was also seen to symbolize England's inability to tackle both social problems and widespread criminality. It was time, argued politicians, to say 'enough'. 'Do we have the determination to confront the slow-motion moral collapse that has taken place in parts of our country these past few generations?' asked the Prime Minister, David Cameron.[5] Cameron repeated the lines that had helped ensure his election. Britain, he said, was 'broken' and in urgent need of repair.

The Labour leader, Ed Miliband, also spoke of moral decline but of a still broader nature. 'It's not the first time we've [recently] seen this kind of "me first, take what you can" culture. The bankers who took millions while destroying people's savings: greedy, selfish, and immoral; the MPs who fiddled their expenses: greedy, selfish, and immoral; the people who hacked phones at the expense of victims: greedy, selfish and immoral.'[6]

This narrative of decline resonated across the world, reflecting global anxieties about criminal disorder and moral collapse. Pessimism about the trajectory of morality found its way into political debate as the US geared up for its 2012 presidential election. Running to become the Republican Party's 2012 presidential candidate, Senator Rick Santorum noted that 'Satan has his sights set on America.'[7] Many Americans shared Santorum's pessimism, if not his rhetoric, with nearly three quarters believing that moral values in the country as a whole were getting worse.[8] Crime lies at the heart of concerns about morality, so it's no surprise that Americans also think that crime is far from under control: more than two thirds believe that crime is rising, and they are not alone.[9] The same is true across most English-speaking countries and has been for decades.[10] Crime, we generally think, is a steadily growing problem, not a diminishing one.

There are many reasons, of course, why some might want us to believe that crime is spiralling out of control. Those espousing our Heroes and Villains view regard crime as a selfish choice encouraged by excessive social tolerance. Might it be that some people, concerned about increasing social liberalism in other spheres, for example in relation to sex, feel that rising crime is proof that such tolerance leads to general social breakdown? Those in the Victims and Survivors camp believe that crime is a result of inequality and social injustice. Might they likewise see crime increases as evidence that society is being run in favour of a small minority and that unrest demonstrates the need for social change?

It is certainly noticeable that high crime rates also reflect badly on whoever is in power. Highlighting crime increases is therefore a useful way of undermining incumbent governments, as well as advancing particular views of crime's causes. In January 2010, shortly before winning back office for the Conservatives, David Cameron explained: 'We have had rising violent crime and it's wrong to say that each of these incidents comes along and somehow there is no connection to what is going wrong in the rest of our society.'[11]

Such arguments resonate, partly because when we look around we can often find reasons to be fearful. Episodes like those of the London riots shake our faith both in humanity and in the state's ability to maintain order. And there are plenty of other examples of widespread unrest. A few weeks before the London riots, for instance, Canada witnessed its own social breakdown. On 15 June 2011, the Boston Bruins ice hockey team won the Stanley Cup after beating the Vancouver Canucks in the final game of the seven-game series. Residents of Vancouver, where the game was played, were restless. Even before the first quarter had finished, eyewitnesses claimed a group was chanting: 'Let's go riot.'[12] And after the home town's defeat they acted on their promise. First, bottles were thrown at the big screens that had been erected to show the game, then windows were smashed and looters emerged from the crowd to take advantage of the situation. As a young man casually smashed yet another window, a visibly upset woman despaired at her city's decline: 'This is our city. What the f**k is wrong with you people?'[13]

Only after millions of dollars of damage, nine police officer injuries and over 100 arrests was order eventually restored. But the sense of pessimism endured. As one forlorn shopkeeper summed up: 'The people who want to do good are vastly outnumbered by people who want to do bad and just don't care.'[14]

Is this correct and is crime really continually increasing? This is a question we need to answer both because it underpins many of the arguments we hear about crime and because it's relevant in finding clues as to the true causes of criminality. If crime has indeed been rising steadily, then a number of theories about its causes might be severely undermined. It becomes, for example, much harder to argue that poverty is the main cause of crime if crime has been escalating while countries have been getting wealthier. Other theories might become more attractive. Many countries have experienced soaring inequality in the last twenty years as the incomes of the wealthiest have grown much faster than the rest. Could rising crime be the result of this shift?

A GLOBAL CRIME WAVE

When the economists Stephen Moore and Julian Simon wrote an account of twentieth-century advances in the US, *It's Getting Better All the Time*, the subject of crime was a notable omission. It contains full chapters on health, wealth, education, technology, the environment, culture and sport but virtually no references to law-breaking. The nearest we get is a chapter on 'safety', which only refers to dramatic declines in accidental deaths at home and work and, in a bout of pre-9/11 optimism, a mention of waning terrorist activity.

The omission is no mistake. Crime was in fact on the rise for much of the twentieth century; indeed, a look at its most extreme manifestation reveals a depressing picture. While roughly one person was murdered for every 100,000 US citizens in 1901, by the year 2000 homicide rates were over five times as high.[15] Nearly 19,000 people were murdered in the US that year and a staggering 1.8 million people visited accident and emergency departments as a result of assaults.[16] Victims paid a heavy price, and so did taxpayers. By the end of the twentieth century, the US government was spending over $100bn each year on the criminal justice system, while the total costs of crime to the US economy were estimated at an astonishing $1tn.[17]

Such a collapse in standards of behaviour poses a fundamental challenge to the idea that economic and social progress will reduce crime rates. Bafflingly, crime flourished in the same period that America grew to its position as the most prosperous and 'advanced' nation in the world. As crime spiralled, GDP, literacy rates and educational achievement all soared.[18]

Intriguingly, this alarming fact that crime can intensify even as economies grow has been replicated across Western democracies. Again, there has been great progress in most areas of our lives over the last century. By 2000, GDP per capita had probably quintupled in real terms, twelve times fewer people died before the age of six and literacy rates in Western Europe had risen so much (to around 99 per cent) that most countries stopped measuring them.[19] Yet despite being richer, better educated and healthier, people were still usually as – or more – likely to be the victims of serious violence at the end of the twentieth century as at its beginning. Murder rates more than doubled in England and Wales between the 1910s and the 1990s.[20] And while homicide rates in Europe fared slightly better, this was only due to big falls in the first half of the century that were reversed afterwards. Between the 1960s and the 1990s, European murder rates also spiked.[21] Likewise, Canadian murder rates went up in the 1960s, almost tripling between 1961 and 1975 before slowly dropping.[22]

These dramatic rises in post-war murder rates are not as bad as they may first seem. They are far, far *worse*. Improvements in communication, transport and healthcare should have transformed thousands of would-be murders into attempted homicides or assaults. Democratic Congresswoman Gabrielle Giffords would never have survived her attempted assassination in January 2011 if it had occurred fifty, let alone 100 years earlier.[23] A bullet passed through her skull, entering at the back-left side and exiting at the front. But just eight months later she was voting in the House of Representatives.

In theory, the benefits of medical advances might have been undone by increasingly lethal weaponry. But in all likelihood better weaponry had only a limited impact on murder rates. Murders aren't always committed with firearms – in many countries only a tiny fraction are – and publicly accessible killing technologies have not (fortunately) improved at anywhere near the same rate as healing ones. Experts looking at both sides of the equation have estimated that US murder rates in the late 1990s might have been up to three times higher than they actually were – or eighteen times those of 1900 – had medical technology remained at the same level as it was in 1960.[24]

This stark rise in lethal violence across the post-war West is not simply a statistical blip. Murder records tend to be reliable, as dead bodies are difficult to hide and most people will report a corpse to the authorities when they find one. But it's harder to work out what happened to crime rates in general. Some crimes other than murder are well recorded. Around 90 per cent of UK vehicle thefts are registered, for example, largely because a police 'crime number' is a prerequisite for insurance claims.[25] But many crimes go largely unreported – either because people aren't confident it will make any difference or for fear of revealing their victimization. Reporting of sexual offences has increased after steady efforts to remove the stigma of victims, but it is still the case that only around a third of US rapes are reported.[26] What's more, police recording practices vary greatly across countries and change frequently – and there are enough stories of 'massaging' of figures by officers under pressure to hit targets to suggest that caution is required.

Fortunately – at least from our point of view – the post-war period has seen governments invest millions of pounds in conducting confidential surveys that ask people about their experiences of crime. Surveys don't cover all types of crime or every country, but they have provided information on crime rates from the 1960s. This information has had far-reaching effects. Vitally, it has prompted a far greater focus on previously 'invisible' crimes like sexual abuse. But most importantly, perhaps, the evidence from these surveys allows us to be reasonably confident that the post-war crime wave applied to a wide range of crime types, not just murder.

In the (relatively few) countries where surveys are regularly carried out – the US, Canada, England and Wales, and Australia, for example – property crime rose significantly from the 1960s to the 1990s.[27] Trends are slightly less clear than those for murder, and different crimes increased in fits and starts and at different speeds. But there are few exceptions to the long post-war property crime wave, and this reinforces our central point: post-war rises in wealth and living standards did not lead to reductions in crime and disorder.

EBBING TIDES

By the 1990s, the level of fear was palpable. In 1995, the US Attorney General commissioned a report on crime trends and the lead author, Professor James Alan Fox from Northeastern University, issued a stark warning. Crime would, he said, continue its steady rise – and teenage crime could be expected to more than double over the next ten years.[28] In 1996 John DiIulio, then at Princeton University, issued a similarly pessimistic warning: 'By the year 2010, there will be approximately 270,000 more juvenile super-predators on the streets than there were in 1990.'[29]

Then something started happening. Crime fell. At first everyone thought the change would be just a temporary reprieve in an ongoing downward spiral. But the improvement continued. For the countries where we have reliable data, many types of crime dropped by half by 2010. Since 1995, burglary in England and Wales is estimated to have fallen by two thirds and violent crime by nearly as much.[30] The US experienced similar reductions and several of its crime 'hotspots' have been cleaned up. Murders in New York City have fallen to a quarter of early 1990s levels – and the city went from accounting for 10 per cent of US homicides in 1993 to just 4 per cent in 2008.[31]

The crime decline – like the crime rise that preceded it – took place in almost all developed countries, though to differing degrees.[32] European countries that had experienced less of a crime spike from the 1960s to 1990s, for example, also experienced less dramatic falls. And the US and Canada have led the way in the great crime decline, theirs starting earlier than those of Europe, Australia and New Zealand. Another interesting difference is found in variations between crimes. Intriguingly, robbery rates fell far more slowly than burglary rates and in some countries actually rose, for example. This is most likely due to the rise in the value of portable electronic goods, which made muggings a more attractive option than getting past ever-improving home security.[33]

The drop in crime was even more dramatic than the rise that preceded it. But, oddly, few have noticed it. Only one in five Americans or English people believe crime is decreasing, even after twenty years of steady reduction.[34] Similar scepticism is found worldwide. In Japan crime has fallen dramatically, yet just 4 per cent of the Japanese feel that public safety is improving and only 35 per cent are positive about the nation's public safety, even though it's probably the safest country in the world.[35]

Our failure to appreciate real changes in crime rates has many causes. Media representations are likely to play an important role. When asked why they think crime is rising, the main reasons people give are television (57 per cent) and newspapers (48 per cent).[36] And there even appears to be some relationship between length of exposure to media and views on crime: 85 per cent of people in England and Wales who watch TV for more than three hours a day think crime is rising nationally, compared to just a third of those who don't watch any.[37]

A glance at front-page stories certainly doesn't encourage optimism. As I write this, the five previous consecutive editions of the *Irish Mirror*, a widely read Irish paper, lead with:

9 September: 'Body in wardrobe horror. Stabbed 40 times for

€300' – which reports the murder of a 53-year-old man murdered for an unpaid debt.

10 September: 'Alps massacre: I'm so scared' – which recounts the fear of a young British girl who had witnessed the contract killing of her father, mother and sister while on holiday in France.

11 September: 'Crying eyes. Freed Collins searching for work as millionaire boyfriend ditches her' – which tells the story of a woman released from detention after the attempted murder of her multimillionaire boyfriend.

12 September: 'Hillsborough: After 23 years of lies and smears . . . the truth' – which reports on police corruption after the tragic sporting accident.

13 September: 'Black Widow tries to make a killing: Trial re-run in bid to grab husband's €1 million estate' – which returns to the story of Collins, reporting her attempt to overturn her conviction.

Other newspapers may not be quite as crime-obsessed, but every single UK or Irish newspaper has displayed a front-page crime story in the past five days and television news bulletins are often dominated by reports of crime.

As we've already seen, the media are attracted to cases that are particularly shocking – ones with archetypal innocent victims and unambiguously evil wrongdoers; but this is likely to distort our judgement of crime trends as well as our view of criminals and their crimes. In the 1970s, Paul Slovic and his long-time collaborator Sarah Lichtenstein started to investigate how well people estimated the likelihood of different events happening.[38] What they found is that we have a good understanding of the everyday risks to human health and happiness, but we are not very good at all at estimating probabilities of infrequent events. Intriguingly, Slovic and Lichtenstein found that we are particularly bad at estimating the likelihood of dramatic events – especially so in relation to violent crimes such as murder. Those who took part in their study thought that people were actually more likely to be murdered than to die of either stomach cancer or diabetes – despite the fact that the latter are considerably more likely.[39]

Psychologists often explain our overestimation of the likelihood of dramatic events as being a result of an 'availability bias'. Our brains apparently confuse the ease with which we can remember something with the frequency of that event, how 'available' it is to our memories. Studies have shown that the pervasiveness of media coverage can therefore influence our estimation of different risks, including violent crime. Professor Slovic and another colleague, Barbara Combs, found that the more coverage any dramatic event got in local newspapers, the more likely it was for people to overestimate its likelihood.[40] Could this explain why in 2010 around 15 per cent of people in Britain thought they were very likely to be victims of burglary in the coming year when the actual likelihood was nearer 2 per cent?[41] And why 15 per cent thought they were very likely to fall victim to violent crime, when the true figure was 3 per cent?[42]

Intriguingly, studies have shown that even fictional representations can have a major impact on our assessment of risk, demonstrating again that fictions affect our perceptions of reality. When the film *Jaws* was first screened in 1975 the number of swimmers off the coast of California plummeted.[43] Shark attacks had not risen, water safety had not declined, and yet thousands of people refused to go for the swim they would have a year earlier. Many still mustered the courage to go to the beach but decided not to enter the water, perhaps imagining the ominous *Jaws* theme tune – and failing to consider the reality that the journey to the beach was far more dangerous than the swim they were refusing to take.[44] I know of no studies that assess whether fictional representations of crime have a similar impact, but it seems to me feasible that our obsession with crime fiction might contribute to our inflated estimation of crime rates.

Our ease in remembering events affects our perceptions, then – so it is clearly plausible too that our misconceived view that crime is rising is due partly to the ease with which we can recall recent (as opposed to distant) crimes. Another factor is the way in which crime stories are told. Editors recognize our attraction to the dramatic, so problems are presented as 'spiralling out of control' for added impact. Children have 'become feral', implying that any incident will only be the first of many more. Images are selected to be quickly identifiable with the reported topic – pictures of knives, guns, balaclavas and police officers are stock favourites. And pictures can be used to amplify the drama of the story too, presenting a mother's grief, a judge's indictment, a victim's suffering. Tight deadlines contribute to the clichés as writers struggle to go beyond the predictable.[45] The time taken to produce news stories has fallen dramatically as broadcasters and newspapers have cut costs and increased their output to serve twenty-four-hour news stations and free online news platforms.[46]

That emotive language and imagery matter is again proven by psychological experiments – and companies do not spend billions on finding just the right image for their brand if it did not have some effect. Imagery affects our behaviours. People are more willing to pay for cancer research if they are told about the suffering caused by the illness, for example, and more likely to take up airplane insurance if terrorism is mentioned or there has been a recent terrorist incident.[47]

Of course, another reason why we overestimate crime is simple misrepresentation. Crime statistics can be a source of political advantage so it's perhaps no surprise that they are frequently misused. In 2010, the then Shadow UK Home Secretary, Chris Grayling, asserted on the radio that violent crime had doubled under the Labour government – totally ignoring more reliable statistics indicating that violent crime had in fact fallen considerably. The year before, Grayling had also compared life in the Moss Side area of Manchester to that depicted in *The Wire*, the US crime drama. In reality, Manchester experienced nearly 100 times fewer fatal shootings than the far smaller city of Baltimore, where *The Wire* is set. The whole of Greater Manchester (population well over 2.5 million) suffered just two gun fatalities in 2009, while Baltimore (population 637,000) experienced 196.[48] Grayling spoke of 'urban war', but the statistics showed that gun crime was not just rare; it was also falling.

Newspapers often collude in such attacks, selectively highlighting bad news, choosing statistics that best suit their purpose and picking misleading imagery. The 2006 story taken from the *Sun* shown in Fig. 2 is certainly not reporting just the facts. Its headline 'Cops Losing Fight on Violent Crime' is very much at odds with the verdict of UK statisticians, who said: 'The number of violent crimes experienced by adults showed no statistically significant change between 2005/6 and 2006/7', a repeat of the previous year's verdict.[49] The paper also fails to refer to the longer-term trend of falling crime. Graphics highlight the negative and then show a man with a gun next to the words 'violent crime' and 'robbery' – implying (entirely incorrectly) that this

Fig. 2: 'Cops losing fight on violent crime': *Sun*, 27 January 2006

image is in some way representative of the average violent offence. And we should note again that there are myriad assumptions behind the wording used. Saying that it's the 'cops' who are losing the fight on violent crime suggests that it's the police whose actions largely dictate crime rates (see Myth 8). The idea that there is a 'fight' also implies the need for a combative, physical response to crime.

The fact that many of us forget that crime is falling – and are encouraged to do so – is important because the crime decline, like the rise that preceded it, provides further clues to the causes of crime. Just as post-war crime increases show that it doesn't automatically fall as countries become richer, better educated and healthier, rapid falls in crime since the 1990s reveal something vitally important. Crime and violence are not a necessary price for modernization, as some had started to suggest by the 1990s. And crime is not spiralling

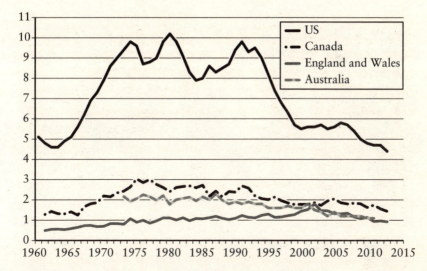

Fig. 3: When is the next crime wave coming? Murders per 100,000 in the US, Canada, England and Wales, and Australia[50]

out of control, as we are often asked to believe by those urging particular actions to check crime's 'advance'. The often-ignored drop in crime also gives us reason for hope: we are entitled to be optimistic that we have learnt at least some of the ways in which we can control crime.

Finding what has led to falls in crime requires a much better understanding than we have so far acquired, however. We do not yet know the secrets that explain the ebb and flow of crime over the past century. What is the strange moon that has been exerting its influence on tides of crime across the Western world?

UNKNOWN CURRENTS

There are many people who will tell you that they can explain what lies behind the great twentieth-century crime wave or its rapid ebb. A number of books have broken through to mainstream public debate about crime and its causes and the ones with the widest readership are often those that make the most assertive arguments. In his exhilarating best-selling book *Freakonomics*, the Harvard economist Steven Levitt teamed up with a journalist, Stephen Dubner, to share the findings of Levitt's 2001 research paper, written in collaboration with John Donohue, which argued that legalized abortion was a major contributor to falling crime.[51] Levitt's idea was that 1970s abortions brought down the number of unwanted children and this in turn reduced crime twenty years later – because, he argued, the children not born would have been much more likely to go on to become criminals.

Other studies make equally assertive claims. Several academics have argued that, in the US at least, a large part of the drop in crime was the result of increased use of prison. A study by the lawyer-sociologist Thomas Marvell argued that 'current crime rates would be approximately six to nine times what they are now' were it not for the vast sums the US spent on quadrupling its prison population in the late twentieth century.[52] Meanwhile, in his successful book *More Guns, Less Crime*, John Lott claimed that part of the crime decline (he thought around 3.5 per cent) was due to new laws introduced in some states to allow people to carry firearms.[53] Lott claimed that his findings were not so counter-intuitive once you recognize that it's generally only law-abiding people who get permission to carry weapons and that criminals are as scared of someone holding a gun as the next person.

Despite vast differences in their conclusions, these studies have at least two things in common: their ability to capture headlines and their method of analysis. This method – generally known as econometrics – sounds intimidating. It results in papers filled with equations, data tables and the results of various 'tests' run through powerful computer programs which can make even the mathematically minded feel insecure.

Of course, it's tempting to defer to the wisdom of those clever enough to wield this startling array of tools, rather than seek to understand them. But the basics of econometrics are reasonably easy to grasp. Essentially, econometric studies look at a number of different trends or events and try to understand the relationships between them. To create models explaining shifts in crime, our dispassionate scientists must therefore first identify the main factors that might influence crime. Then they must find the data that measures these factors. Then they must discover how all these factors interrelate, translating their questions into equation form and applying their formulae to their neat rows of data. Results will tell researchers whether there is a relationship between crime and the factors identified, how 'confident' researchers can be of the relationship, and the likely magnitude of the relationship. This is the process that allows authors like Levitt and Donohue to say 'legalized abortion appears to account for as much as 50 percent of the recent drop in crime'.[54]

Such methods and the arguments that rest on them appear superficially plausible. But a deeper examination soon reveals that what looks like dispassionate science is in fact a messy art. Even where there is a sincere intent to find the truth, econometric models are typically underpinned by myriad assumptions. Take the factors that people think might influence crime. These vary vastly between different models. Levitt's include abortion laws; most don't. John Lott's include gun laws; most don't. Levitt, Lott and Marvell do not regularly look at factors such as drug consumption, social values or marriage – which other studies do examine. Almost all studies include variables such as police numbers – but virtually none bother to examine the number of people working in private security companies, even though the US, for example, has significantly more security guards than police officers.*[55]

Once people have developed their ideas about which factors might influence crime, they then have to find ways of measuring them – and, of course, they must choose the ways they choose to measure crime itself. There are choices as to whether to use police force figures for recorded crime (which are more plentiful) or data from victim surveys (which are often more meaningful), for example. At this point, many factors that we are pretty certain have an impact on crime rates are usually excluded from the statistical study because there is no

---

* As well as dozens of potentially important variables being omitted, many of the variables that are included in econometric models are also of questionable explanatory value. Race, for example, is commonly used in these models 'explaining' differences in US crime rates, but while it's certainly true that young African American men commit more crime than young white American men, it's far from clear exactly what sort of causal theory is being proposed.

reliable information. It's certain, for instance, that what the police spend their time doing matters at least as much as how many of them there are (see Myth 8); but most studies prefer to include in their models the more measurable statistics on the number of police officers. As importantly, I have never seen an econometric model that includes 'the number of well-positioned street lights' or 'good transport out of urban centres at night' as variables – even though we know from small-scale studies that these can have an impact on crime rates.

The process of deciding which data should be used also requires a high degree of precision as to what exactly is being tested. Many people think that inequality matters in assessing crime rates, but in order to model such a relationship you need to decide which types of inequality you are going to include: differences between incomes, differences in wealth, or how unequal people feel their society is, for example? And if the latter, what survey question gets to the heart of the matter, if any? Again, choices must be made – and they are choices that are constrained by the limits of our ability to measure complex phenomena in our complex world.

Even after data has been collected, there are many judgements to be made when specifying the lengthy equations used to generate results. One major problem is that having too many variables in a model creates mathematical complexity and confusion – so modellers go through a process to narrow down to the variables that appear to 'matter'. As factors that show an apparently 'weak' relationship with crime over the period examined are excluded, the mathematical relationships between crime and those factors that remain grow stronger. Our econometricians also use a range of techniques to assess whether factors are causal or simply relate to each other. They might ask, for example, is it that crime falls when we increase police numbers or might it be that police numbers rise and fall in response to changing crime rates? And they might create some new formulae to 'correct' for the impact of crime on policing numbers.*

---

* Classic problems are endogeneity (when the two factors examined – say crime and sentencing practices – might both be affected by a common third factor, such as inequality); simultaneity (when two factors affect each other in different ways – for

In the process of creating a model, it's often surprisingly easy to persuade yourself that this vast array of omissions and assumptions aren't that important and that the conclusions you come to are still highly meaningful. As an old economics joke puts it, 'Econometricians, like artists, tend to fall in love with their models.' Russ Roberts is an economist who interviews other famous economists for a living. As he describes it, results are 'presented as objective science but . . . what actually goes on isn't. You don't just sit down and say I think these are the variables that count and this is the statistical relationship between them and I'm going to do my analysis and then publish it. If you do that and you don't get anything that's significant, which happens tons of times, you convince yourself rather easily that you must have had the wrong specification, you left out a variable or you included one that you shouldn't have included or you should have added a squared term to allow for a non-linear relationship until eventually you craft, sculpt a piece of work that is' – he pauses – 'a *conclusion* and you publish that and you show that there is a relationship between a and b, x and y.'[56]

The findings of these studies show just how much the assumptions of those wielding the statistical tools can affect their results. An astoundingly thorough study looked at thousands of publications that examined the impact of policing and prison on crime using these statistical methods and found that results were outlandishly inconsistent.[57] Twenty per cent of the studies examining the impact of tougher sanctions, for example, reported that their econometric models made them strongly agree that tougher sanctions would reduce crime, but an almost identical number argued that their data clearly disproved the idea that tough sanctions reduced crime.

The statistical guru Professor Ed Leamer from the University of California, Los Angeles, is unusual for an econometrician in that he admits to being highly sceptical as to whether statistical analysis really is the path to objective truths. In a 1983 paper he demonstrated that, even using *exactly the same data*, methodological assumptions make vast differences to studies' conclusions. He used data on a range

---

example, when leaders and followers adjust styles based on behaviour of others); measurement error; and common-method variance.

of trends to estimate the impact of capital punishment on murder rates – but varied his statistical techniques to reflect what he considered might be the 'reasonable assumptions' of people with different political viewpoints. The results are striking. Using the same data, a 'right-winger' might estimate that each execution prevented twenty-three murders, presumably through deterring would-be killers, while a 'bleeding heart' might estimate that as many as thirteen lives would be lost for each execution carried out, perhaps because of the violent precedent that execution sets.[58] Leamer summarizes: 'Economists have inherited from the physical sciences the myth that scientific inference is objective, and free of personal prejudice. This is utter nonsense.'[59]

Leamer advocated that academics both own up to the uncertainty of their conclusions and publish the results that they get from other ways of analysing the same data to show the vulnerability of the results to the specific methodology used. Yet although Leamer was writing in 1983, little progress has been made since and academics continue to publish results with false certainty.[60] Self-delusion may be a factor, but individual and institutional self-interest certainly push against intellectual integrity. 'The more exotic and dramatic your finding,' Leamer says, 'the more likely it is that you'll be featured in the *New York Times*. And, as a result, the university likes that so there's a real bias towards shocking claims, contrarian claims.'

Journalists, policymakers and politicians are often quite easily persuaded by these studies. Correlations are not proof of causation, as shown in Fig. 4, but we seem to be in awe of techniques we do not understand. Studies have shown that those without a mathematical or scientific background actually rate work as being considerably more credible when an entirely arbitrary and unrelated mathematical equation is woven into the text.[61] The other factor at play is again expediency. Policymakers – like everyone else – are drawn to research that confirms (with certainty) their own views, and it is certainly not unusual for media outlets to select contributions based on their fit with editorial stances. John Lott, producer of the 'more guns, less crime' theory, appears frequently on Fox News, has been a columnist for FoxNews.Com and has recently written a book called *Debacle: Obama's War on Jobs and Growth and What We Can Do Now to Regain Our Future*.

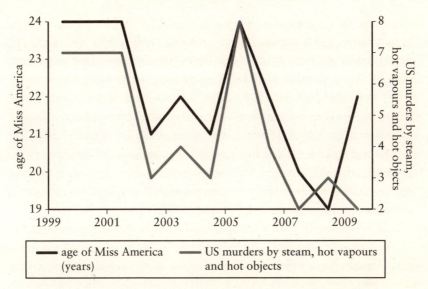

Fig. 4: The risks of over-interpreting your data – Miss America's youthfulness causes murders by steam, hot vapours and hot objects? (Correlation = 0.87)[62]

Academia is not free from politics, of course, so it is not surprising that all of the studies claiming to explain twentieth-century crime trends have been challenged since their publication – usually by authors who use similar statistical tools to 'disprove' them. Levitt (more abortion, less crime), Lott (more guns, less crime) and Marvell (more prison, less crime) have all countered their critics, though Levitt to his credit downgraded his estimate of the impact of abortion dramatically when it was pointed out that he had made a basic coding error in his research, which he found 'personally quite embarrassing'.* Lott has, meanwhile, gone to extraordinary lengths to maintain that more guns mean less crime, despite the fact that his results change considerably with even minor tweaks to time periods, methods and datasets used.[63] He has even taken Steven Levitt to

* Levitt did not, however, apologize for a range of methodological choices that I find difficult to understand, including the decision to focus on changes in crime rates over a twelve-year time span, ignoring fluctuations within those years.

45

court after the Harvard professor wrote that 'when other studies have tried to replicate his [Lott's] results, they found that right to carry [gun] laws don't bring crime down' and accused Lott of paying for a journal to publish work by him and those supporting his views.[64] Levitt was forced to retract the latter accusation but not the former.

All this simply serves to reinforce the point that the results of such analysis remain *opinions* and not pure facts. And it confirms that we should be highly sceptical of claims that increases and reductions in twentieth-century crime have been 'explained'. We simply cannot rely on these methods alone to draw robust conclusions, and we must certainly not accept their conclusions at face value.

This is not to say that statistical studies have produced nothing of worth. Indeed, I see the wild differences in the conclusions of these many studies as confirming an important truth, which is that arguments which attribute rises and falls in crime to just one or two easily measurable factors are likely to be wrong. If the world were simple and our behaviour determined by just a few factors, these models would after all produce far more consistent results. If crime were a result of just poverty or tough sentences, for example, models would have picked this up quite regularly. But they have not. Crime is not simply related to poverty and inequality: the mathematical relationship between these and twentieth-century crime is far from clear-cut even at first glance (see Myth 6). And neither is crime straightforwardly related to police and prison numbers (see Myths 8 and 9). This is a great disappointment to many of us as we appear to prefer bold, simple answers to ones that are more nuanced.

The other value of econometric studies is that they have contributed to the development of statistical techniques that can be used for more robust analysis. As mentioned, small-scale experiments are much better at revealing crime's causes because they allow us to isolate the impact of specific changes on crime rates and compare these with similar areas where changes don't take place. Such experiments – which we will examine frequently – do reveal some of the many, often small-scale factors that can influence crime.

As we shift from small- to larger-scale interventions, though, we often become less certain. This is partly due to the practical and political difficulties of creating genuine experiments to test the impact of factors like police numbers or poverty. So here we must use our judgement, being careful to test our theories against the findings of smaller-scale studies and the wealth of information we now have on the lives of individuals who commit crime (and those who don't). Occasionally, so-called 'natural experiments' can help us too. For example, Finland reduced its prison population while its neighbouring Scandinavian countries increased theirs – and this does help us to understand the impact of tough sentences on crime rates (see Myth 8).

Crucially, it is only by piecing together the evidence that we can develop our own plausible explanations for the ebb and flow of crime in the twentieth and twenty-first centuries. My own theory – based on these much wider sources – is that it had relatively little to do with 'moral decline', poverty or inequality. Instead, it seems likely that the period of economic expansion from the 1960s saw a dramatic increase in criminal opportunities. High-value consumables became a tempting target for theft and at the same time shifting social values brought ever-increasing numbers into situations where violence was a risk: for example, the mixed-sex urban settings where intoxicated men could be tempted to prove themselves through violence. Crime only fell as society adapted to these changes with better policing and home security and far more effective supervision of social spaces. We may also have benefited from technological advances, which made computer games much better than they used to be and kept more teenagers indoors and out of trouble – and from the decline in the use of highly addictive drugs like heroin and crack cocaine, which are now less fashionable than they were in the 1990s.

But it is hard to conjecture in this way without feeling somewhat dishonest. The truth is that these are perhaps the most plausible reasons for rises and falls in crime but they are no more provable than the theories proposed by our bold econometricians. As we'll see, we know with great certainty some things that do affect crime rates, but explaining the complex trends of the past is very difficult.

Instead, we must content ourselves for now with knowing that the simplest arguments about shifts in crime rates – which we hear frequently – have flaws. By seeing how crime has ebbed and flowed over past years and decades, we understand that crime is not after all the price of social and economic progress but neither is it inextricably tied to economic and social advance. We realize that our Heroes and Villains and Victims and Survivors views are both far too two-dimensional to be trustworthy. We know that crime is unlikely to have a single cause. And we know that sometimes the beauty of models is only skin-deep.

Remember this, because you will frequently be asked to forget it. In every recession, for example, people still confidently predict crime waves based on varying degrees of scientific endeavour. After the financial crisis of 2008, the Police Federation of England and Wales asked their researchers to come up with estimates of what would happen to property crimes as the recession bedded in. Using econometric analysis (cue alarm bells), they argue that 'In the current economic climate . . . the model suggests a probable surge in such property crimes. Our calculations showed that crime could rise by anything between 6.1 per cent and 15.7 per cent in 2009 to 2010.'[65] How, the Police Federation asked, could it make sense for the government to be cutting police numbers at a time like this?

Unsurprisingly, the predictions did not prove accurate. In England and Wales robbery levels continued to fall slightly in the late 2000s and burglary levels were roughly stable, albeit with a slight spike in 2010–11 from which the country quickly recovered. US crime rates

Fig. 5: Illustration from a Police Federation briefing[66]

similarly proved somewhat recession-proof. As *The New York Times* reported with surprise in May 2011, 'the nation has endured a devastating economic crisis, but robberies fell 9.5 percent last year, after dropping 8 percent the year before'.[67]

Once again, we should query the motives of those relaying strong messages and scientific-sounding predictions.* After all, alongside the Police Federation's confident proclamation of doom we were also treated to an archetypal representation of criminals (Fig. 5). This prompts a question. If we have been misled about levels of crime and changes in crime rates, have we also been misled about those who commit crime?

* The Police Federation only examined three recent recessions, looking at what happened to crime in those periods and then predicting that another recession would prompt similar changes. But these recessions all occurred during a period when crime was rising, not just in England but across the world. Their 'model' also included only a few of the economic and social trends that might matter for crime rates.

Myth 2: Taking up a life of crime

He felt a wild longing for the unstained purity of his
boyhood . . . He knew that he had tarnished himself, filled his
mind with corruption and given horror to his fancy.

Oscar Wilde's Dorian Gray[1]

LIFE CHOICES

Lee Kildare was a man who felt he had few options in life. He had
struggled at school and, suffering from dwarfism, was under four feet
tall. In 2008, at the age of twenty-two, he was convicted of a string
of burglaries in Newcastle. He described his reasons clearly: 'it's what
I have to do for money because I couldn't get a normal job. It's a tall
man's world.'[2]

Kildare had particular talents that made him confident he was
good at what he did. 'People come to me for help with burglaries
because I'm small and can get through small holes,' he said. 'But they
are not taking advantage of me. I'm well-known and well-liked and
no one picks on me.' After his conviction, he made it clear that he was
unlikely to give up crime. Notice the present tense in this statement:
'I have shoplifted in the past and it is easy as no one would ever suspect me. I normally get away with it because of my height . . . Now I
burgle derelict houses for metal so I can sell it on as scrap.'[3]

Kildare's attraction to crime as an alternative career does not at
first sight appear unusual: it is often presented as the preferred entre-
preneurial option of the greedy or the needy. As one newspaper
headline reported in 2006, 'Crime is the "career" of choice in the

inner city.[4] And newspaper clips from December 2010 (a month I selected at random) show the persistence both of skilled and less skilled criminals: 'DNA links 72-year-old career criminal Frank (Frankie Bones) Boehme to 2008 bank break in,' reports one story; 'Career criminal back behind bars after burglary,' announces another; 'New York crime boss arrives in Montreal, bodies begin to fall,' states a third.[5]

In film too we find career criminals in abundance. Few of them are easily persuaded to give up crime until they have either reached a natural retirement age, earned so much that crime is no longer necessary, or have been prevented from committing crime by prison or death. Take the bank robber John Herbert Dillinger, portrayed by Lawrence Tierney in the 1945 film *Dillinger* and by Jonny Depp in *Public Enemies* (2009). His pursuit of money (and later fame) leads him to turn to crime, and there is no going back. His ever more professional crimes are only curtailed when he is betrayed and his career is cut short by a police shoot-out. Take the master thief Neil McCauley, played by Robert De Niro in the 1995 film *Heat*. He is on the brink of retirement but is persuaded to commit one final job, partly out of professional pride. Or Frank Lucas, the central character of *American Gangster* (2007), played by Denzel Washington, whose success is only checked by a lengthy prison term. That two of these heroes, Lucas and Dillinger, were true-life criminals further suggests that crime can be perceived as an alternative career choice.

Most media accounts emphasize increasing criminality as people age. Serial killers provide an extreme example: most FBI profilers describe their patterns of criminal and abnormal behaviour as escalating before their first murder. Then, after their first murder, the killers' urges become irrepressible and the body count rises until they are caught. The motivations of serial killers vary in subtle ways, but one famous profiling system highlights four 'types': 'visionary' killers (who are usually compelled to kill by forms of delusional mission); 'mission-oriented' killers committed to ridding the world of certain types of people such as prostitutes and homosexuals; hedonistic killers (who kill for the thrill); and 'power/control' killers (who gain satisfaction from their complete power over their victims).[6] None of these motives suggests that murderers' offending will tail off.

Violent and non-violent crimes can clearly be habit-forming – a reason why parents and religious teachers so often warn of the 'slippery slope' that leads to long-term corruption. In the Bible, Jesus warns us of the need to be vigilant to eliminate even sins of the mind due to the risks of habit-forming immorality: 'if thy right eye offend thee, pluck it out, and cast it from thee: for it is profitable for thee that one of thy members should perish, and not that thy whole body should be cast into hell'.[7]

The idea that criminal behaviour, once learnt, becomes hard to shake off clearly supports both our Heroes and Villains and our Victims and Survivors views of crime. The notion of the incorrigible career criminal and remorseless serial killer lends credence to the Heroes and Villains argument that we must pull out all the stops in the fight against crime – both to ensure that it doesn't pay and to protect the public from people who have decided to pursue their own happiness whatever the cost to others. And, from the Victims and Survivors viewpoint, the idea of crime as a career choice forced on those excluded from the labour market is equally important. As Robert Merton, the Columbia University criminologist who later advised President Lyndon B. Johnson, wrote in the late 1940s, 'The moral mandate to achieve success exerts pressure to succeed by fair means, if possible, and by foul means if necessary.'[8]

The perception of crime as an enduring life choice has influenced policy decisions too. For many decades, policymakers have paid special attention to teenagers, for example, based presumably on the assumption that this is the age when criminal habits become irrevocably ingrained: dozens of programmes have made efforts to deter teenagers from crime, either before or after their first offence. 'Scared straight' programmes and 'boot camps' for first-time offenders, which we examine in Myth 9, are obvious examples.

Concerns about career criminality have prompted wider changes too. Longer sentences – a trend seen in most English-speaking countries since the 1960s – are an understandable way of dealing with people we believe to have been dangerously corrupted. And many countries have introduced legislation that aims to punish offenders not just for their specific crimes but for the risk they pose to others – presumably again fearing that the corrupted are hard to help. In

2003 the Home Secretary, David Blunkett, introduced an Indeterminate Sentence for Public Protection, which allows the state to incarcerate for life people who have committed any offence deemed worthy of a two-year prison term if they are considered a serious risk to the public.

How accurate is it, though, to see crime as a long-term career option? Is it true that criminal habits – even when not motivated by money – are hard to shake off? And are we right to concentrate our crime reduction efforts on those years when teenagers must make their life choices?

AN ODD KIND OF CAREER

Pick a career, except sport perhaps, and you expect people to work harder and more successfully as they reach middle age. In most developed countries, people do not embark on full-time jobs until their late teens or early twenties and then their careers take off. Average hourly earnings of twenty-year-olds are about half those of forty-year-olds, and the fifties and sixties become the coasting or wind-down periods, except for the most driven.[9]

For some reason, however, the pattern of criminal 'careers' seems different. The first thing that stands out is that people opt into their criminal careers rather early. One famous example is Colton Harris-Moore, the Barefoot Bandit. He was arrested aged sixteen and sentenced to a three-year custodial sentence after a spate of burglaries and thefts. Shortly afterwards he escaped from a halfway house in Renton, a small town in Washington State, and then became further immersed in his life of crime. On the run, his crimes grew ever more brazen. In addition to burglaries and car thefts he stole a series of small aircraft, gaining ever more notoriety and a nickname that resulted from him leaving footprints at the scenes of one of his crimes.

The Barefoot Bandit is not in many ways that unusual. Both police statistics and anonymous surveys show that most people who commit crime carry out their first offence before the age that most start work.[10] And indeed, according to surveys, the age when people commit most crimes is actually between fourteen and seventeen.[11] The image of the stubbled prowler that for some reason springs to my mind when I hear the word 'burglar', for example, appears to be unhelpful. Staggeringly, in many areas of England the most common age of burglary offenders is a mere fourteen years old.[12]

This highlights another oddity of criminal careers. Teenagers are our most prolific offenders because, unlike those in mainstream employment, criminals appear to 'work' less, not more, as they get older. Criminal careers tail off remarkably early for almost every crime type. Teenagers and men in their early twenties are on average far more likely to commit crime than those in their thirties and forties – and this holds true even for the most serious crimes. In the US, murder rates are usually highest among eighteen- to twenty-four-year-olds and in Europe people are most likely to commit murder in their twenties.[13] And this pattern holds for other types of crime too, including bank robberies and muggings.[14]

A very small proportion of people stick at crime for a long time. In 2008 Richard Blaylock, a British man, was sent to prison at the age of seventy-six after receiving the sixty-eighth conviction of his life.[15] But these cases are very much the exception, as the vast majority of people dramatically reduce their offending – or stop entirely – rather early in life. There is variation in the length of criminal careers, but those convicted of serious crimes at the age of eighteen seem to give up crime on average six years later, according to one study.[16] As a result, English and Welsh men in their forties are an astonishing twelve times less likely to be convicted than eighteen-year-old boys.[17] And more British eleven-year-olds are cautioned or convicted each year than 45-year-olds.[18]

This is not simply because older criminals get better at their trade and so don't show up in arrest records, or because they have been prevented from committing further crimes by permanent imprisonment. Older people who continue to commit crime do get a *little* better at not getting caught.[19] But a range of carefully conducted anonymous surveys have confirmed that most people have dropped out of frequent offending by the age of forty.[20] In other words, the long-term corrupting effect of committing crime appears rather small – and most people stop offending reasonably early in life.

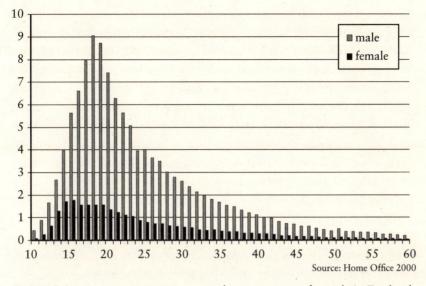

Fig. 6: Crime as a young man's game: the percentage of people in England and Wales found guilty of or cautioned for a crime at every age[21]

The unusual pattern of criminal careers applies both to men and to women. But it is clear that crime is predominantly a young man's game. You may already be beginning to doubt whether crime really should be seen as part of a career, but if it is a profession, then it's as male-dominated as it gets, being apparently less open or appealing to women even than policing. In England and Wales at the turn of the twenty-first century, teenage girls were responsible for nearly six times fewer offences than men of the same age – and similar differences are found across the world.[22]

CRIME'S PRODIGIES

The frozen image from the television security footage shows two boys walking quietly out of the shopping centre in Bootle, near Liverpool, in 1993. The younger boy is a toddler, holding the hand of the other boy. And they follow closely behind a third young boy, making his way out of the building. The image is mundane. But it is haunting too in light of the events that followed. The two older boys are ten-year-olds, Jon Venables and Robert Thompson, and the toddler is a two-year-old, James Bulger, known by his family as Jamie. Having lured him away from his mother during a routine shopping trip, Jon Venables and Robert Thompson took James to a nearby railway station. After throwing bricks and other items at him, they killed him. It was a planned attack and excerpts from police interview footage revealed the details of the crime.

Hearing the killers' own testimony evokes the most visceral reaction. An unbroken, almost babyish voice softly responds to calm police questioning:

'What was it you told us?' the officer says.

'That I killed James,' Jon Venables answers.

'Right. Now I know that took a lot of doing . . .'

'I can't tell you anything else,' Venables interrupts, distressed.

'Why?'

''Cos that's the worst bit,' Venables says.

'I know that's the worst bit,' the officer continues 'but you know what you did. Think about it and just tell us what happened.'

'We took him on the railway tracks and started throwing bricks at him . . .'

The case understandably shocked the nation. Children – not teens or hardened career criminals – had committed a horrific crime and the natural reaction to the tragic case was shock and anger. When the two boys were convicted, the media's relief and satisfaction that the 'Evil, brutal and cunning' children would be locked away was palpable. 'How do you feel now, you little bastards?' asked the *Daily Star*'s front page.[23]

Other child killers have gained similar notoriety. In 1968 Mary Bell, an eleven-year-old English girl from Newcastle, was convicted for strangling two boys, a three- and a four-year-old. And echoes of the Bulger case were heard across the North Sea just a year later, in 1994, when a five-year-old and two six-year-old boys kicked and stoned to death a girl of five in Norway. Every few years another tragedy occurs. In 2000, a Michigan boy obtained a firearm to lethal effect, using a semi-automatic handgun to kill a female classmate at kindergarten. And in 2006 a twelve-year-old Canadian girl was an active accomplice in the murder of her parents and eight-year-old brother.*

We are drawn to these cases partly because they are unusual. But they also fascinate us because they simultaneously contradict the prevailing view that children are life's innocents and affirm childhood innocence through the portrayals of the perfectly helpless child victims. The murderers are usually depicted as aberrations, the victims as representatives of childhood as a whole. As the *Daily Mail* headline put it, the Bulger murder was a case of 'The evil and the innocent'.[24]

If there's one author who has done most to contribute to the prevailing view of children as life's innocents it is Charles Dickens. In novel after novel he depicts children resisting the corrupting forces of the outside world, only occasionally relenting after sustained pressure. Here is Oliver Twist when he realizes that the rough rogues Bill Sikes and Toby Crackit are planning to involve him in a crime. Twist, despite having been surrounded by cruelty, violence and thievery for most of his life, could never countenance such evil:

> 'Oh! For God's sake let me go!' cried Oliver; 'let me run away and die in the fields … pray have mercy on me, and do not make me steal. For the love of all the bright Angels that rest in Heaven, have mercy upon me!'

For young innocents, death is preferable to crime, even if sustained exposure to the evils of others can eventually corrupt. Fagin, the leader of a ring of child pickpockets, even gets close to corrupting Oliver as he has done the Artful Dodger, Nancy and others. As Dickens puts it, 'having prepared his [Oliver's] mind, by solitude and gloom, to prefer any society to the companionship of his own sad thoughts in such a dreary place, he [Fagin] was now slowly instilling into his soul the poison which he hoped would blacken it, and change its hue for ever'.

The fact that murders can be committed by children suggests that they can be corrupted very young. But it also raises another

---

* Jasmine Richardson, twelve, admitted she had choked her brother to make him unconscious, while her boyfriend, Jeremy Steinke, stabbed her parents multiple times and slit her brother's throat.

possibility that Dickens and others rarely encourage us to think about. Could it be that those who commit crime do not start out in life being instinctively opposed to law-breaking? Could it be that, rather than gradually learning the skills of a criminal lifestyle, many people are born with antisocial instincts which they eventually learn to shake off?

Thanks to a series of studies we now know the answer to this – and those attached to the idea of childhood purity should look away now. In the 1980s and 1990s, a Canadian team of investigators led by Richard Tremblay studied boys from deprived areas in Montreal in an effort to understand when children were at their most aggressive.[25] Over a period of ten years they asked teachers to report on the boys' aggression at school. They found, perhaps surprisingly, that children were using physical aggression most often when they were in kindergarten between the ages of five and six, and at their least aggressive at fifteen, the oldest age group observed. Far from an upturn in violence in the often angst-ridden teenage years, there was an almost universal decline in aggression as the boys moved up the school. Four out of five of the boys studied became less aggressive as they grew older, while most of the rest had never shown any aggression in the first place. Just four in every 100 boys maintained high levels of aggression throughout their school lives – and these boys usually exhibited a wider range of behaviour problems. Remarkably, none of the children observed were found to have become violent later in their school careers if they had shown no signs of aggression in their first years of schooling.

When Tremblay and his team turned to the pre-school years to find out when children start to be physically aggressive, they found that children are even more physically aggressive before they enter education. Research from North America, Scandinavia and the UK shows that the 'terrible twos' are aptly named – because this is the age at which levels of physical aggression towards others often appear to be highest (see Fig. 7). And even the under-twos are frequently aggressive. In one study, close to nine in ten mothers reported that their seventeen-month-olds were sometimes physically aggressive towards others.

These studies of childhood aggression also revealed some interesting facts about parental memories. Researchers found, for example,

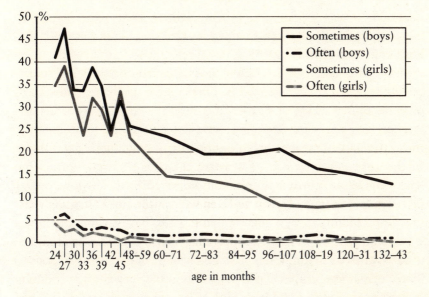

Fig. 7: Learning all the time: the frequency of hitting, biting and kicking from two to eleven years of age[26]

that it was absolutely imperative that they asked parents about their children's recent behaviour and then kept track of the parents' responses as their children grew up rather than asking them about their children's past behaviour – mainly because parents demonstrated a startling inability to recall their offsprings' past transgressions. A similar phenomenon has been found with older children who are behaving aggressively, as most parents report that the adolescents' aggression had only emerged in the past couple of years, whereas deeper investigation almost always revealed earlier problems.[27] Could it be that our idealized view of childhood is making us forget that our children's antisocial behaviour usually starts in the home and not when they are exposed to malign influences outside it?

These findings are initially highly surprising, and yet they become increasingly intuitive once you get used to them. If, as I have, you ask young parents about their toddlers, you will most likely find attempted murder (particularly of siblings) to be surprisingly common. Kicking and punching (not purely for exercise) is similarly typical, with little evidence of guilt emerging in the aftermath. Young children are prone

59

too to relatively frequent shoplifting and trickery – the placing in supermarket trolleys of all those items that they want but their parents don't is a favourite.

We excuse much of this behaviour, of course, because we believe young children aren't aware of the harm they might cause and are less able to control their urges or less aware of the boundaries of socially acceptable behaviour. But this should not be allowed to obscure the fact that while criminal behaviour peaks in adolescence, the (more numerous) antisocial acts of younger children often take place in a context where they are not deemed criminal. Hitting a fellow toddler in a playpen is rarely considered a police matter, nor is stealing a fellow pupil's lunch money. The very young also have few opportunities to engage in more complex and harmful criminal behaviour: they are closely supervised and often lack the physical or cognitive abilities to carry out serious crimes. Eight-year-olds aren't very good at climbing fences or entering locked buildings, even on the rare occasions when their parents allow them out alone. As the fourth-century philosopher Saint Augustine put it, 'the feebleness of the infant's limbs is innocent, not the infant's mind'.[28]

When I speak to Professor Tremblay over the phone, he is quite clear that the findings of his studies should encourage us to focus on different questions from those to which we currently pay most attention. 'Many people, including specialists in child development, seem to think – like the philosopher Jean-Jacques Rousseau – that we are born good and that we learn bad behaviour from our environment. But all the evidence shows that's not the case.'[29] 'There's been too much focus on outside influences that encourage crime such as antisocial peers or television. We need to focus not on why people take up crime but why it is that some children never learn to stop the behaviours that most of us work out aren't useful or appropriate.'[30]

HIDDEN CHILDHOODS

One reason we have focused on the wrong questions is that we have created two entirely different languages to describe the antisocial behaviour of children and that of adults. Adults are regarded as self-directing agents; we treat their acts as moral choices and respond with legal sanctions. Children, meanwhile, are seen as reacting to their circumstances, and their behaviour as part of a process of learning and experimentation about how to succeed in life.

Where society draws the line between these two attitudes towards behaviour – and how sharply that line is drawn – appears to vary considerably. The United Nations Committee on the Rights of the Child concluded that 'a minimum age of criminal responsibility below the age of 12 years is considered by the Committee not to be internationally acceptable', but their recommendation is not universally shared. Until 1963, Britain's age of criminal responsibility was eight years old; today it is ten. In Egypt and Lebanon, it is just seven.[31] Other countries take a wider view of childhood. The age of criminal responsibility in Russia is fourteen and in Brazil it is eighteen.[32] Meanwhile there is huge variety within the US, varying from seven in Oklahoma to fifteen in New Mexico.[33]

Such age thresholds are not an entirely reliable guide to how punitive countries are towards their young people, as they all have alternative mechanisms to deal with antisocial acts below the threshold. But they are still significant, denoting different views of the age when children should be assumed responsible for their actions and subject to the same punishment-focused regime as adults. And they still influence – and in a way distort – crime statistics. In the UK, for example, even the most violent and unruly child will not be charged with a criminal offence until the age of ten, so it is perhaps not surprising that policemen, parents and social workers associate that initial criminal conviction with a 'worsening' of behaviour.

Vivid recollection of an individual's recent crimes can contribute to perceptions that their conduct is deteriorating when it isn't, and also mislead us as to when the criminal behaviour began. Superficial coverage of the Barefoot Bandit, for example, suggested his teenage spree was a form of flamboyant rebellion, an attempt to carve out a more glamorous and rewarding lifestyle. Yet as the case received more attention, investigative journalists had time for more considered examination. They found not the teenage onset of criminal behaviour but a young man who had suffered behavioural problems since early childhood. Colton Harris's mother reported that he had displayed 'a sort of disconnection' from an early age, and from the age of seven our Barefoot Bandit was said to have been spending long periods of time living outdoors and committing thefts from holiday homes in the area. His first court conviction came at the age of twelve, but this was certainly not his first crime.[34]

Legal definitions of childhood do not just mislead us about the onset of antisocial behaviour. They also fail to reflect the reality of social learning, which is a gradual and complex process that continues throughout childhood and the teenage years – and indeed into adulthood. Most people learn to behave socially before the criminal justice system becomes interested in their behaviour. Children learn that they can get what they want without violence or theft by co-operating with others (for example, by sharing toys) or by using verbal skills of persuasion and negotiation. But some children learn more slowly than others, continuing to exhibit troublesome (and criminal) behaviour into their teens, as they explore how best to interact with their changing world. As we've seen, unlike long-term criminality, youthful crimes are relatively common. Around a third of the population receive a criminal sanction at some point in their lives and one in seven ten- to 25-year-old British males assault someone each year.[35] But the statistics show that most of these people eventually figure out that crime is not worth persisting with and that only a tiny proportion – probably smaller than the 4 per cent of continually troublesome children in Tremblay's study – continue to offend for many decades.

In the following chapter we will examine why some people learn more slowly than others. But it is worth pointing out here that antisocial behaviour can fade even in people who have committed extreme acts of violence. Mary Bell, the ten-year-old who killed two young children in 1968, spent much of her youth in various forms of institution but was supported with counselling services. She committed a range of teenage misdemeanours, including shoplifting, but her conduct eventually settled down, her biographer, Gitta Sereny, reporting that the birth of her child when she was in her late twenties was an important point of stability in Mary's life.[36]

Other child killers have reformed too – though some continue to be prone to serious offending. Despite their young age, James Bulger's killers, Jon Venables and Robert Thompson, were tried as adults and originally sentenced to be detained 'at Her Majesty's pleasure' and serve a minimum of eight years in prison. A 280,000-person petition organized by the *Sun* calling for a longer term was supported by the then Home Secretary, Michael Howard – but judged illegal by the European Court of Human Rights, allowing both boys to be given new identities and released after less than ten years. Jon Venables has developed alcohol and drug problems. In 2010 he was convicted of possessing pornographic images of children and in many ways appears to belong to the small group who persist in antisocial behaviour rather than learn their way out of crime. Robert Thompson, however, seems to be following the more typical pattern, despite the seriousness of his childhood crimes. His former social worker now describes a well-adjusted and popular young man whom he recently spotted working as an usher at a public event. 'I don't think he has reoffended since his release, that would be very hard to imagine . . . He will hate what has happened with Venables, because it will bring it all flooding back, and once more put his name in the spotlight.'[37]

The fact that people can learn their way out of crime does not, of course, excuse their behaviour or suggest that they should not be held morally or legally culpable. But it does help to confirm that the long-term criminal career is very much the exception rather than the rule. And it highlights again that many of the behaviours that are later deemed to be criminal are present – and indeed often more acute – very early in people's lives. Studies time and again find that only a tiny minority buck the general trend towards better behaviour throughout childhood.[38] And we usually see that adolescents who engage in more crime as they are given increased freedom and opportunities already have some history of behavioural problems. Gang membership, for example, can lead to more teenage crime – but those with a history of bad behaviour are far more likely to join gangs in the first place.[39] Similarly, the (very rare) individuals who make most of their money from crime do sometimes progress from smaller to bigger jobs as they build connections and learn; but most persistent criminals start their pilfering at a very young age indeed. It is even rarer to develop dysfunctional, sadistic urges like those of James Bulger's killers without a history of serious childhood antisocial behaviour – a fact that raises important questions about the influences of biology or very early upbringing on future criminality which we will explore in Myth 5.

DEALING WITH CRIME'S ORIGINS

The possibility that people can learn their way out of crime and anti-social behaviour is a powerful and encouraging concept. But our discoveries should prompt us to ask more questions. In addition to looking at why people take up crime, we must ask why it is that most children *stop* exhibiting bad behaviour early in life. We must ask why some people don't seem to learn to avoid crime. And we should ask why it is that we treat adult and childhood behaviour so differently – and which solutions produce the best results.

These ideas also provide us with further clues about the nature of crime and what works to prevent it. They suggest that some of the factors we are led to believe have a great influence on criminal behaviour may not be the most powerful ones. Most people, after all, learn not to commit crime without coming into contact with the criminal justice system and tough law enforcement. And we have many reasons to doubt the concept of crime as a career option, suggesting that we should be wary of expecting dramatic results from attempts to reduce crime through improving employment prospects. A criminal career does not appear to be remotely attractive, given that most people who commit crime as teenagers or young adults soon give up offending so quickly.

We have also made an important shift by focusing not on legal definitions of crime but on the behaviours that we find unacceptable. What 'counts' as crime is, after all, sometimes as much to do with how society interprets a particular set of actions as with the motivations or personalities behind those acts. That similar actions are treated differently when they occur in different places or are carried out by people of different ages is significant: we clearly need to look behind the classifications of 'crime' to spot patterns of behaviour that societies want to curtail or encourage. And we need to recognize the importance of criminal opportunities, appreciating the key fact that crime increases as children and teenagers are allowed more autonomy to explore the adult world.

The question all this invites, however, is why is it that a small group of people persist with crime into their teens and beyond? Could it be that they find they are good at crime and it offers them the best chance of the wealth and status to which they aspire? Or could there be other reasons? We have found that our Heroes and Villains and Victims and Survivors views both overstate the degree to which crime is the result of deliberate career choices. Now it is time to examine why a small minority do persist in crime.

Myth 3: Criminals will stop at nothing

Not being able to govern events, I govern myself.

Montaigne[1]

PERSEVERANCE

Everyone thought the Antwerp Diamond Centre was impregnable. Diamonds could only be accessed by their owners and the vault which contained them was supposed to be impenetrable. There were ten security features, including cameras, infrared heat detectors, Doppler radar, a magnetic field, a seismic sensor and a lock with 100 million possible combinations – roughly one combination for every euro's worth of diamonds stored in the vault's safety deposit boxes.

Yet on Monday, 19 February 2003, the area's diamond traders were shocked to discover that the vault had been robbed over the course of the weekend. One hundred and twenty-three safety deposit boxes had been emptied, though the robbers appeared to have been forced to leave thirty-seven boxes unopened, presumably unable to carry off more than their estimated $100m haul. Papers and even diamonds were found scattered across the vault's floor as the perpetrators had rushed away. 'It is impossible and yet it happened,' said one of the victims, a diamond merchant, Marcel Fuehrer.[2]

Initially, there was no trace of the thieves. But shortly after the crime police received a call from a familiar source. August Van Camp had dedicated much of his retirement to protecting the local habitat and often reported cases of fly-tipping and littering in the strip of forest that ran alongside the E19, the road which connects Antwerp in northern Belgium to Brussels in the south. His calls were often ignored, but this one was different. He had found rubbish again – but strewn amidst the debris were unusual items, and none more so than dozens of diamonds and rolls of Israeli and Indian currency.

Within hours, the police were swarming across the scene collecting evidence. Receipts, half-eaten food with DNA evidence and video-tape all pointed towards the involvement of Leonardo Notarbartolo, a lifelong thief and confidence trickster, and three other men. Each was known to have a criminal speciality. And after their arrests and conviction, Notarbartolo gave an interview and revealed their apt nicknames – the Genius, the Monster and Speedy – and also mentioned the King of Keys, a possible fifth conspirator who was never found.

But for the discovery of the dumped rubbish the thieves might have got away with it. The crime was planned over eighteen months with seemingly immense care. Notarbartolo claims to have received help from a diamond trade insider who not only inspired the idea but supported it with financial backing and by producing an exact replica of the vault for the thieves to practise on.[3] Each security device was dealt with through subtle trickery. Video evidence showed Notarbartolo disabling the vault's heat sensor with hairspray when he visited the day before the crime. The one-foot-long vault key was reportedly copied from videotape footage. A polystyrene block was used temporarily to block the heat sensor until it could be disabled.[4]

The existence of such capable and determined professional criminals is cause for concern. But the motivation of greed is far less worrying than that of revenge or sadism. Attendees at the seven-month-old Tyler Shanabarger's funeral in Johnson County, Indiana, reflected on his tragic death, struggling to imagine the remorse that his parents, Ronald and Amy, were experiencing. The autopsy had revealed that Tyler had been a victim of Sudden Infant Death Syndrome, more commonly known as cot death, and his mother Amy had had to suffer the horror of checking on her son one morning and discovering the fatal accident.

The ordeal became even more harrowing a few days later, however. Ronald Shanabarger suddenly confessed to Amy that he had in fact murdered their son, suffocating the child while she was away at work.

He stated that he had killed the infant in an act of planned vengeance against his wife, who had refused to cut short her holiday to comfort him when his father died three years earlier. As the prosecution reported, 'Shanabarger said he planned to make Amy feel the way he did when his father died. He married her, got her pregnant, allowed time for her to bond with the child, and then took his [boy's] life.'[5]

Such cases of meticulous planning fascinate us, because they involve deliberate cunning and cruelty that we find hard to comprehend. Men like Notarbartolo and Shanabarger frighten us because they seem unstoppable, committing their crimes in a cold and calculating way. We reserve some admiration for the ingenuity behind robberies, but people intent on revenge and physical harm are generally despised. We describe them with words like 'predator', a term which distances the accused from humanity and emphasizes their desire to prey on others. Both types of criminal are people who don't care how they get what they want – and derive satisfaction from hurting or outwitting others.

We've seen that it is generally misleading to view crime as a lifelong lifestyle choice made in adolescence or early adulthood: most people who commit crime behave badly throughout infancy and childhood. But these cases prompt the disturbing thought that we may be seeing a strange kind of natural selection. Perhaps those who continue to commit crime beyond youth find they have a real knack for troublemaking, and gradually the amateurs are weeded out by fierce competition. Leonardo Notarbartolo, speaking to the journalist Joshua Davis, said he still remembered the details of his first theft. He was just six years old when his mother sent him out for milk and he returned with far more money than he'd set out with. When he had found the milkman sleeping, he had rifled through his possessions and made off with the proceeds. He was beaten by his mother but, Davis observes, 'he had found his calling'.[6]

Criminals are often presented as both determined and effective. Our Heroes and Villains and Victims and Survivors views of crime both, after all, imply criminal determination. The Victims and Survivors approach holds that those who commit crime are strongly driven by the need to compensate for the wages which poverty and social inequality deny them. And the idea of determination is especially central to the Heroes and Villains concept: politicians of this persuasion frequently refer to criminal resolve as a reason for tougher penalties. One of the main arguments used by opponents of gun control is that making guns harder to own legally will not stop determined criminals and will just impede law-abiding citizens. As the US Tea Party movement put it, 'Criminals ignore gun restrictions. Strict gun laws won't stop those with intent.'[7]

The belief in determined criminality is particularly deeply embedded in the language of law enforcement. As the United Nations Interregional Crime and Justice Research Institute reports, 'Modern crime is increasingly organized, sophisticated and able to infiltrate our daily lives, we thus have a collective responsibility to develop new and innovative interventions to cope with the emerging and complex problems it poses.'[8] The image of the determined criminal is thus used to justify specific approaches to tackling crime: criminal sophistication must be matched by increased law enforcement expenditure and more severe sanctions.

IMPATIENCE

The researchers at Bing Nursery School on the campus of Stanford University found a small room and placed in it one desk, one chair and a little bell. One at a time, the nursery's four- to six-year-olds entered the room and met Dr Walter Mischel, a friendly man with a Brooklyn accent. He asked them to play a game which was based on a simple proposition. They could eat the fluffy marshmallow, Oreo cookie or pretzel that Dr Mischel gave them (just one was provided, according to their preference), or they could resist temptation until he returned fifteen minutes later and then be rewarded with an additional goodie. If they wanted to eat their treat, all they had to do was ring the bell so Dr Mischel could record the time of their capitulation.

Mischel taught at the university's Psychology Department and had devised the test after seeing his own young children undergoing rapid changes as they grew older. In a recent media interview, he explains in a warm, gravelly voice: 'I . . . saw the dramatic transition that they seem to go through in the third and fourth and fifth year of life when they go from these rather impulsive, non-rational, highly immediate creatures to actually being able to regulate their own thinking, their own intentions, their planning and so on. And I became fascinated by the process of "how they do it", [and that] became my question.'[9]

The 'marshmallow test', as it became known, was therefore devised at the Mischels' kitchen table before being introduced at the Bing Nursery, which his children also attended. The task was sufficiently probing as to reveal different levels of childhood impatience in his own young children – though psychologists have naturally had to devise harder tests to assess the ability to delay gratification in older children and adults.[10]

Replications of the experiment reveal that children's love of sweets remains as great today as it was in 1968 when Mischel first conducted his tests. The strategies children employ to resist temptation are diverse. Some hit their heads; others kick at the underside of the table; and a few (rather unwisely) stare purposefully at the object of their desire. As time ticks on, the temptation becomes harder to bear: children stroke and sniff their marshmallows and even nibble the edges, hoping this doesn't count. Most succumb. In Mischel's original experiment, barely one in three children was able to endure the fifteen-minute wait and many ate their treat almost immediately.

The most striking finding of the study, however, was how closely the behaviour of the children related to other problems in school. Those who gobbled their marshmallow seemed to be the same ones who were having trouble sitting still and concentrating in class, and who were most likely to break rules and get into fights. Older children, unsurprisingly, generally performed better – but again those children who did badly for their age were the ones who more regularly had problems with discipline and school performance.

The results were intriguing and prompted Mischel to focus on why some children performed better than others. As well as natural variations in their ability to resist temptation, he noticed that children who did better adopted different strategies. And he even found that letting children cover the marshmallow or telling them to imagine it as, for example, 'a fluffy cloud' helped impatient children to hold out for longer. Effective strategies also varied as children aged. As Mischel puts it, 'If you're working with six-year-olds it's already a somewhat slightly different story. If you're working with nine-year-olds it's a different story and so on. But at the age where they're first really learning . . . how to do this [aged three or four], what makes this a lot easier for kids is when they work out that they can spontaneously distract themselves . . .'[11]

Yet it was not until a few years later that Mischel began to wonder whether the test might have wider ramifications. Curious to know how the children he had come to know during the tests were now getting on, he would ask his children about their friends and make notes on their progress. A pattern started to emerge. Those who had struggled with the test seemed more likely to be doing less well in school or having other difficulties.

Intrigued, Mischel decided to investigate further. He followed up his original study by sending surveys to the parents, teachers and academic advisers of his 300-plus original subjects. The findings appeared to confirm the hunch. Those who had succumbed quickest to temptation struggled in stressful situations and found it difficult to maintain friendships. Convinced he was onto something, he obtained further grant funding and a bigger, more representative sample of children was tested and followed up every ten years. As time passed, their problems increased. 'The main things that we found,' he reports, 'were that seconds of delay time [before eating the marshmallow] were predicting things like cocaine drug use in adolescence and later in life; things like body mass index; years of education.'[12] Later replications of the study suggested something even more interesting – that marshmallow guzzlers might be more likely to end up in prison.

Knowledge of the marshmallow test and its findings spread just as a number of new experiments into child development kicked off. In Dunedin, New Zealand, researchers successfully secured funding from government and a range of other sources for a project that tracked all of the 1,037 babies born at the Queen Mary Maternity Hospital between 1 April 1972 and 31 March 1973. Early tests assessed their physical and mental health but also tracked psychological well-being and, drawing on research from Mischel and others, their self-control. As the babies grew, wider data was collected too – on employment records, income and educational achievement – but also on antisocial behaviour and offending. Avshalom Caspi, a psychologist at London

University, examined the data once the study had been running for long enough to see if Mischel's results with Californian children also held true in the antipodes. They did. Caspi found that children who were 'undercontrolled' (those who were restless and impulsive and had poor attention spans) were much more likely to be aggressive and commit crime later in life.[13]

As more surveys of this kind were conducted, the evidence mounted further. A study of Pittsburgh youth found that those children who said they were 'unable to delay gratification', whose teachers said they were likely to 'act without thinking', and who were fidgety and easily distracted in videotaped observations were also much more likely to commit crime in adolescence and young adulthood than their less impulsive peers.[14] Poor self-control was a strong predictor both of behavioural problems and of criminality at the time of the test and later in life. Most tests, in fact, find that impulsiveness in early childhood is one of the best predictors of future criminality.

The Dunedin study showed that children who are unable to delay gratification also seem to suffer greater health problems – including, perhaps unsurprisingly, obesity and drug addiction. And they are more likely to become pregnant or father children as teenagers, and do less well at school or in work.[15] There were two other factors that seemed to matter for all these outcomes. First, studies found that lower IQ was associated with future criminality.* And second, social class mattered. Kids with low self-control and low IQ from a poor family background were most likely to be the ones engaged in anti-social behaviour and to go on to commit crime as adults.

The fact that lack of self-control is so strongly linked to criminality gives us reason to pause. For it seems that, far from being determined, criminals are in fact often characterized by their lack of determination and their unwillingness to forgo short-term pleasures for long-term gains. And it appears that those who commit crime

---

* A Swedish study measured children's IQ at age three and followed the children throughout their lives. The researchers found that those who ended up committing the most crime had an average IQ of 88, whereas non-offenders had an average IQ of 101. Similar studies in Michigan, Philadelphia, Copenhagen and Cambridge, UK, have had similar results.

may not be particularly clever either, with on average (though certainly not always) lower IQs.

FRUSTRATION

These suppositions are reinforced when we look at the facts of criminal cases: most incidents lack the rational calculation you might expect from someone carefully weighing up risks and rewards. Countless statements testify to offenders 'snapping' after a series of frustrations, often experiencing genuine remorse after their crimes. Stresses which provoke crime range from common disappointments (such as missing the bus) to major and infrequent crises (such as being evicted from one's home). There can be dramatic consequences even for relatively minor upsets. Incidents of domestic violence spike noticeably when strong favourites lose American football matches, for example.[16] Similarly, domestic violence in England peaks when England loses big football games. At the more harmless end of the spectrum, researchers have even found that drivers honk their horns more aggressively in intensely hot weather.*[17]

It is impossible to see inside people's minds to understand the thought processes that occur when they commit terrible crimes. But there is no doubt that murder, for example, is rarely calmly and carefully conceived. Where the circumstances in which US murders took place were recorded, nearly half turned out to be the result of an argument – and a further quarter took place in the course of another crime, often as a result of robbers panicking in the face of resistance from the victim.[18] The desire for immediate action, however senseless, appears too strong to resist for many who face disappointment or adversity. Take gang violence, for example, where many killings are presented as being rational acts to protect 'turf'. Some are, but most detailed studies conclude that the majority of tit-for-tat gang killings are better seen as exaggerated responses to friends' deaths.[19]

Murder may have some rewards, but it's hard to look at even

---

* For those wondering, excessive use of a car horn during daylight hours is indeed a criminal offence in most countries, albeit one that is not often enforced.

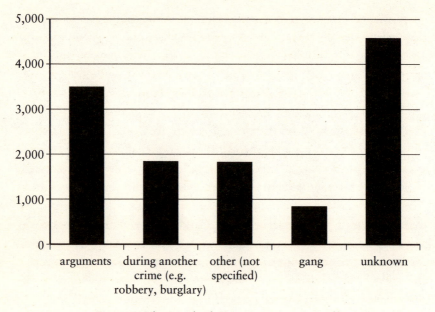

Fig. 8: US homicides by circumstance, 2012[20]

partially planned murders and understand their logic. In 2009, Shakilus Townsend was beaten and stabbed to death by members of a
London street gang sometimes known as Shine My Nine. The victim
was reported to have had gang ties, prompting media speculation
that the killing could be related to the drugs trade – but the story that
emerged was far from a case of simple economics. In fact, the victim
was lured to his death by his girlfriend, Samantha Joseph, a troubled
fifteen-year-old who was desperate to regain the affections of a Shine
My Nine gang member who had left her when he found out that she
had been unfaithful to him with Shakilus. The hasty, ill-planned
crime brought no gain to the seven teenagers, who were predictably
jailed as a result.

If they had considered the odds, perhaps the tragedy could have been
avoided. For, unlike those who commit non-violent crime, would-be
murderers should know that they are very likely to be caught and
punished severely, with well over half of murders solved in all
developed countries I have seen statistics for. Indeed, in the UK around
90 per cent of murders are usually solved and in Germany around

95 per cent.[21] There are black spots in less developed countries, particularly when the police are overwhelmed by the sheer volume of wrongdoing, and it remains true that murders involving victims from certain groups – such as prostitutes – are less likely to be solved. But perpetrators of serious violence are still typically rewarded for their crimes with a sentence of life imprisonment or even death: hardly a smart choice.

OPPORTUNISM

Even in non-violent crimes, the pursuit of short-term advantage appears regularly to override long-term considerations. We see few traces of Notarbartolo's careful planning in action, and strong indications that it might be the impulsive among us who succumb most readily to criminal temptation.

We are drawn to the most spectacular cases, but few robberies are even basically planned.[22] Interviews with British burglars found that less than a third of those questioned said that they went to the area in which they committed their last burglary with the purpose of carrying out the crime, and the main reasons they gave for selecting their most recent target were 'chance' or that they were 'passing and the target looked easy'.[23] In another British study, less than one in five of those who had committed multiple burglaries (who might be expected to be particularly professional) said that their last job was completely pre-planned – and this proportion roughly coincides with the number who said they chose their target because of a tip-off.[24]

This isn't meant to imply that there's no rationality involved. Burglars target houses on street corners because they are easier to access; an occupied house or the presence of a police officer will certainly be off-putting. But most crimes involve forms of calculation that are at best rudimentary. Crime is clearly not 'accidental': people do make decisions to commit even unplanned offences. It is just that these decisions are often made quickly, with little regard for long-term consequences.

Non-violent crime is rarely as lucrative as we might assume. Burglars, for example, repeatedly fail to spot high-value household items, instead opting for goods that are familiar to them and can be quickly consumed or disposed of, such as alcohol. One thief from Munich returned a stolen violin worth tens of thousands of euros to its owner, with an accompanying note explaining that it was out of tune. Many vehicle thefts have no material reward, partly because buyers for stolen cars are hard to find and partly because joyriders find the immediate thrill of a fast drive tempting enough to forget about the long-term risk of prison.

Even the crimes that we think of as most organized, such as art theft, aren't particularly lucrative. Robert Whitman, a former FBI special agent, has investigated art thefts throughout his career. He has seen numerous botched heists and points out that it's extremely rare for thieves to recoup even 10 per cent of the value of a stolen item: 'There is no place to sell it [high-end art]. It's really not a smart crime,' he reports. 'There's this thought process that these [thieves] are like Thomas Crowne. There's this myth, and I think people find that . . . interesting.'[25]

Similar myths surround the drug trade, with growing evidence showing that most drug dealers earn relatively little. We have already encountered Sudhir Venkatesh's *Gang Leader for a Day* as one of the documentary accounts that portrays crime as a rational response to social conditions. But within his work we also find interesting truths, such as the fact that low-level dealers earn less than the Federal minimum wage;[26] many dealers have legitimate jobs to supplement their income. People who commit crime drift in and out of the legal and illegal economy, confirming our finding in Myth 2 that, for most, crime is more a sideline than a professional career.

Other studies support the view that crime is far from a full-time job, even for serious offenders. In 2000, researchers found that half of prisoners in Quebec had earned on average less than C$2,619 (£1,176) from their crimes, and another quarter less than C$7,291 (£3,273) annually.[27] Only the top 25 per cent made a good living. When first asked, these top earners exaggerated their income, claiming to earn on average C$55,322 (£30,034) per year from their crimes. But when researchers asked them to itemize their crimes and estimated each take, they concluded their earnings were a still considerable but far lower C$32,000 (£14,000) per year. As we'll see, a lucky or skilful few earn still more, but it is clear that crime as a profession is far from the norm even for prolific offenders.

Criminal specialization is also surprisingly unusual. There are not two distinct types of criminal – one less calculating sort that commits violent 'crimes of passion' and another, like Notarbartolo, who avoids violence unless it has a clear business purpose. In Canada, only a tiny proportion of prolific offenders (around 5 per cent) had been convicted only of property crimes, most having been sent down for both violent and non-violent offences.[28] Studies in the UK and US, meanwhile, show that after someone has committed a specific criminal offence, he or she is more likely to go on to a different type of crime than repeat the same offence.[29] In other words, the burglar on one day can be a violent offender the next and a bag-snatcher the following week. Of course, people who commit crime do have 'red lines' that they are reluctant to cross: it would be ludicrous to suggest that once someone has tried shoplifting they'll commit murder. But for those engaged in serious criminality, specialization is rare, which reflects the opportunistic and unplanned nature of many criminal acts.

That offending is usually the result of crime-prone people encountering temptation in their daily lives is vitally important in understanding the bulk of crime in developed countries. In Montreal, a study showed that the average distance travelled by offenders committing burglaries was just over a mile, UK data revealed that half of British offences were committed less than a mile from where the offenders lived, and in Melbourne half of burglaries were committed within one and a quarter miles of the offender's home.[30] And two British researchers, Paul Wiles and Andrew Costello, found that when offences weren't carried out near home, they were usually perpetrated in locations the offender travelled through on a routine basis, such as schools or shopping centres.[31] Given this, it's no surprise that heroin addicts overwhelmingly commit burglaries in just two areas – near their homes or near the places where they buy drugs.[32]

Temporal patterns of crime also reflect the routines of daily life. Across developed countries, crime peaks in summer holidays when risk-taking teenagers are under less supervision and are more likely to be outdoors. Rioting is a summer special too: only a tiny fraction of recent northern-hemisphere riots have taken place in winter, and almost all of these were associated with some kind of public festival, like the Mardi Gras riots in Philadelphia and Seattle in 2001. Violent crime peaks after payday, when young men congregate to drink in bars and nightclubs. And rates of theft and criminal damage often soar once children have gone home from school, as seen in Fig. 9. Seeing crime as being influenced by daily life helps to explain differences in age profiles or different types of crime too. Fraud, for example, is usually committed by older offenders because few teenagers have the requisite opportunities for this kind of law-breaking. And the importance of opportunity is seen starkly in the relationships between victims and perpetrators. 'Stranger danger' is a myth, as the threat of serious crime comes less from 'other people' than from people we come into contact (and conflict) with. In Canada, nine in ten solved homicides were by a person the victim knew.[33] In the UK, nearly half of all female murder victims are killed by partners or ex-partners and two thirds of serious sexual assaults on women are committed by current or former partners (52 per cent) or family members (10 per cent).[34] Robbery and burglary are less personal affairs, but at least a third of US burglaries (and potentially as many as half) are by people who know their victims.[35]

The way in which crimes are committed is likewise affected by circumstances. Gun availability is clearly linked to gun fatalities, for example. The US has by far the highest levels of gun ownership and Switzerland the second most: they rank numbers one and two in terms of developed-country gun-related deaths, though the majority of these deaths are in fact the result of suicide, not murder. In the US around seven in ten murders are gun-related, a far higher proportion than in countries with tighter gun control such as England and Wales (one in ten) and Canada (roughly one in five). Countries like the UK, which enjoys a ban on domestic handguns and a range of other restrictions, are no less violent or criminal than the US except in terms of gun fatalities.* How many fewer murders there would be in the US if gun availability were far lower is difficult to

---

* As an aside, firearms are sufficiently hard to get hold of in the UK for the majority of gun crimes to be committed with converted replicas. Even when guns are owned,

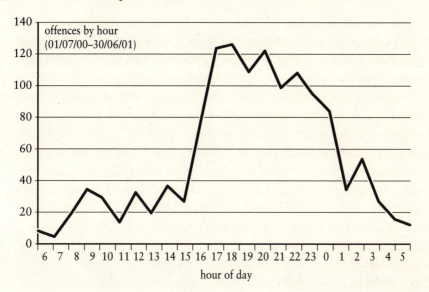

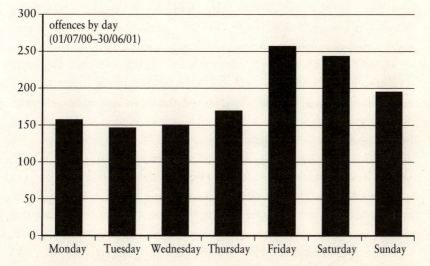

Fig. 9: Criminal opportunities: criminal damage in Copeland, a semi-rural area of England (2000–2001)[36]

_____

obtaining ammunition is difficult and I know of several anecdotal examples where such difficulties have prevented crimes from being carried out.

determine – and given that the country has an estimated 300 million domestically owned firearms, the feasibility of reducing ownership rapidly is unclear. But to me these figures point to the obvious benefits of reducing easy access to firearms.

That the majority of crimes are carried out without careful planning does not make them excusable. But it is clear that we must be wary of the concept of the determined criminal and be cautious of those who present crime as an exception to everyday life, rather than an ever-present risk which ebbs and flows in harmony with our patterns of daily existence. We should recognize that there is a degree of rationality in crime, but also that it is not perfect rationality, as crime is often the result of impulsive action, someone seeking short-term satisfaction and ignoring possible long-term hardships.

PROPULSION

Jeffrey Hill is a powerfully built African-American man.

'My drug of choice was crack cocaine.' Hill speaks slowly and deliberately, pausing after each sentence. 'In the beginning it kind of helped me deal with what I was going through [his father's death]. And it seemed like the more I did the better I felt. It was the easy way for me to escape my feelings.'

A woman's voice breaks in, speaking tentatively: 'Tell me about, ah, the hours before. What led you to kill your mother?'

This is an interview on death row and Hill is a man who has confessed to stabbing his mother to death while stealing $100 from her home.

'The hours before . . .' Hill pauses. 'Well, I wasn't aware of what I did the hours before.' Another pause. 'A lot of people have told me a lot of different things, you know, like how I was, where I was, what I did, this that and the other. Months went by and I didn't remember what I did. I don't wan' to remember that. Ah, you know. I forced myself not to remember that. That's the day that I constantly wish I could take back.

'I don't make excuses for my actions. You know, I've tried from day one to take responsibility for this – because it's the right thing to do. Erm, regardless of whatever the outcome woulda been. This has always been about me taking responsibility, ah, and letting people know I care and I loved my mother as deeply as I possibly could. Did I want to go in there and take her life? No. Did drugs play a part of it? Yeah. But I don't hide behind that. It's easy to say "I snapped". It's, you know. I don't know. I don't know why I snapped. I don't know why we're here today. All I know is, I don't have a mother. My kids don't have a grandmother. My uncle don't have a sister. And so on and so on. You know, that's what I know and – that's what I deal with every day.'

Hill had asked his family whether he should challenge the sentence.

'If they wanted me to die, I would die,' he says. 'If they wanted me to fight, I would fight.' He is close to tears. 'I just didn't [pause] want to hurt 'em any more. So whatever they wanted me to do I was going to do it . . . I didn't want them to be hurt again.'

Sympathy for someone who has killed his mother is something we are instinctively uncomfortable with – and it's probably not the case that any one of us could commit such a crime under certain circumstances. But it's also hard not to recognize the remorse as Hill speaks, and not to conclude that he has made a terrible choice. In fact, he has not just made one terrible choice: his life was a sequence of bad decisions, hastily made, that led him to where he is today, death row in an Ohio prison.

Mischel's marshmallow test is significant not just because it shows that people who act impulsively may commit impulsive crimes. Mischel's and others' tests demonstrate that self-control affects all sorts of life decisions which in turn may affect whether or not people commit crime. Those with poor self-control are more likely to get into financial difficulty, for example, and to experience drug and alcohol addiction. The path from weak self-control to crime may sometimes be straightforward – a simple tendency to lash out and act without thinking – but there are more subtle connections.

It is striking that most people who regularly offend engage in other behaviours that might make for a risky lifestyle, being more likely to misuse drugs and alcohol and have unprotected sex. Across the developed world, around two thirds of those arrested are under the influence of drugs, usually cannabis or amphetamines.[37] And in many countries around half of all violent incidents are believed by victims to have been committed by people under the influence of alcohol.[38]

There is no doubt that drug addiction can increase the amount of crime that people commit – many addicts have to fund habits costing over £100 per day.[39] Yet there's little to suggest that drugs regularly entice previously law-abiding citizens into a life of crime. When addicts do commit crime, their criminality usually precedes their drug use. In the 1980s and 1990s two separate Australian studies found that nearly three quarters of heroin users committed their first crimes before they had ever taken heroin.[40] A few academics have deployed this evidence to argue that crime leads to drug problems, as criminal activity makes drugs more affordable and brings people into an environment where drug-taking is more common. But the reality is usually more complex. Rather than drug addiction causing crime or crime causing drug addiction, it's simply that these behaviours are attractive to certain types of people. Crime, substance abuse and risky sex have a lot in common. They all offer short-term pleasure but in the longer term are usually poor choices in terms of health, wealth and happiness. These are life's snares – traps some people avoid and others fall into according to their ability to make considered decisions.

The ability to avoid such snares depends both on our personality traits and on the degree of temptation to which we are exposed. We all have a tipping point when short-term pleasure becomes irresistible, but most of us can also resist temptation when the benefits of doing so are obvious enough. When Mischel was designing his marshmallow test, he experimented by making the long-term rewards bigger. He found that if he told children they'd get a whole bag of marshmallows rather than just an additional sweet if they could wait fifteen minutes, almost all of them were able to resist temptation. The size of the immediate prize and the length of the wait also mattered, with the most tempting upfront offers making resistance extremely difficult.

I was aware of the difficulties of resisting certain pitfalls many times when visiting UK prisons. One of my favourite questions was to ask what people would do on release – not just in the longer term, but immediately. I particularly remember one conversation in a prison in south-west England in 2006. A skinny young man with a shaved head was talking openly.

'I'm in here for driving under the influence of cocaine, you see. And some other stuff. Me and my mates got into a bit of trouble. There was some fights. I'm not planning on coming back here now.'

'So what are you going to do when you get out?'

'Do you mean right away? Well, first of all I'm going to meet up with all my mates and have a massive mash-up. We'll probably go into town.'

As Mischel observed the children at Bing Nursery, he refined his views on why some people were so much better than others at controlling their marshmallow-eating urges. 'I was very interested in the actual process of resisting temptation,' Mischel says. 'Not merely deciding to resist temptation, but what happens when you're in the hot seat? What happens when you're actually there?' In asking this question, Mischel revealed an important insight – that intentions do not entirely dictate behaviour. Rather, we must both establish our intentions (deciding not to eat the first marshmallow immediately) and then find ways of making sure we act on these intentions. Mischel talks of 'hot states' and the 'cooling strategies' that help people under pressure to act based on long-term interests. And while his findings and those of other researchers show that people who struggle with self-control early in life often end up having problems later, he points out that people can change and, he believes, self-control can be developed. As he puts it, 'It's not simply that life does things to us, it surely does, but we in turn do things to it.' He continues: 'It is very important for parents not to misinterpret this [marshmallow test] as if it were a fortune cookie that actually could predict for the individual child [whether they would go on to have problems in life]. We are talking about predictions that are based on group data . . . To me the most interesting are the people who started low and went high, those who started high and went low.'

REAL-LIFE CRIMINALS

During his discussions with the journalist Joshua Davis, one of the many revelations Notarbartolo made was that he was undone by his own compassion.[41] His co-conspirators had been firmly opposed to Speedy's involvement in the Antwerp heist but he refused to listen. Yes, he knew Speedy's behaviour could be erratic, but he was a lifelong friend and Notarbartolo couldn't bring himself to exclude him from the score of a lifetime. Speedy would, he assured the others, stay calm under pressure. And indeed he performed his duties admirably. As they sped along the motorway away from Antwerp, Notarbartolo was starting to relax. He and Speedy had barely slept in two days but the gems were on their way to Milan and the task left to them was simple: they were to burn the incriminating evidence, hide the diamonds and divide up the proceeds once the furore had passed.

Yet Speedy was, according to Notarbartolo, getting restless and starting to sweat. When they pulled up to burn the rubbish, Speedy totally lost it. He started madly throwing the rubbish into the forest in what Notarbartolo described as a full-blown panic attack. In the half-light there was no time to hide the incriminating evidence. In any case, this was a quiet strip of forest and surely it was unlikely that the debris would soon be found. They did not count on August Van Camp's crusade to protect the local environment. Months of painstaking preparation were undone by a fit of irrationality.

Examination of crimes that appear to have been carefully planned often reveals less than perfect rationality. Ronald Shanabarger's case notes, for example, certainly give pause to those assuming that his crime was an act from which he could have benefited. Shanabarger confessed his crimes and remains in prison, but there are questions about his state of mind when he killed his son and the degree of forethought involved. While the prosecution vigorously pushed for a sentence of life without parole, emphasizing the careful planning of the crime, the judge sentenced Shanabarger to forty-nine years in prison, meaning he would be eligible for parole in twenty-three years. The factors that counted in Shanabarger's favour included 'his diminished mental ability' and the fact that the prosecution might not have been able to prove the murder without his confession.[42]

That there may be elements of irrationality and impulsiveness behind even apparently carefully plotted crimes should not be a surprise given what we have seen about the people most likely to commit them. And it is striking how quickly myths of legendary, determined criminals can dissolve on close examination. Possibly the world's most famous bank robbers, Bonnie and Clyde, are now regarded as experts, with strong morals to boot. Yet when they first met, Bonnie Parker, nineteen, was the wife of an imprisoned murderer and Clyde Barrow, twenty-one, a petty thief and vagrant. Their biographers are far less impressed by them than cinemagoers. As Jeff Guinn puts it, 'Clyde and Bonnie were never criminal masterminds or even particularly competent crooks.'[43] Their 'gang' was a loose and fluid group which impulsively stole, engaged in sporadic violence and robbed from liquor stores as often as banks.

John Dillinger, another famous bank robber immortalized in film, was scarcely more professional. The product of a broken home, he was a school bully who was in and out of work and prison.[44] He was prone to bouts of impromptu violence and petty theft as well as the bank robberies that eventually brought him celebrity in the 1930s. And, though he did occasionally travel outside Indiana, his home state, most of his crime was carried out within its boundaries. Dillinger's impulsive and risky behaviour was not limited to crime either. When he was first admitted to prison he was diagnosed with gonorrhea. Indeed, his taste for prostitutes eventually led to his downfall, a Romanian madam tipping off the Federal agents who shot him dead in 1934.

DEALING WITH
DISORGANIZED CRIME

There is something both encouraging and disconcerting about the idea that criminals seldom carefully calculate the risks and rewards of their actions. Encouraging, because it may be easier to prevent crime than we might have assumed: if people rarely plot their crimes, we may be more able to steer people away from criminal behaviour. We've already seen how introducing a requirement to wear a helmet contributed to major falls in motorcycle theft. And we will see further examples of how crime can be prevented through small changes. One anecdotal example from a UK police officer I know related to a problem with antisocial teenagers in Wapping, East London. A small group of friends would sit on top of a bus shelter and from that height shout at and intimidate passers-by, harassing residents and bus users in particular. They could climb onto the top of the shelter easily from a wall next to the bus stop, so the officer contacted the council and conducted a small experiment. If they moved the bus stop to a place where it was harder to climb onto the roof, would the behaviour continue? In this case, no. They found another spot to hang out at and the trouble ended.

On the other hand, impulsive law-breaking becomes hard to prevent simply by ensuring that criminal acts don't pay. People seem remarkably willing and able to commit crimes with few long-term rewards, so the effectiveness of making the consequences of crime ever more harsh is questionable (Myth 9). Similarly, crime is unlikely to be eradicated through improving people's economic situation: a significant amount of violent crime has no economic motivation and employment does not appear to create a major obstacle to continued offending, as we'll see in Myth 6.

Instead, we might have more success in reducing crime if we recognize the real nature of the triggers that lead to it. People do respond to incentives, but at best imperfectly, being much more likely to react to changes in their immediate environment. And people who commit crime are on average less likely than most to make measured, long-term calculations.

We might do well to recognize that understanding the real world makes straightforward condemnation of crime a little more difficult. Like many others, George Bush believes in a 'simple truth'. 'Each of us,' he says, 'faces the innate temptation to succumb to evil and yet always has the freedom to instead choose to do good.'[45] The idea is appealing and reassuring. But it ignores the fact that some people are faced with – and less able to deal with – more stressful circumstances than others and, more importantly, find making considered choices far harder than most. Many criminals were, after all, once like the small children in Walter Mischel's test – the ones who wanted to wait for two marshmallows but couldn't.

Myth 4: Organized crime is big, bad and booming

Power does not corrupt. Fear corrupts . . . perhaps the fear of a loss of power.

John Steinbeck[1]

FIRST EXPOSURE

In October 1963, Joe Valachi became part of a drama that gripped a nation. The US Senate's Permanent Subcommittee on Investigations inquiry into Organized Crime and Illicit Traffic in Narcotics featured on national television for almost a month. The public hearings brought organized crime into the spotlight to a greater degree than ever before. They drew on the most significant body of casework yet amassed by the FBI and the Justice Department and featured the compelling testimony of Robert 'Bobby' Kennedy, who had been pursuing Italian-American organized crime with ever-increasing vigour since his appointment as US Attorney General in 1961.*

Valachi was undoubtedly the centrepiece, however. Newsreels show him, stocky and chain-smoking, sitting calmly in a suit and tie. His demeanour gave few clues that he was a self-confessed Mafia enforcer with a history that made him the focus of national attention – his conviction for heroin trafficking; a falling-out with a New York mob boss, Vito Genovese, his boss and Atlanta penitentiary cellmate; and

---

* The 1951 Kefauver Committee had highlighted to the US public the existence of a Mafia that was 'world-wide in scope' but the absence of corroboration from mob insiders somehow diminished its impact. Here at last was a star witness.

the prison murder that left Valachi facing two death sentences, one for murder and one from the mob.

The footage shows Valachi responding straightforwardly to the questioning of the Subcommittee's Chairman, Senator John McClellan, and other committee members.[2]

'When did you become a member of this organization?' asks McClellan.

'1930,' Valachi replies, leaning forwards slightly.

'Nineteen hundred and thirty,' McClellan echoes.

'What is the name of it?' McClellan continues.

'Cosa Nostra, in Italian . . .'

McClellan echoes again, 'Cosa Nostra, in Italian.'

'"Our thing" and "our family" in English,' Valachi explains.

Valachi confirmed the worst fears of the Subcommittee and the US public. And his revelations went far beyond proving the existence of a powerful and secretive Mafia organization. In what he described as an act of vengeance against the man who had ordered his death, Valachi explained the organization's inner workings. He told of the now famous 'Omerta' or vow of silence; the rites of initiation that marked his entry into 'the family'; his relationship with his Godfather and mentor, Joe Bonanno; and the trades in which Cosa Nostra members were involved – gambling, prostitution, loan-sharking, narcotics and infiltration of legitimate business. Most importantly, he named names: first, the leaders of the five New York 'families' – Vito Genovese, Carlo Gambino, Giuseppe Magliocco, Joseph Bonanno, Gaetano Lucchese; then over 130 members of the Genovese crime family to which he belonged, along with dozens of mafiosi from other Cosa Nostra families.

Charts were drawn up and pinned against the pillars in the grand Senate Committee room. These charts revealed the strict hierarchy of each of the five families, with a boss, a 'consigliere' or senior adviser, an under-boss, captains or 'capos', 'lieutenants' and then 'soldiers' beneath them.

'About how many soldiers would usually be under a "boss"?' a Committee Senator asked.[3]

'Well, Vito Genovese has about four hundred and fifty. In and around that. About four hundred and fifty. Could be even five hundred.'

Valachi told of the power of those heading these organizations, with a special focus on his former boss. 'Senator,' he stated, 'I happen to know Vito's power. He not only controls the power in our family. He also controls the power in the Gambino family and the Lucchese family.'

The scale of the organization nationally was more difficult for Valachi to estimate due to his relative lack of seniority. But he pointed to Cosa Nostra operations across the United States and had no doubt about the organization's reach and sophistication. 'This Cosa Nostra, it's like a second government,' he said. 'It's too big.'[4]

Attorney General Bobby Kennedy, after years of Justice Department investigation into the Cosa Nostra, concurred. 'The picture is an ugly one,' he summarized. 'It shows what has been aptly described as a private government of organized crime, a government with an annual income of billions, resting on a base of human suffering and moral corrosion.'[5]

As the nation watched, Kennedy explained the ramifications of Valachi's testimony. He cited the successes that had resulted from the Justice Department's increased vigour, but emphasized the resilience of organized criminals and the need for constant vigilance. As Kennedy put it, 'We have been able to make inroads into the hierarchy, personnel and operations of organized crime. It would be a serious mistake, however, to overestimate the progress federal and local law enforcement has made. A principal lesson provided by the disclosures of Joseph Valachi and other informants is that the job ahead is very large and very difficult.'

Kennedy continued: 'Organized crime not only becomes more refined in its activities, but also takes advantage of modern developments in transportation and communication. As it does so – and grows richer and more powerful in the process – it can more easily elude law enforcement efforts.' The threat, Kennedy argued, was a growing national problem, one that threatened to undermine the fabric of US society. As he put it, 'Racketeers bore their way into legitimate business,' 'corrupt law enforcement' and pose an 'urgent national problem'.[6]

For Kennedy, the first step in tackling organized crime was to raise awareness of its scope and scale. As he explained, 'In case after case ... where there is little public interest, the cash registers of organized crime clang loudly. Where public interest is aroused – and stays aroused – racketeers are driven into bankruptcy or prison.'

The second step was to increase national oversight and enforcement efforts. Between 1961 and 1964, when Kennedy stepped down from his post to run for the Senate, the number of specialist organized crime agents in Washington DC's FBI office soared.

The third step was to level the playing field in the fight against organized crime. The mob were, he argued, using ever more sophisticated 'techniques to frustrate investigating officers who must attempt to obtain evidence of violations legally', and new powers were needed to overcome this. Kennedy made an impassioned plea to the Subcommittee.[7] 'While the new legal weapons Congress has already given us have been extraordinarily effective, as I indicated earlier, one major purpose in my appearing here is to seek the help of Congress in the form of additional legislation – the authority to provide immunity to witnesses in racketeering investigations; and reform and revision of the wire-tapping law.' The ability to gather intelligence was vital to the prosecution of senior Cosa Nostra figures. In Kennedy's words, 'Our principal problem is insulation. The kingpins of the rackets – our main targets – are often far removed from their illegal activities.'[8]

Valachi's and Kennedy's descriptions of the Cosa Nostra and its activities helped to frame public perceptions of organized crime and government responses for many decades, not just in the US but also across the English-speaking world. The need to combat the threat of highly organized, violent, wealthy, expansionist and sophisticated cartels became a staple of speeches by politicians and law enforcement agency leaders. And heightened awareness, tough enforcement and sanctions for organized crime bosses and new legal powers remained the primary tools for tackling the threat.

Subsequent developments appeared to prove the resilience and flexibility of organized criminality. *Time* magazine's cover story reported that the Mafia was still 'big, bad and booming' in 1977, but in the 1980s and 1990s biker gangs, African-American groups and expansionist South American cartels also came to the fore. Law enforcement officials argued that this was partly because the Cosa Nostra increasingly 'outsourced' their dirty work, but also because a series of convictions had suppressed their power, leaving space for new criminal groups. Increased drug consumption in this period created vast incomes which were seen to spawn a proliferation of organized crime rings. By 2009, an FBI 'National Gang Threat Assessment' describes some 20,000 violent gangs operating in the US with nearly one million members. 'Many', the report says, 'are sophisticated and well organized; all use violence to control neighborhoods and boost their illegal money-making activities, which include robbery, drug and gun trafficking, fraud, extortion, and prostitution rings.' 'Criminal gangs commit as much as 80 per cent of the crime in many communities, according to law enforcement officials throughout the nation.'[9]

Globalization was thus believed to have provided new income streams and opportunities to evade law enforcement. President Clinton, in his 1996 address to the United Nations General Assembly, argued that organized crime groups could undermine national security and called for international co-operation to counter the threat posed by money laundering, narcotics trafficking and terrorism.[10] Barack Obama in 2011 was no less worried. 'Criminal networks', he explained, 'are not only expanding their operations, but they are also diversifying their activities, resulting in a convergence of transnational threats that has evolved to become more complex, volatile, and destabilizing.'[11]

Criminal groups also appeared to confirm Kennedy's fear that their ability to respond to new tactics would make them ever harder to pin down. In 2012 John Lawler, CEO of the Australian Crime Commission, argued that organized crime was in fact becoming 'the fifth estate – one that rivals . . . institutional authorities, as the most powerful estate of them all'.[12] 'We are seeing organized crime walking the halls of power in failing states. And in Australia, we are seeing organized crime increasingly hiding clandestine activities through legitimate business enterprises.'

It should be no surprise, then, that today international organizations, increasingly active in the fight against organized crime globally, talk of a worrying threat. Shortly after being established in 1997, the United Nations Office on Drugs and Crime estimated that drugs markets alone account for 8 per cent of total international trade and it now rates transnational organized crime as a 'US$870 billion a year business'.[13]

Bobby Kennedy's predictions that organized crime would adapt to environmental change seem at first glance to have been confirmed, and his three-step approach to fighting organized crime has become the new standard. Politicians continue to increase public awareness of the threats we face, ably helped by journalists' voracious appetite for stories of alarming criminal sophistication.

Governments also continue to centralize policing. New FBI-style operations are springing up across the world – the UK National Crime Agency (2013) being the most recent example – and international crime-fighting bodies such as Europol, Interpol and the Financial Action Task Force, which was set up in 1989, are growing in size and scope.

And legislation to enable the disruption of organized crime groups and ever-tougher penalties for them continues to flow. Many new laws are based on the approach of the 1970 US Racketeer Influenced and Corrupt Organizations (RICO) Act. This was designed specifically to tackle the Cosa Nostra threat and aimed to criminalize membership of and association with crime groups; to make sentences tougher; and to create new ways of seizing criminal assets: for example, by allowing civil actions which could penalize crime groups 'on the balance of probabilities' rather than 'beyond reasonable doubt'.* Politicians across developed countries continue to advocate mandatory minimum sentences, particularly for drug trafficking, and to target the 'proceeds of crime'.† The fight against crime is also

---

* RICO allowed the government to charge members of any 'enterprise' linked to two or more serious crimes with racketeering, even if members of the enterprise could not be directly connected to the crimes in question. There are currently over thirty named offences that could lead to a charge under RICO. They range from murder, kidnapping, extortion and arson through to illegal gambling, obstruction of justice, embezzlement and securities fraud. And it created tough sentences for racketeering. Courts could imprison members of criminal enterprises for up to twenty years and impose fines of up to $25,000. RICO also allowed citizens to file civil suits if they believed they had been harmed by racketeering enterprises. Organized crime figures could therefore be punished financially when juries believed them guilty. Plaintiffs could receive 'treble damages', or three times the harm caused by the racketeers.
† And across the English-speaking world penalties for organized criminals have increased. In 1997 the UK put in place a seven-year minimum sentence for third drug-trafficking offences while similar mandatory sentences for organized-

increasingly international. In the 2000s the US government was spending hundreds of millions of dollars each year on Plan Colombia, a programme focused on stabilizing Colombia, reducing its dependence on coca cultivation and disrupting the drug supply.[14]

These approaches clearly accord with the Heroes and Villains view of crime, which calls for us to pull out all the stops against shadowy but powerful forces. And they have had a major impact. They have led to vast quantities of taxpayers' money being spent, both on enforcement operations and on housing prisoners for far longer periods. In the US alone, the number of prisoners being held for drug-related offences rose from 41,000 in 1980 to a staggering 507,000 in 2010. Regulation has also changed the way that companies do business, with tighter financial accountability requirements than ever before. And countries now even interrelate in new ways. The Financial Action Task Force, for example, regularly names and shames 'high-risk and non-co-operative jurisdictions' in order to reduce their appeal to investors and to spur diplomatic negotiations.

But all this leads to obvious questions. Is organized crime really big, bad and booming? Is it really the case that large, sophisticated and hierarchical organized crime groups have come to run lucrative illegal trades with virtual impunity? And how helpful have governmental responses to this diagnosis really been?

THE BUSINESS OF CRIME

When he signed up for his Ph.D. in Economics at Yale, Peter Reuter hadn't decided which areas he would specialize in. He had already taught Economics at the University of New South Wales and had developed a range of problem-solving skills and an enquiring mind, but had no idea that his life would be dedicated to understanding the murky world of illegal gambling, drugs and organized crime.

It was gambling that got him hooked, Reuter explains, as he talks

---

crime-related offences were also introduced in Canada (recently reinforced under Prime Minister Stephen Harper's Omnibus Crime Bill) and Australia (most recently for people-trafficking).

to me while driving from his home to the campus of the University of Maryland, where he is now a professor.[15] After starting his Ph.D. he was asked to help a historian friend with research into illegal gambling, and shortly after that he began work on a project commissioned by the research arm of the US Justice Department. It was an exciting assignment. As the FBI was targeting Mafia leaders in the mid-1970s, Reuter would be looking in detail at the illegal industries the Cosa Nostra were believed to control – numbers games,* bookmaking and the loan-sharking business – in the heartland of their operation, New York City. 'I found myself intrigued,' Reuter comments.

It was not just the topic that was appealing. Reuter was excited – and somewhat surprised – by what his work gradually revealed. Government reports and film dramatizations all suggested that illegal businesses were essentially dominated by organized crime groups which eliminated competition through violence and corruption. These organizations were thought to be large and hierarchical, with orders cascading down various layers of management, and numerous street-level employees. Reuter, however, found 'numerous, relatively small, often ephemeral, enterprises', frequently involving just a few individuals. In all three sectors – loan-sharking, bookmaking and illegal numbers games – there was no evidence of a Cosa Nostra monopoly, or for that matter of any criminal organizations carving up geographical areas of total control.[16] Almost anyone with access to customers, a few contacts and the essentials of the trade (for example, the capital needed to run an illegal lottery) could set up in business. And Reuter found that they could usually do so without facing threats of violence.

Instead of geographical monopolies, Reuter found vigorous competition. Plenty of people were making money out of their involvement in illegal trades but the profits were rarely spectacular, as indicated by the fact that many of them had other jobs. Prices were competitive and attempts to exert control over these illegal trades usually failed. For example, one effort at price fixing in the sports bookmaking

---

* 'Numbers games' or 'numbers rackets' are the terms most commonly used to describe illegal lotteries, where results are often tied to published figures, such as the last three digits of the amount racetrack bettors placed at a particular racetrack.

business was an abysmal failure, with those involved exerting great efforts but finding themselves unable to identify and coerce either the wide range of bookmakers or their numerous customers.[17]

The Cosa Nostra appeared in Reuter's study but their role was distinctive and, once again, it was very far from what the Valachi hearings might have led one to expect. 'The Mafia was involved in gambling,' Reuter explains, 'but it wasn't so much in the provision of gambling services. Sure, there was some of that – but they were more involved in dispute settlement. They offered to act as a guarantor for bookmakers who might deal with bettors who intended to cheat them,' in effect becoming the enforcers of contracts which couldn't be secured through usual legal channels.

These surprising findings prompted Reuter to investigate whether the pattern he saw held true in other illegal markets – and, in particular, whether the booming trade in illegal drugs operated on similar principles. What he found challenges the idea that all-powerful crime groups control entire illegal trades. 'What I'm struck by,' Reuter explains, 'is how small are the firms in illegal markets, and that is a real *structural consequence* of product illegality . . . your principal cost – at least if there's any enforcement – is the cost of risk associated with the activity. And if you make the firm larger, then the number of people that can inform against you goes up. So you want to keep it pretty small. Drug organizations are almost always quite small.'

Reuter is now in full swing. He is approaching Maryland campus and hurrying to get thirty years of research findings across in just a few minutes. 'Another consequence of product illegality,' he continues, 'is [that] information is fairly poorly distributed. You can't advertise. You can't have product protection. So every market [meaning each area of the US] has heroin that is labelled 777 because they are lucky numbers but there is no information that the 777 in Detroit is the same as in San Francisco because there's no way you can protect the brand. Being big is very useful for a coffee company – brands are protected, brand recognition is valuable and there are big economies of scale in advertising. But these benefits just aren't there in drug markets. What's more, it's very difficult to control the staff. In this shady world, people trust individuals and not brands and, assuming they can access the means of doing business (for example, wholesale drugs), then middlemen usually get little benefit from being part of a large operation. Mid-level operators can easily go it alone.'

Reuter races on to explain other reasons why illegal trades work differently. 'Not a lot of highly educated people want to work in illegal markets and they're commonly associated with violence so people with a higher tolerance for that [violence] . . . are more likely to be there. That's not to say that . . . all illegal markets are highly associated with violence . . . but you have to take into account the threat of violence when deciding whether to do this.'

Organizational skills certainly don't come naturally to many working in illegal trades. Reuter describes a conversation with a detective who had spent a year undercover working in a numbers operation and had risen to being the right hand of Jimmy Mac, a well-known crime figure, in just twelve months.

'After a while,' Reuter recounts, 'I said [to the detective]: "How do you make sense of this? I mean here's a system which ultimately depends on trust. You're a stranger and yet you make this meteoric rise."

' "Remember," the detective said, "this is a world in which the capacity to turn up in a specified place at a specified time makes you a star performer." '

This pithy anecdote is worth remembering when estimating the organization and sophistication of drug 'kingpins'. Numerous cases show that it is certainly easier to become a 'major player' than one might think. Reuter cites the case of one of the biggest heroin dealers in Los Angeles, who just twelve months before had been selling $20 packets of the drug by hand. Chance encounters can transform the scale and nature of an operation, because knowing someone who can buy significant quantities of drugs and someone who can provide them to you immediately makes you a major player.

It helps, of course, if you can trust the people you're dealing with – a reality which explains not only the small scale of criminal groupings but why it's so common to find that certain ethnic groups are disproportionately represented in particular illegal trades. Turks and

Albanians play an important role in UK heroin importation, for example, but this is not because they are particularly 'sophisticated' or part of a single Mafia-style organization; it's because Turkish and Albanian immigrants who are willing to sell drugs can quite easily make contacts with relatives and friends who live in places where drugs are grown or readily available. The limited contact between law-abiding would-be informants in immigrant communities and the police and other public service providers can also minimize the likelihood of detection.

This world of chance encounters and connections is in stark contrast with the traditional view of criminal 'recruitment', which suggests that criminal organizations hire outsiders who start off doing the 'dirty jobs' before rising up a criminal hierarchy.*[18] And we can see how misleading it is to conflate the concept of illegal markets with that of large, sophisticated criminal groups. For Reuter the terms 'illegal market' and 'organized crime' are – and should be – entirely distinct. After all, he has shown that thriving illegal markets can – and usually do – happily exist without large, sophisticated organized crime groups. In many respects, illegal trades are inimical to hierarchical structures. In almost every illegal trade that Reuter has examined it is a distinct disadvantage to be big, tricky to find good enough workers for even small-scale operations to last long, and almost impossible to gain monopoly positions, largely because transient customers and goods make it easy to move outside the monopoly for cheaper or better wares. Bigger is better only where there is widespread corruption or state collusion that allows criminals to operate entirely unchecked. Reuter highlights as a good example the case of Miami's bookmaking business in the 1940s and 1950s, when the police force effectively controlled illegal industries and recruited

---

* As Edward Kleemans, a Dutch professor and organized crime specialist, writes: 'People get in touch with organized crime through their social relations; over time their dependency on the resources of other people (such as money, knowledge and contacts) gradually declines; finally they generate new criminal associations, which subsequently attract people from their social environment again. In our view this "snowball effect" better characterises the development of the analysed cases than the traditional view of "recruitment".'

Mafiosi to collect rents on them. In normal circumstances, however, small is beautiful – or at least necessary.

Reuter's analysis has given us a new understanding of illegal markets and the role of organized crime groups within them. And the dynamics he has discovered recur in the findings of other experts examining illegal industries across the world. Chinese people-trafficking, Albanian heroin distribution and US marijuana trades have all been shown to share similar characteristics.[19] Yet for some reason, the fact that illegal markets are not dominated by large, hierarchical groups, that violence is not pervasive and that it is easy to become a drug dealer rarely breaks through into mainstream discourse.

THE CRIMES OF BUSINESS

David Sweanor is Adjunct Professor at the University of Ottawa's Faculty of Law and almost none of the things that you would associate with that. He spends a lot of time outdoors cycling, enjoys bench-pressing competitions with his son and has a way of talking that is very far removed from the language of the courtroom. He has spent as much of his life campaigning as being studiedly impartial, mainly with the goal of reducing the harms of tobacco consumption. And he is a man who likes stories and attracts the private confidences that generate them.

Professor Sweanor sits with me in a spacious office at the Institute for Government and describes his process for discovering dirty secrets.

'I did some work with some former CIA and DEA guys and the CIA guys were terrific. They'd say, "You've probably heard the things the CIA can do. You know, we can be listening through your window from a block away and know what you're saying. We can follow your car with you having no idea that it's happening" – and, you know, all the kinda hi-tech stuff. And that's all true. But, you know, the single most effective way of getting information is to drink with somebody in a bar.'

Sweanor continues: 'You need to find two points of contact, two points of connection with somebody. So I might say, "Oh Tom, you're interested in crime too. That's one of my areas of great interest." And then, you know, find something else like some sport that we both enjoy. We've now got two points of contact. So then you just have something to drink, be friendly and everybody wants to tell you their story . . . even people who really shouldn't.'[20]

One day, Sweanor was sitting with a tobacco executive in a bar. The executive knew that Sweanor was an active anti-smoking activist, but it was not long before he was revealing the finer details of an illegal venture sponsored by his own company. The trigger for the enterprise was the company's growing frustration that they were losing out on market share: not in the legal market for cigarettes but in the growing black market of smuggled cigarettes. Those people who didn't want to pay full price were buying smuggled brands – and not the company's brand.

At first, selling into the illegal market was a relatively straightforward business. The company had found a local gangster who was willing to buy a cargo of untaxed cigarettes (officially for export outside the UK) and then divert them into the UK black market. The first shipment was a success. But problems arose at the point of re-negotiation. As Sweanor's drinking partner explained: 'You're used to somebody coming in and trying to knock you down on price . . . You're not used to someone coming in and telling you they know what route your daughter takes to school and you don't want anything bad to happen to her.' As Sweanor puts it, 'The company was using business logic but this was a whole different way of thinking.' It prompted the company to get out of the arrangement, realizing that dealing directly with gangsters was perhaps not the best route to a smooth and profitable partnership.

Yet Sweanor can provide dozens of other examples of big tobacco companies sponsoring black-market trade. Usually they maintained a degree of distance from those actually smuggling the cigarettes, and in doing so they successfully created a booming international black market which generated phenomenal levels of profit.

Sweanor spotted it first in Canada. In the early 1990s he was working as counsel for the Non-Smokers' Rights Association, campaigning for tax increases to reduce tobacco consumption and improve public health. The tobacco companies he was up against put forward an array of counter-arguments, including the point that higher taxes would almost certainly increase black market sales. Sweanor said it was scaremongering – yet, as he and others won the argument and taxes rose, so too did illegal sales.

Sweanor had been wrong. A trickle of cheap, smuggled cigarettes soon became a steady flow. Sweanor was asked to document what was happening. The first thing he found was that the cigarettes flowing into Canada were all Canadian brands and were almost all coming into the country from the US. But the strange thing was what was happening to Canadian exports to the United States. This is odd because Americans don't generally like Canadian brands, mainly because they have a different taste but also due to brand loyalty. As taxes in Canada rose, however, Americans appeared to develop an appetite for Canadian exports. As Sweanor explains, 'We got to a point where somewhere around a third of cigarettes produced in Canada in 1993 were being exported to the US, where there was virtually no market for Canadian cigarettes.'

What Sweanor was looking at was widespread tobacco smuggling. Major Canadian brands were exporting cigarettes to US subsidiaries, who were selling to wholesalers and distributors, who would then either smuggle them back across the US–Canadian border or sell them to people who would. The Canadian companies were shipping vast quantities of cigarettes to the US, apparently legally, but with full knowledge that they would somehow find their way back across the border.

The smuggling was straightforward due to a bizarre and politically problematic vacuum in Canadian–US border control. Akwesasne, a First Nations reserve, straddles the border. Tobacco could enter the south (US) side of Akwesasne and not have left the States. And then it would leave the north end of the reserve and be in Canada. 'Those people were engaged in the smuggling and they would say, "No, we are a First Nations community and we can move stuff across our land if we want to. And if it then ends up on trucks going to Montreal or Toronto that's not our problem."' As Sweanor explains, 'Up to a certain point it's legitimate until you get into the idea of conspiracy. Everybody ultimately knew what was going to happen.'

There can be little doubt that Canadian tobacco companies were being at least wilfully blind to the fact that they were facilitating smuggling activity. At one point one reservation was receiving 5 billion cigarettes a year, enough for the 2,800 Native Americans living on it to smoke nearly 5,000 cigarettes per day.

Blindness affected not just Canadian companies but tobacco companies across the world. Legal action by the Canadian authorities and others has now forced companies to disclose a range of documents. And, in a misguided attempt to swamp prosecutors with an unmanageable quantity of material, a number of tobacco companies provided investigators and journalists with an array of incriminating evidence.

British American Tobacco (BAT) documents now stored in Guildford, UK, show that senior executives repeatedly used special euphemisms for contraband – in particular the terms 'duty not paid' and 'general trade'. The terms crop up time and again. When foreign tobacco companies were still excluded from Vietnam in the early 1990s, for example, BAT's marketing department nonetheless carried out analyses of their prospects in the Vietnamese 'general trade' segment. Working with a regional distribution partner, Singapura United Tobacco Limited, meant that BAT effectively had a route to the market. 'SUTL,' they wrote, 'with its strong networks of customers in [neighbouring] Cambodia have been able to capitalise on the demand of the Vietnamese customer despite the ban.'[21]

BAT stresses, naturally enough, that it has never been directly involved in smuggling nor actively facilitated it, but it is impossible not to question this when reading certain documentation. What's more, dubious strategies by BAT and other tobacco majors abound. Alarmingly, a range of tobacco companies spent significant sums on local advertising campaigns in countries where their cigarettes were not legally sold. To circumvent advertising restrictions in closed markets, companies used their branding on non-tobacco products, including clothing.

Tobacco companies presented these practices as an attempt to build brand awareness prior to being legally permitted to enter the country. But the approach was partly a more straightforward way of increasing sales and profits. As a former BAT Finance Director, Keith Dunt, put it, ' "Duty not paid" is part of your market and to have it exploited by others is just not acceptable.'[22]

The approach was also a means of influencing public policy. As Sweanor explains, 'Companies could use contraband as a way of opening a market – getting cigarettes into a country which was not open to their brand being sold and then saying, "Look. You really should allow us to come in and build a factory and create some local jobs ... and then get the tax revenue."' Intriguingly, several studies have even suggested that illegal cigarettes have been used to influence tax policy. By pointing to the illegal trade, companies were able to make the argument that tax increases would simply lead to more smuggling, and on several occasions, including in Canada, illegal trade has spiked in the run-up to and immediately after tax changes.[23]

Companies distanced themselves from direct criminality through the use of subsidiaries and distributors, but it is hard to disagree with Sweanor's assessment. 'I don't think the companies were even that cautious. It just seemed part of doing business: this is another way to channel product. Until of course the walls came down once they started facing serious threats, they had to figure out what to do, which in many cases was blame someone else.'

The archetypal fall guy was Les Thompson, a salesman in R. J. Reynolds's Canadian office who was moved to their North Carolina headquarters in Winston-Salem in 1992 in order to set up a subsidiary called Northern Brands International. The subsidiary was a roaring success, making millions of dollars almost exclusively by selling cigarettes to distributors who were channelling untaxed cigarettes back across the US–Canadian border.

As the trade across the border came under increasing scrutiny, however, so did Northern Brands and Thompson. Investigations and prosecutions followed – but the brunt of the blame fell on Thompson. Northern Brands paid a $15m fine, a fraction of the operation's estimated profits, while Thompson, encouraged by his R. J. Reynolds-appointed lawyers to sign a statement, was sentenced to nearly six years in prison.[24] R. J. Reynolds, the holding company, agreed to take steps to avoid similar actions in future.[25]

Sweanor was – and remains – incredulous. 'I was looking at this and saying, if he's a lone rogue he's got to be one of the greatest criminal minds in history as well as being superman because it meant he was responsible for over 40 per cent of the sales of those companies and no one noticed; he was entering into binding legal contracts ... selling to new distributors that have to have been vetted by their lawyers and Les isn't a lawyer and nobody noticed that and the equipment got from Montreal to Puerto Rico ... and then with all the tens of millions of dollars he put it all into the companies' bank accounts and the companies didn't notice. And he did all this from the Headquarters of Northern Brands that just happened to be located in the R. J. Reynolds North Carolina head office.'

Thompson himself now testifies to the role of R. J. Reynolds in supporting the operation. 'A lawyer on the company's board tells me in a meeting in my vice-president's office that "This is a legal business. It's a loophole. Nobody likes it but we've got to be there." '[26] 'We were told to keep no paperwork in this business,' Thompson says. 'I've been charged with money laundering $72 million, I don't have $72 million. I'm going to be paying a $100,000 fine very shortly at my sentencing. I am cashing in my pension in the United States to pay that fine. R. J. Reynolds has that money. I do not have that money.'[27]

Sweanor and others did not give up the chase, however. In 2008 Canada's largest cigarette manufacturers all pleaded guilty to aiding and abetting tobacco smuggling and agreed to pay over C$1bn for defrauding the Canadian government of unpaid taxes. In 2010, R. J. Reynolds paid C$325m and Northern Brands a further C$75m.[28] Meanwhile, Philip Morris International and Japan Tobacco International agreed to pay a combined C$1.65bn in the largest settlement to date.[29]

Sweanor says the money is less important than the undertakings companies took to prevent further smuggling. 'The agreement included undertakings as to what the companies would do to prevent further smuggling: so how they would be monitoring the product, how they would be responsible [and fined] if their product showed up illicitly in a country. And that had been the policy goal from the beginning in the work that I was doing. The companies can be your biggest enemy if they think that there's a profit to be made from engaging in facilitating contraband. If they can only lose from contraband, they're excluded from the market so that anyone selling illicit cigarettes is taking revenue away from them, they go from being your worst enemy to being your best friend because their vested interests have now entirely changed.'

Progress was rapid. From its peak in 2000–2001, illicit trade has fallen dramatically, with Her Majesty's Revenue and Customs estimating that the UK illegal market has shrunk by more than 50 per cent.[30] Of course, some ground is harder for the companies to recover. As Sweanor explains, 'The companies created the market for the contraband product . . . and now they've cut off the pipeline and others are stepping in to meet the demand that's been created for cheap cigarettes . . . The supply lines are established and then someone else steps in to fill them.' Proving this, many Native American reserves straddling the US–Canadian border now have their own small plants and operations and increasingly illegal brands (rather than brands being sold illegally) are coming to the fore.

The case of cigarette smuggling undermines the idea that 'organized crime' is somehow always an external threat, resulting from what Kennedy and many others describe as criminal groups 'boring into the legitimate economy'. In reality, we can see that threats from within the 'legitimate' sphere can be as much of a problem. Frustrated in their commercial ambitions, tobacco companies have effectively promoted criminal activity and recruited criminals to achieve their ends. And their effectiveness has been greatly increased by the sophistication of their business practices and the high skill levels of those facilitating the illegal trade: complex pricing strategies, underhand marketing tactics and political influencing strategies were all at play.

Tobacco is not of course an isolated case. Italian-American crime groups grew in power in the US in the early to mid-twentieth century at the time of prohibition. Then, overseas alcohol producers without buyers again forged alliances to distribute their products, and the perceived 'harmlessness' of alcohol allowed several police forces to maintain relatively clear consciences as they regularly ignored the illegal trade in return for payments. Illegal gambling flourished due to a similar dynamic, with several corrupt police forces effectively taxing the illegal trade, and hiring the most reliable shady characters they could find to collect on debts.[31]

Today, companies are regularly tempted to do business with dubious operators in order to trade in new markets. The Swedish researcher Nils Bagelius looked at thirteen Swedish companies venturing into Baltic countries and Russia in the 1990s. Eight used local 'wise guys' to negotiate deals and the other five used police and security services.[32] Such grey areas lead to complex ethical questions, but they certainly challenge the idea that organized criminal groups are somehow neatly separate from 'legitimate society'.

Often, industries that are perceived as being controlled by organized crime groups are in fact more generally characterized by corrupt and harmful practices. As the Italian Commissione Parlamentare d'Inchiesta, looking at the involvement of the Italian Mafia in waste management, pointed out in 2000, 'It would be a serious mistake to relate all illicit activities in the waste disposal industry to the so-called "ecomafia", as the data gathered by the Commission in its hearings clearly demonstrates. There are, in fact, companies not related with organized crime that however seem to found all their activities on an incorrect management of waste.'[33]

The concept of a distinct 'underworld' is reinforced by notions of a criminal career ladder, but it is worth reiterating that even major crime figures have rarely worked their way up 'criminal hierarchies'. Not only can success come quickly, but it can come with little prior criminal involvement. Some of the biggest cocaine imports to Italy in the late 1990s were organized by a former bank manager from Naples who had no Mafia involvement.[34] Similarly, those who facilitate illegal activity, including underground bankers and money exchangers, often also provide legal services. And investigations show time and again that the most sophisticated 'organized crime' operations benefit from corrupt or negligent business practice.[35]

Ambiguity even exists within the role of the state itself. Many Western foreign policy interventions have supported individuals and administrations with clear links to illegal trades, as was the case when the US assisted Manuel Noriega to rise to power in Panama, despite knowing that he was a major cocaine distributor. And similar ambiguity is found in the role of citizens. The illegal markets that we are told are run by 'organized crime' are ultimately supported by the wilful blindness of citizens. Many of us are extremely relaxed about smoking an untaxed cigarette and taking drugs, ignoring the illegality of both.

CRIMINAL ESTIMATES

As well as misrepresenting the nature of the organized crime threat, media, political and law enforcers' accounts often exaggerate the scale of the problem. Many in these groups believe that bigger is better. After all, impressive drug seizures and evidence of large criminal organizations make money for media groups; they justify police expenditure; and they provide greater justification for policy changes, ranging from tougher sentences on the one hand to legalization of prostitution and drug distribution on the other.

Time and again, however, the figures quoted in reports fall apart once examined closely. Take, for example, this recent headline from the Canadian Broadcasting News: 'Canadian Naval Bust Worth $150m happened peacefully.' Or this one from the *Daily Mail*: 'Now even drug barons are going green as police raid solar-powered cannabis factory growing £500,000 worth of plants.'[36] Both reports imply that dealers become extraordinarily wealthy from their trade. But the reality is that even the leaders of these operations would never be paid anything like those amounts for the drugs they sold. The vast majority of drug seizure estimates are inflated by the use of a slippery little concept known as 'street value'. Street value is calculated by taking the price a user would pay for the drug in the country of seizure and then multiplying it by the total weight seized. If the average punter can buy cocaine in the US at $100 per gram, then a seizure of 10 kilos (which would easily fit in a rucksack) quickly becomes 'worth' $1,000,000. Police sometimes go a bit further too. The purity of drugs on the street is famously variable, so many estimates add on a bit extra to take that into account. An assumption of 50 per cent purity would mean doubling the estimated seizure value to $2m, for example.

This initially seems reasonable and obviously results in totals that sound impressive. But street values do not represent what the drugs will be sold for by those caught producing or transporting them. Drugs in producer countries are worth far less than in those where production is limited. And wholesale prices are far lower than retail prices. Even once drugs have arrived in their country of sale, there are often several intermediate layers as they are parcelled up into

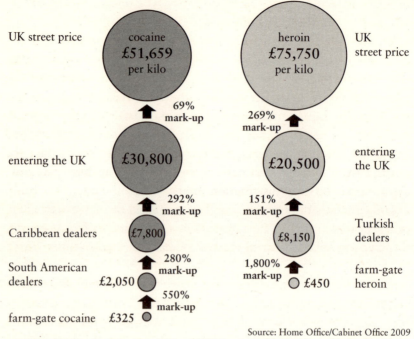

UK street price   cocaine £51,659 per kilo   heroin £75,750 per kilo   UK street price

69% mark-up   269% mark-up

entering the UK   £30,800   £20,500   entering the UK

292% mark-up   151% mark-up

Caribbean dealers   £7,800   £8,150   Turkish dealers

280% mark-up   1,800% mark-up

South American dealers   £2,050   £450   farm-gate heroin

550% mark-up

farm-gate cocaine   £325

Source: Home Office/Cabinet Office 2009
Note: Directional only, based on 2001 and 2007 data and analysis; purity assumptions not known

Fig. 10: Estimated drug values and mark-ups at various stages of the UK's cocaine (left) and heroin (right) supply chain[37]

ever-smaller packages and sold on, with each dealer taking a cut of the profits in return for their time and risks (see Fig. 10).

To state the obvious, the value of the drugs at each stage is, in fact, only the amount that someone would be willing to pay for them in their current condition and volume. In the case of the 'Canadian Naval Bust Worth $150m', the value of the seizure would actually be more like C$10m–20m.* This is undeniably a large sum, but it is still ten times less than the C$150m declared in the headline; and pretending that the value of the seizure is C$150m is the equivalent of seizing

* This estimate is based on approximated wholesale prices of C$26,000 per kilo (C$26,000 × 500 kg = C$13m), the 2005 estimated Canadian wholesale price per kilo from World Drug Report, 2006: http://www.unodc.org/pdf/WDR_2006/wdr2006_chap5_cocaine.pdf.

ground coffee and calculating its value based on the price you could get selling it as espressos in a coffee shop.

The actual value of the plants in the solar-powered cannabis factory would also be considerably less than the £500,000 stated. Not only have 'street prices' been used once again, but estimates involving whole cannabis plants often include the weight of stalks and seeds, which produce only minuscule amounts of cannabis's active ingredient, tetrahydrocannabinol, or THC. These examples of inflated valuations after drugs busts are not isolated: they are in fact the norm. Peter Reuter explains: 'We want to know how much this [any] seizure cost the drug-distribution industry, and the answer is probably a quarter of the retail [price].' Estimating the street value is 'a different concept and I don't think it's a relevant one'.[38] Of course, 'It's perfectly understandable why they do it . . . it makes them [those seizing drugs] look important.' [39]

Such systematic misrepresentation distorts public perception, suggesting organized drug production and distribution on a vast scale. But individual cases of misrepresentation can also have more immediate effects. Judges sometimes use similar calculations, for example, to tip the scales of justice and ensure that mandatory minimum sentences apply. Some of the worst abuses of this kind have now been curtailed – but until 1993, US courts could, for example, include the weight of the blotter paper on which LSD is usually sold when considering sentencing options. The Supreme Court had effectively ruled that someone possessing a tiny 0.005 gram of LSD (worth well under $100) could receive the mandatory thirty-year sentence for possessing 5.7 grams (including the blotter).[40]

In some cases, inflation has been written into law. As Richard Miller, a campaigner against drug prohibition, highlighted, US sentencing guidelines for cannabis specified a bizarre way of calculating the weights that would inform cannabis-related offences. Those guidelines read: 'In the case of an offence involving marihuana plants, if the offense involves (A) 50 or more marihuana plants, treat each plant as equivalent to 1KG of marihuana; (B) fewer than 100 plants, treat each plant as equivalent to 100G of marihuana. Provided, however, that if the actual weight of the marihuana is greater, use the actual weight of the marihuana.'[41]

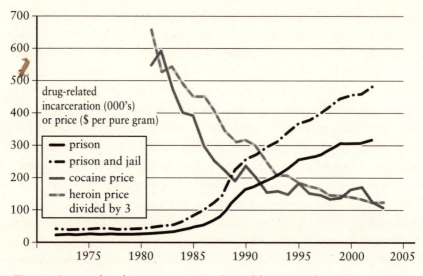

Fig. 11: Drug-related incarceration and retail heroin and cocaine prices in the US

In other words, judges were not to be guided by the actual quantity of drugs unless these were greater than the (inflated) rule-of-thumb estimates. This may be one reason why the war on drugs has had much more impact on prison numbers than it has on the availability (and therefore prices) of drugs. The graph in Fig. 11, which Reuter presented to a 2009 government inquiry on drugs, demonstrates that the retail prices of US heroin and cocaine have fallen roughly fivefold since 1980, whereas the numbers in prison for drug-related offences have *risen* fivefold.[42]

REAL-WORLD 'KINGPINS'

Estimates of criminal wealth can be equally misleading. Crime can be lucrative, particularly in comparison to a minimum-wage job. But criminals often collude with law enforcement, journalists and drama-tists to exaggerate their power and means.

Frank Lucas, the subject of the Hollywood blockbuster *American Gangster*, has been described as 'a wildly successful businessman.

His business just happened to be running one of America's biggest heroin empires.'[43] After moving to Harlem as a youth, Lucas claims to have worked for fifteen years as a driver to the well-known Harlem drug dealer Bumpy Johnson, before a 'takeover' of Johnson's 'drugs empire' when he died in 1968. Lucas describes how from that point he 'owned Harlem' and made $1m per day selling heroin there, sometimes disguised and sitting in his own nondescript car in order, he says, to supervise the operation more effectively.[44] The key to his success, Lucas argued, was that he managed to cut out the middleman. At a time when most dealers in Harlem were thought to be buying their drugs from Cosa Nostra figures, he claims to have created his own supply line – by setting up the infamous Cadaver Connection, the catchy name given by journalists to an audacious method of transporting heroin from Southeast Asia in the coffins of dead American servicemen.[45]

In a 2000 *New York Magazine* interview Lucas estimated that he once possessed 'something like $52 million', largely located in Cayman Islands banks. Added to this, he claimed to have 'maybe 1,000 keys [kilos] of dope on hand' and to own 'Frank Lucas's Paradise Valley', described as 'a several-thousand-acre spread back in North Carolina on which ranged 300 head of Black Angus cows, including a "big-balled" breeding bull worth $125,000'.[46]

The film *American Gangster* and the *New York Magazine* interview with Lucas on which it is largely based are so compelling that it feels churlish to check the facts – particularly as the story itself appeared to dispel the myth that African Americans were incapable of developing crime organizations as sophisticated as the Mafia.* Nonetheless, sense-checking leads to dozens of immediate questions. There seems little doubt that Lucas was a drug dealer who earned considerable sums of money for a brief period of time. But a freelance journalist and film producer, Ron Chepesiuk, has tried to get to the truth and has found more uncertainty than certainty: 'Frank Lucas, the self-styled American gangster, bragged that he was making a million dollars a day in Harlem in the early 1970s peddling smack. First of

---

* As one comment below an online documentary on Lucas reads, 'Anything whites can do blacks can do better. Blacks can do an'thing better than whites.'

all, can you imagine trying to haul away in a car $1 million a day in street money? Also, Lucas was on welfare when they published that *New Yorker* [*sic*] article that caught the attention of Hollywood. So what happened to that million bucks a day? I know for a fact from sources that Lucas was in constant trouble with La Cosa Nostra because he owed them money. Do you know how much a kilo of smack was selling for at the time? About $25,000 a kilo. Is that the kind of price that leads to a million dollars a day in drug-peddling profits?'[47]

Most of the information we have about Lucas comes from his own testimony – but reading his interview in full it is hard not to detect the distinct possibility that Lucas is more image-conscious fantasist than calm, calculating and ruthless entrepreneur. Certainly, the evidence clashes with the suave, Machiavellian figure Denzel Washington portrays. As Sterling Johnson, a New York judge, points out, 'Frank was illiterate, Frank was vicious, violent. Frank was everything Denzel Washington was not.'[48] 'Frank would do things on the spur of the moment. He was one with a temper.'[49]

Lucas's arrest and conviction record challenge the image of him as a particularly sophisticated criminal. The raid that brought Lucas's first major conviction revealed drugs and drug money all over his house, hardly a marker of a professional criminal enterprise. Contrary to the Hollywood version, Lucas actually only served five years of his initial sentence for drug trafficking, but a few years after his release he was rearrested and convicted of another drug offence, caught by a sting operation trying to exchange money and a small quantity of heroin for a kilo of cocaine. In December 2011, even after his Hollywood portrayal had secured him a source of fame and income, Lucas was charged with another crime – cashing in his son's benefit cheques.

Vast swathes of Lucas's story don't check out. It is, for example, not possible that he worked with Bumpy Johnson for fifteen years, given that Bumpy had only been out of prison for five years before his death. Bumpy's wife vehemently denies that Lucas was in any way her husband's protégé. Ike Atkinson, who Lucas claimed helped him transport heroin to the US from Thailand, denies that the Cadaver Connection ever existed.[50] Instead Atkinson, who was eventually convicted for leading a smuggling operation, argues that he transported drugs from

Bangkok to the US in cargo designated as furniture. And he accuses Lucas of inventing stories by embellishing bar room conversations he overheard when visiting Atkinson. Even ignoring evidence that Lucas was indebted, the claim that Lucas had $250m of assets is entirely unfeasible given that total US Federal asset seizures per year barely reached that amount.

Yet the minority who question the myth of Frank Lucas are rarely heard and still more rarely sought out. Why? Marc Jacobson, Frank Lucas's most famous biographer, provides a clue. After reporting Lucas's words as gospel for several pages in his now famous *New York Magazine* article, he wrote: 'But what did I think? . . . Frank was a conman, one of the best. He'd been telling white people, cops and everyone else, pretty much what they wanted to hear for decades, so why should I be different? It was true: I liked him. I liked the fuck out of him. Especially when he called his 90-year-old church-lady Hulk Hogan-fan mother, which he did about five times a day. But that wasn't the point.

'Braggart, trickster, and fibber along with everything else, Lucas was nonetheless a living, breathing historical figure, a highly specialized font of secret knowledge, more exotic, and certainly less picked over, than any Don Corleone. He was a whole season of the black *Sopranos* – old-school division. The idea that a backwoods boy could maneuver himself into position to tell at least a plausible lie about stashing 125 kilos of *zum dope* on Henry Kissinger's plane – much less actually do it – mitigated a multitude of sins.'[51]

Credit is due to Jacobson for at least nodding to his deliberate blindness, unlike many others who write in the genre of criminal biography. Chroniclers rarely let facts get in the way of a good story and those who engage in sceptical analysis seldom succeed commercially. Exceptions such as Robert Lacey's *Little Man: Meyer Lansky and the Gangster Life* are all too scarce.[52] Lansky's death in America in 1983 was front-page news and gave the nation an opportunity to re-rehearse the story that he was the Mafia's banker, who amassed a personal fortune of $300m and claimed, 'We're bigger than US Steel.' Lacey's study, however, reveals Lansky as an egotistical small-time crook and unsuccessful businessman who did not enjoy a happy life and died at liberty, leaving his crippled son living on welfare.

The absence of a criminal's wealth or convictions is never sufficient to persuade believers in stories of vast, sophisticated criminal organizations that criminal masterminds might not be that sophisticated – or that criminal. Indeed, most will follow Bobby Kennedy's logic that an absence of evidence is in fact a marker of criminal sophistication. As Kennedy put it, 'When we see that one of our subjects has become operational, we know he is no longer a kingpin.'[53] Such arguments are clever because they are circular – and therefore impossible to disprove. But once we shift the burden of proof onto those attempting to prove criminal sophistication and organization it becomes evident that many accounts of criminal conspiracy are highly speculative.

Facts are furiously interpreted to fit the dominant images of 'organized crime' spread by Hollywood. If a person suspected of being involved in crime knows someone else known to have committed a crime or suspected of it they become a 'criminal associate', making them therefore guilty by association; if someone is killed, we are told it is most likely an 'execution' in a 'business dispute'; if someone starts dealing drugs after someone else stops, we are told of a 'takeover' or 'inheritance' of business.

The extent of these contortions is remarkable. Take this extract from the Wikipedia entry on Vito Genovese, the Cosa Nostra member described as all-powerful by Joe Valachi: 'On August 24, 1964, Ernest Rupolo's body was recovered from Jamaica Bay, Queens . . . It was widely assumed that Genovese had ordered Rupolo's murder for testifying against him in the 1944 Boccia murder trial. Genovese had not ordered Rupolo killed immediately for turning on him, but instead forced him to live the last 20 years of his life in terror.'[54] These kinds of assumptions are not simply unverified, they are highly implausible – not least because they require us to believe that the best way to maintain a reputation as a brutal and all-powerful mobster is to wait around twenty years for vengeance. Yet the fiction is maintained because it fits with the received image of an all-powerful crime lord. And, once written, fiction can become fact, irrespective of the existence or credibility of sources.

A PROBLEM OF SCALE

Given the plethora of invention and exaggeration surrounding criminal activity, wealth and sophistication, it will be no surprise that evaluations of the scale, harm and costs of 'organized crime' overall are equally exaggerated for effect. Illegality clearly makes it practically impossible to generate robust estimates of how much money people make from criminal activity, and it is equally hard to calculate the harm done by organized crime and therefore its costs to society. Nonetheless, many estimates are made, presented with unjustifiable certainty, and are often both exaggerated and meaningless.

In 1997, the United Nations International Drug Control Progam published the first UN World Drugs Report stating: 'Many estimates have been made of the total revenue accruing to the illicit drug industry – most range from US$300 billion to US$500 billion. However, a growing body of evidence suggests that the true figure lies somewhere around US$400 billion. As demonstrated in Fig. 4.1, a US$400 billion turnover would be equivalent to approximately 8 per cent of total international trade.' The number was used for various purposes. The UN itself saw it as a reason for the creation of the UN Office on Drugs and Crime that year; law enforcement agencies across the world pointed to it as justification for increased funding; and in South America the number was even used by workers' rights activists to show what a tiny share of the money spent on drugs was going to producers.

Of course, the hastily estimated figure was not remotely credible. After criticism by a number of academics, the UN's Financial Action Task Force (FATF) finally hired Peter Reuter to check the estimate. His valuation, one of the most thorough to date, in fact put the value of the 2001 world drug market not at $400bn but at somewhere between $45bn and $280bn. The wide estimate reflects the significant amount of estimation required, but the FATF were not happy. As Reuter explains to me, 'They didn't publish it in the end. And there were two things. One was I pointed to the very high range you have to put around these estimates . . . [they wanted one number]. And, secondly, the figure I came up with was much lower than they wanted.'[55] Reuter's own calculations of the 'value' of illegal narcotics are arguably contentious – because, as Reuter himself points out, a high proportion of the market value comes from the very fact that drugs are illegal.[56] Drugs such as cannabis, cocaine and heroin are essentially simple agricultural products that are straightforward to grow and process, but because of the high risks attached to drug trafficking, import prices are vastly inflated. Colombian cocaine export prices were estimated at $1,050 per ton in 1997, whereas US import prices were $23,000: the mark-up is an amazing 2,190 per cent. Compare this to the average 12 per cent difference between export and import prices in taxed legal commodities such as coffee or sugar, and we see that the 'value' of the world drugs market would be dramatically lower were the commodities legal.* Indeed, depending on taxation and levels of demand, we might expect heroin or cocaine to cost little more than other processed agricultural products and the 'value' of world drug markets to fall accordingly.

Different but equally serious problems exist in the realm of 'money laundering'. What counts as money laundering is heavily dictated, after all, by government definitions. Many governments now count as money laundering the division of large bank deposits into smaller ones to avoid extra reporting requirements, irrespective of whether the money was gained illegally or whether the purpose of spreading it out is to avoid taxation.

Estimates of the total costs of organized crime are perhaps the most problematic, however. Again, they include all manner of sums that are not so much a measure of criminal activity as of our responses to it. For example, estimates are higher in the US than elsewhere, not because its problems are necessarily more serious but because the US tends to have far tougher sentences for drug possession and distribution – the expense of which often appear in estimates.† Policing spend, healthcare costs and all manner of other government policy choices are also frequently factored in. Estimates can also include rather slippery concepts such as

* Demand might increase somewhat if drugs were legalized, but it is hard to envisage any world in which it would rise by 2,000 per cent.
† Interestingly, this also means that US rehabilitation programmes appear to be more cost-effective than those in Europe. Any reduction in reoffending in the US will save more money because average sentences are longer.

'lost tax revenue'. This is odd enough for legal products that are being distributed for the black market, but for illegal activities it seems to imply that governments want drug dealers to pay more taxes, rather than stop dealing drugs.

What's more, estimates of the costs of organized crime ignore some offsetting benefits. Many illegal activities are a source of income for individuals and increase overall consumer spending. And because some criminals launder the proceeds of crime – passing it through legal channels – they will pay taxes on it. A reasonably high proportion of the income from some illegal businesses is in fact taxed. For example, a significant proportion of the sex trade is conducted from legal 'massage parlours' which accept cheques and credit cards.

Perhaps the grossest form of inflation derives from the way in which organized crime has come to be defined. In the 1960s the term was used reasonably tightly to refer to groups like the Cosa Nostra, and formal definitions tended to cover monopoly control, hierarchy and continuity.[57] But as the focus of law enforcement expanded to other areas, the definition has become increasingly vague, referring to more general concepts such as 'illicit enterprise', 'illegal activities' and, more recently, 'networks' causing 'harm'.[58] Today it is very easy to be caught in the 'organized crime' net. As the United Nations Office on Drugs and Crime explains:

The UNTOC [UN Convention on Transnational Organized Crime] does not contain a precise definition of 'transnational organized crime'. Nor does it list the kinds of crimes that might constitute it.

This lack of definition was intended to allow for a broader applicability of the Organized Crime Convention to new types of crime that emerge constantly as global, regional and local conditions change over time . . .

The Convention does contain a definition of 'organized criminal group'. In Article 2(a):
- a group of three or more persons that was not randomly formed;
- existing for a period of time;
- acting in concert with the aim of committing at least one crime punishable by at least four years' incarceration;
- in order to obtain, directly or indirectly, a financial or other material benefit.[59]

Even this classification, which clearly allows the scale of the 'organized crime' threat to balloon, was, oddly, insufficiently broad for some. UK policymakers and police like to include serious individual crimes, for example, into their estimates of costs and harm, further muddying a murky quagmire.

RESPONDING TO MYTHOLOGY

Loose definitions are not simply misleading. The spectre of a vague but vast threat has been used to justify ill-planned action which has generated considerable collateral damage.

The attempt to deter drug dealing and other involvement in illegal trades has led to lengthy (and costly) prison sentences, which many feel have become disproportionate. Most of those affected have not been violent organized crime lords because, as we've seen, illegal trades are often neither violent nor organized. People who want to fight 'organized crime' at all costs view someone trading small amounts of a drug as part of the organized crime threat and as morally repugnant as a violent gang leader. As the Royal Canadian Mounted Police put it: 'Before you've decided that pot is a pretty harmless drug compared to others, consider this: organized crime is involved in just about every aspect of marihuana production, trafficking and exporting due to its high profitability, profits that are then filtered into a litany of other crimes.'[60]

In reality, trades in illegal goods are problematic partly because they are morally ambiguous. Most drug trades, for example, are essentially consenting transactions which buyers and sellers enter into happily. This differs vastly from 'traditional' crime, which is not of mutual benefit because one person is simply appropriating something of value – cash, property or status – from another, usually by force.

Drug deals also differ from what we might term 'commercial crime', where the goods traded (such as tobacco) are legal, but the manner in which they are produced or distributed breaks state rules. The distinctions are important as there are gradations in morality with different types of offence. This is why some communities come to tolerate and occasionally support local drug dealers, in particular when they do not engage in community violence, offer (or more usually claim to offer) protection from 'traditional' crime or contribute to local community infrastructure. But the distinctions are also important because different types of crime have different harms and underlying dynamics. Surely they should face specific and appropriate penalties rather than be lumped into an 'organized crime' bucket for equal treatment?

Ironically, tough punishments have much more effect on highly informed and calculating rational agents like the multinational corporations who for decades effectively evaded sanctions for their involvement in cigarette smuggling. But players in fluid and fragmented trades in illegal goods are much less likely to respond to ever-tougher penalties, as we see in Myth 9. More importantly, the effective prosecution of those involved in illegal markets is dramatically diminished by the fact that newcomers quickly take their place to meet the demand. We forget this because we assume that they must invest significant time and have high levels of skill to attain the status of 'international drug lord' when in fact a few relationships suffice. And we can see that the vast number of drug arrests has had a limited impact by the fact that tougher penalties have not led to reduced availability of drugs, nor even the increases in drug prices one would expect if supply had been cut.

Because 'organized crime groups' of the kind targeted by ever-broader law enforcement definitions are so common, it is not clear whether the focus on 'organizations' and their leaders has been helpful. Arguably it was with Cosa Nostra, a rare example of a group that developed a standardized set of practices, a relatively strong hierarchy and some capacity to challenge state power in certain communities. But more generally the focus on 'groups' is harder to justify. In illegal trades most groupings are short-lived 'marriages of convenience' and the question 'Who did it?' is any case much less important in the context of a competitive market. Street gangs, meanwhile, have their own distinct dynamics and there remains a vigorous debate about whether treating a gang as a single entity deters membership or actually reinforces the sense of group identity. Certainly, some of the greatest successes in tackling gang crime have resulted from emphasizing to individual members that they have other, more productive, sources of identity.[61]

The win-at-all-costs approach to organized crime has had other perverse consequences. Civil liberties have been eroded as measures have been applied without due care. In certain hands, new legal powers can become tools to persecute groups whose lifestyle those with authority might disapprove of and associate with criminality. There is a difference between an organization which contains criminals and an organization that exists to commit crime, but when government officials are frustrated in their attempts to secure individual prosecutions, the group is usually the next target. This dynamic explains the numerous costly – and usually unsuccessful – attempts to pursue biker gangs such as the Hell's Angels Motorcycle Club under RICO and civil forfeiture laws.

Legislation is now frequently used for purposes for which it was never intended. RICO was designed to tackle a specific problem (the Cosa Nostra), but its powers increase punishment and lower burdens of proof and therefore make it attractive for other purposes. It is now regularly deployed in legal disputes between companies (notably, the Montreal Expos, a baseball team, recently filed charges against Major League Baseball). RICO is used to tackle corruption too, the Key West Police Department having been successfully prosecuted under RICO in 1984.

US asset seizure laws have now evolved to a stage where they can be applied whether or not there is any proof of illegal activity. One famous 1970s case saw the seizure of a US hire yacht by Puerto Rican officials when a small quantity of marijuana was found on board, even though the leasing company was 'in no way . . . involved in the criminal enterprise carried on by [the] lessee' and 'had no knowledge that its property was being used in connection with or in violation [of Puerto Rican law]'.[62] The seizure was, extraordinarily, upheld by the Supreme Court in the first of many such cases.

Pursuing 'facilitators' and 'proceeds' rather than profits compounded problems. Where minor drug dealers lacked cash (as they often do!), courts went after their possessions but, perhaps disappointed by their hauls, they dragged innocent civilians into the mix. Thousands of cars and homes used for drug transactions have been seized, whether belonging to dealers or not. A brilliant exposé by Sarah Stillman in *The New Yorker* highlights the case of an elderly couple, Mary and Leon Adams, whose house was nearly seized after an undercover officer tempted their son into selling small quantities of marijuana on their front porch.[63] Only the delay in their eviction necessitated by Leon's ill-health gave them the time they needed to seek legal advice and contest it. Others have not been as lucky. Stillman's investigation suggests that in Philadelphia alone hundreds of houses have been seized without being linked to an underlying conviction for a drug-trafficking offence.[64]

Police forces around the world can see that many US police departments are now running at a profit and they are actively lobbying for their governments to pursue a similar course. They argue that the collateral damage is worth it; they point to the vast threat of organized crime as evidence of the need for such powers and conveniently forget that both drug seizures and asset appropriation appear to have at best a limited impact on drug markets fuelled primarily by users' demands. Some types of appropriation do make a difference. In some areas, for example, street gangs use ownerless cars to avoid being linked to crimes, and it makes sense to impound these. The key point, however, is that judging what should be seized and how should not be left to a group of people who have strong professional and financial vested interests in appropriation.

No-holds-barred 'fights' against organized crime have also imposed regulatory burdens. Several experiments have proved so catastrophic they have quickly been reversed. In 1969, Operation Intercept saw the US subject every vehicle crossing the Mexican border to a three-minute inspection but was curtailed after two weeks when it was recognized that the delays were having a major impact on legal trade across the border. And it is noticeable that penalties can fall not on the groups most linked to illegal activity but on those without the power to protest effectively. There is no evidence, for example, that those countries named and shamed by the Financial Action Task Force as being 'havens' for money laundering have more illegally earned currency passing through their financial sectors than elsewhere – less, in fact, than that likely to be found in Western banks, according to the small amount of evidence there is. After all, it's in the West, with its higher consumer spending, that most illegal income is made, and the vast majority of criminals keep it either in ready cash, property or possessions or in local bank accounts.[65]

In other words, while some government action to target organized criminals has worked, much appears to be based on flawed theory with little supporting evidence. Only one of the standard approaches to tackling organized crime – centralizing law enforcement – appears to have had a truly positive impact by reducing local police corruption. Scrutinized by new national agencies, US police forces have become less inclined to facilitate criminal activity in return for a cut of the action, and criminals are far less likely to be tempted to corrupt local law enforcement personnel when they know it does not protect them from national agencies. Such successes show the importance of effective checks and balances on state power, and illustrate why an independent judiciary, government transparency and parliamentary and public accountability are so important. But they must not be heralded without considering the ineffectiveness of other measures, nor the serious collateral damage that ill-conceived government actions have inflicted on society.

FLASHBACK: FIRM FOUNDATIONS?

In 1966, Joe Valachi was found hanging by a rope in his prison cell. Only swift intervention from guards saved his life. His actions were in one sense difficult to understand: he had escaped the death penalty, was living in relative comfort and no longer feared mob reprisals.

In another sense, however, the attempted suicide was quite consistent with a pattern of behaviour that had developed early in Valachi's life. Valachi had not been dealt a kind hand and hadn't made much of the cards he got. Having exhibited behaviour at school that would most likely lead to the diagnosis of multiple behavioural disorders today, he battled with depression for much of his life. Those who knew him well noted he had a volatile temperament: he was inconsistent and prone to violent outbursts. During his interrogation by an FBI agent, James P. Flynn, in the run-up to the 1963 McClellan hearings, Valachi often became frustrated and aggressive – to the extent that the interviews had to be paused.[66]

Such behaviour alone might raise questions about Valachi's reliability as a witness. But descriptions of his interrogation process prompt further doubts. Valachi, under threat of a death sentence, was interrogated for three months, four days a week and for on average three hours a day. His testimony was cross-checked on an ongoing basis and he was cross-examined on any inconsistencies. The process may have had the best of intentions, but it is easy to see how a quest for evidence that fitted FBI expectations might have led to a gradual influence over Valachi's later testimony.

Selwyn Raab, author of *Five Families: The Rise, Decline, and Resurgence of America's Most Powerful Mafia Empires*, describes what happened, reserving great praise for the cleverness of Agent Flynn, Valachi's interrogator. 'He [Flynn] was tough,' Raab says. 'He told Valachi, "Listen either you tell us what we want to know or you're no value to us and there's no deal involved." ' 'Flynn bluffed Valachi,' Raab continues. 'He said, what, you know *we* know all about Cosa Nostra. Thinking the FBI had deeper knowledge than they actually did, Valachi began to talk.'[67]

Leading interview techniques are known for their power. People even confess to crimes they did not commit in order to escape the psychological trauma of aggressive interviews. In 2004, the Northwestern University School of Law Center on Wrongful Convictions found that sixteen of 111 US death row exonerations since 1973 related to convictions based on false confessions. Eleven per cent of Iceland's prisoners meanwhile say that they have once falsely confessed to a crime. Informant testimony, however, is still more problematic: where it will benefit them to a great extent, it should be used even more cautiously. Fifty-one of the 111 death row exonerations examined by Northwestern researchers were due to false informants' testimony, making it the number one reason for wrongful convictions.[68]

Unsurprisingly, the biggest problems seem to arise when interrogation is prolonged, interrogators hold strong preconceived views, and informants are either more suggestible (based on psychological tests) or have more to gain from their testimony.[69] Awareness of this is one reason why courts will quite regularly throw out certain types of evidence after calmer deliberation. Valachi's interrogation and hearings clearly meet all of these 'risk' criteria – and it is notable that Valachi was not once required to testify against Cosa Nostra colleagues in a court of law.

Of course, we cannot conclude that Valachi's testimony was false – and other evidential fragments contributed to the conclusions of the Subcommittee's 1963 hearings and subsequent policy decisions. But many are uncertain. Several experts point out that Valachi's testimony was never used in court and are quite clear that Valachi could not have known of the Mafia's operations beyond New York. As Robert Morgenthau, a former New York District Attorney, describes it, 'He was coached and he became an expert on organized crime in Detroit, Cleveland, Chicago, Las Vegas and so on – things he didn't know anything about.'[70]*

Yet Valachi's evidence and that of other Mafia informers is regularly taken at face value and, worse, it is extrapolated wildly. As Peter Reuter explained to me, 'I think the Mafia should be known as the exception and not the rule.'[71] But in many senses, decades of 'fighting' organized crime have been based heavily on the Mafia model. We have too often seen the adversary as fixed, large groups rather than fluid markets; too often overestimated the distinction between criminal and legitimate worlds; too often exaggerated the threat to justify disproportionate and counterproductive responses and to expand state power. It is hard not to conclude that the term 'organized crime' has become a blanket under which to hide a multitude of sins.

---

* Senate committees have been wrong before. The Permanent Subcommittee on Investigations of the Senate Government Operations Committee, which ran the Valachi hearings, was the very same committee (though with different members) that Senator Joe McCarthy had used a decade earlier to proclaim a degree of Communist infiltration of American life that is now largely recognized as fanciful. It is also worth noting that Senator McClellan was a participant in the hearings, but led a Democratic walkout in protest at Senator McCarthy's conduct.

Myth 5: Biology determines criminality

He is a man of good birth and excellent education, endowed by nature with a phenomenal mathematical faculty. At the age of twenty-one he wrote a treatise upon the Binomial Theorem ... and had, to all appearances, a most brilliant career before him. But the man had hereditary tendencies of the most diabolical kind. A criminal strain ran in his blood, which, instead of being modified, was increased and rendered infinitely more dangerous by his extraordinary mental powers.

Sherlock Holmes describes the infamous
Professor Moriarty[1]

I was born with the devil in me. I could not help the fact that I was a murderer, no more than the poet can help the inspiration to sing ... I was born with the evil one standing as my sponsor beside the bed where I was ushered into the world, and he has been with me since.

Dr H. H. Holmes, one of the most notorious mass murderers of the nineteenth century, confessing his crimes in 1896[2]

CRIMINAL MINDS

The Christmas period has always been a peak time for domestic violence in New York City. With people cooped up indoors on bitterly cold days, and often drinking heavily, family feuds resurface and friendly relationships slide into outright conflict. Cases of violence, even when they lead to death, are so commonplace that they usually merit just a brief mention in the small-print pages of *The New York Times*. So it was for a story found in the paper, dated 8 January 1991. Herbert Weinstein had been charged with killing his wife, Barbara, in their twelfth-floor Manhattan apartment. The case, police suggested, was simple. As Officer Werner of the NYPD reported, 'Apparently there was some kind of family dispute. She may have become unconscious and he then threw her out of the bedroom window.' Bloodstains on the floor of the East 72nd Street apartment appeared to seal Weinstein's fate.[3]

But there was something about the case that made it memorable: Herbert Weinstein's brain. More precisely, a cyst was growing in Weinstein's arachnoid membrane, which it was argued was dramatically affecting his brain functions. For the first time in US history, the judge in the case allowed defence attorneys to use brain scans in court – and the scans showed that Weinstein had abnormalities in his left frontal lobe, an area that neurologists believe is central to rational thought, planning and self-control.[4]

The Weinstein case was reminiscent of others. In 1966 Charles Whitman, an engineering student and former Marine, killed his wife and his mother before climbing the main tower in the University of Texas campus armed with hunting rifles, a semi-automatic carbine and a sawn-off shotgun. As he made his way to the twenty-ninth floor of the building, he killed a further three people. Once he had successfully barricaded himself on the observation deck, he shot dead ten more from a distance, before finally being halted by the accurate shooting of an Austin police officer. Friends simply couldn't understand what caused the recently married student to snap, but Whitman had formulated his own theory. His handwritten note from the day of the massacre note read: 'I wish an autopsy on me to be performed to see if there is a mental disorder.'[5] Suspecting nothing would be found, his instruction was carried out. And, to the investigators' surprise, the autopsy revealed a tumour which had been placing intense pressure on his amygdala, a part of the brain associated with anger and violent impulses.

Bobby Joe Long, the serial killer better known as the Classified Ad Rapist, raped fifty women and murdered at least nine between

1981 and 1984. In 1994, after he had spent nearly ten years on death row, Long's lawyers realized that the ruling in the Weinstein case might have opened a new way of enabling their client to escape the electric chair. The brain-imaging scans they submitted in court revealed that Long had suffered severe damage to several brain regions, in particular the amygdala – the same part of the brain that had been affected in the Whitman case.[6]

Such cases suggest there are links between our brains' structure and function and our risks of committing crime – an idea that dates back to at least the nineteenth century. It was then that a US physician, Dr John Harlow, chronicled the miraculous case of the railway foreman Phineas Gage, who survived a metal spike passing through his prefrontal cortex but showed 'animal propensities' and became 'fitful', 'irreverent' and 'impatient of restraint or advice when it conflicts with his desires'.[7]

By themselves, of course, these cases prove little. There are, after all, simply too few of them to prove a definite link between brain damage and criminality – and the connection could simply be coincidental. Alternatively, the cases might just reveal an extremely rare syndrome, for example – one affecting very few people and of little relevance when explaining crime in general.

Much has changed since the early 1990s, however. Intrigued by such cases, scientists and criminologists have embarked on a multitude of studies aimed at finding the biological roots of crime and antisocial behaviour. They have been assisted by rapid technological advance. Brain-scanning equipment developed in the latter half of the twentieth century has become more accurate, safe and cheap. By 2003, the human genome project had also successfully mapped our 20,000 genes to a high degree of accuracy – apparently providing a more precise way of testing biological causes of crime. Scientists are developing an increasingly sophisticated understanding of the functions that each gene relates to, and the costs of DNA testing are plummeting, enabling large criminological studies to examine genes as well as the environments in which people live.

News stories now suggest that we have either cracked or are close to cracking the question of how much biology influences crime. Each year the media reports on several new 'landmark' studies. In 2010 the

Daily Mail asked: 'Is a life of crime hereditary?', finishing the piece with the line 'New research suggests that criminal behaviour could be "all in the genes".'[8] In 2011 a story in *The New York Times* with the byline 'Genetic Basis for Crime' reported that 'A small cadre of experts is exploring how genes might heighten the risk of committing a crime and whether such a trait can be inherited.'[9] And in 2012 *Slate*, the widely read US online current affairs and culture magazine, asked 'Should We Screen Kids' Brains and Genes to ID Future Criminals?'[10] The article cited Professor Adrian Raine, a psychologist, who asked: 'if I could tell you, as a parent, that your child has a 75 per cent chance of becoming a criminal, wouldn't you want to know and maybe have the chance to do something about it? . . . We have to start having this conversation now . . . so we understand the risks and the benefits. It's easy to get on your moral high horse about stigma and civil liberties, but are you going to have blood on your hands in the future because you've blocked an approach that could lead to lives being saved?'[11]

Legal professionals have picked up on such reports as swiftly as they responded to the Weinstein ruling. Brain scans are now a standard form of evidence in death sentence cases in the US, but genetic evidence is also gaining ground. In March 2007 Abdelmalek Bayout, an Algerian migrant living in Italy, killed another migrant, a Colombian, Walter Felipe Novoa Perez, during a fight. According to Bayout's original testimony, Perez had taunted him for wearing kohl, an eye make-up worn by both men and (more commonly) women in North Africa, and Bayout had lost control. Bayout confessed and was duly sentenced to nine years in prison, but in 2009 Bayout's lawyers returned to court. They claimed that the initial sentence had been unfair. Their client, they argued, merited much greater leniency because he was simply incapable of staying calm in the face of extreme provocation. To support their case they presented brain scans, but also the results of genetic testing. The judge, Paulo Alessio Verni, appears to have been impressed. Drawing on this evidence, he docked a year from the defendant's sentence, concluding when summing up that Bayout's genetic make-up 'would make him particularly aggressive in stressful situations'.[12]

It matters that lawyers, newspaper columnists and researchers are increasingly convinced that biology plays an important role in determining criminality. A strong biological influence on crime suggests that those who espouse our Victims and Survivors view of crime and argue that social factors such as poverty drive crime rates are very likely to be wrong. Meanwhile, the Heroes and Villains approach would appear to be reinforced. The image of the criminal with strong innate drives is, after all, central to that world view and is used to justify a no-holds-barred approach to dealing with criminals.

The belief that there are strong biological influences on crime might change how we go about preventing crime too. In the past we've used the concept of inheritable criminality to justify approaches that most of us would feel extremely uncomfortable with today. In 1907 Indiana became the first of several US states to permit compulsory sterilization 'to prevent procreation of confirmed criminals, idiots, imbeciles, and rapists'.[13] But should we not at least be more open to incarcerating those with strong criminal tendencies for longer – and perhaps for life – to protect others? Alternatively, is there a more liberal response to a world where biological factors exert a strong influence on criminality? For example, could we use our new-found knowledge to identify those likely to commit crime and provide them with extra support to help them avoid violent and criminal lives?

It is also interesting to think about what this knowledge should mean for our attitudes to criminal responsibility. On the one hand, the belief that some people have strong criminal proclivities encourages a tough stance. But the reason why brain scans and genetic evidence are being submitted by defence lawyers is to raise questions about the degree to which individuals with inherent biological differences can really be held responsible for their actions. Might we in fact be less punitive as a society if we saw highly criminal people as biologically different?

CRIMINAL DESTINIES

It's worth looking in more detail at the research behind the headlines. And we must note that these are not crackpot studies. Professor Adrian Raine, the academic cited in *Slate* magazine, teaches at the

University of Pennsylvania and spent much of the 1990s at the University of Southern California, pioneering the use of brain-scanning technology in the study of criminal behaviour. The university provided Raine with an outstanding opportunity to test whether the cases that showed abnormal brain functioning in murderers were simply anomalies. The university was equipped with a range of brain-scanning technologies, including PET (Positron Emission Tomography) and SPECT (Single Photon Emission Computed Tomography). By measuring levels of blood flow, oxygen and glucose metabolism in the brain, PET and SPECT scans could show how the brain responded to different stimuli, highlighting where patterns of brain activity were unusual.

Moreover, the university was in California, home to more death row prisoners than any other US state.*[14] Prisoners usually have little incentive to take part in medical studies and there are ethical concerns about paying them for their involvement. Yet the judge's ruling in the 1991 Weinstein case had changed everything. By allowing brain-scan evidence in court and then appearing to take it into account in his sentencing, he had given hope to defence lawyers across the country and to California's death row prisoners hoping to have their sentences reduced to life imprisonment.

Forty-one death row murderers making insanity pleas, therefore, signed consent forms to take part in Raine's investigation, and initial safety concerns proved unfounded. As Raine describes it, 'Complete with shackles and guards, they trooped into the PET scanning facility, they looked formidable, intimidating, and ominous, but in reality were co-operative.'[15]

The experiment itself was straightforward. Subjects were injected with the required dose of the radioactive isotope and then asked to complete a basic test. Numbers from nought to nine appeared at random every second on the screen, and test subjects were simply asked to press a button each time a zero appeared. As Raine recounts, 'This goes on for 32 minutes and, believe me, it is a very boring task. It

---

* California seems rather reluctant to execute these inmates. There were only thirteen executions in California between 1976 and 2010, compared to 460 in Texas and 107 in Virginia.

requires the subject to maintain focused attention and mental vigilance for a sustained period.'[16] Yet there was no reaction against the tedium. On completing the test, prisoners proceeded calmly to the PET scanner, still accompanied by guards, where the machine measured which areas of the brain had been most active during the test. Forty-one non-murderers, matched with the murderers in age and sex, repeated the procedures – though without the shackles.

The results were fascinating. Both murderers and non-murderers performed equally well in the test, but in terms of levels of brain activation their results were quite different. The main difference was that murderers generally had far lower levels of brain activity in the pre-frontal cortex area, the very same area responsible for planning, reasoning and problem solving that was shown to be defective in the Weinstein case. Low activity in this area tends to lead to problems with controlling emotional responses, particularly in extreme circumstances. Or, as Raine puts it, 'Reduced pre-frontal functioning can result in loss of control.'[17]

The death row murderers in Raine's sample were clearly a particular type of criminal. But they did suggest a pattern linking brain dysfunction to short fuses and extreme violence. And further investigations produced still more interesting findings. Those murderers who didn't have deficits in the areas of the brain responsible for self-control usually *did* have noticeable differences in other parts of the brain, in particular the amygdala, hippocampus and thalamus, areas that are associated with primitive human urges.

Intriguingly, different brain dysfunctions appeared to relate to different types of violence in Raine's study. Those whose murders were unplanned and involved a high degree of emotion (what FBI profilers called 'affective murderers') were much more likely to have problems in the areas of the brain associated with self-control. Killers characterized by FBI profilers as 'predatory murderers', who showed planning and control in their murders, were, perhaps unsurprisingly, far less likely to have problems in these parts of the brain.

Raine was also impressed by the possibility that these differences might not be due to accidents or disease: he found no correlation between differences in brain activity and history of head injury, medication or illegal drug use. This suggested to him that the risk factors for extreme violence might be present at birth, but he could not test this properly using his methods, not least because he did not have access to genetic records.

This was not the case for Professor Terrie Moffitt of King's College London and Duke University, one of the lead authors of the genetic study that so impressed the Italian judge, Paolo Alessio Verni. Moffitt trained as a clinical psychologist and spent her early career focusing on schizophrenia and antisocial personality disorder, but she has since increased her focus on crime and antisocial behaviour more generally.

Moffitt, often working with her husband, Avshalom Caspi, also a professor at Duke, has been quick to use new technologies in her research and in the late 1990s started to explore the possibility of testing biological influences on crime. Previous research looking at mice and humans had suggested that differences in levels of various neurotransmitters, such as dopamine, serotonin and noradrenaline, might be partly responsible for differing levels of antisocial behaviour; so Moffitt and Caspi focused their research on an enzyme (monoamine oxidase A, or MAO-A), which plays an important role in influencing levels of these neurotransmitters.* More specifically, they concentrated on the 'promoter' region of DNA responsible for transcribing one of the genes involved in determining MAO-A levels.

Moffitt and Caspi understood the technology needed to identify such differences and their relationship to different types of criminal behaviour. And crucially, like Raine, they also had access to the people who would submit to tests. For some years they had been involved with the Dunedin Study we discussed briefly in Myth 3, the vast research programme which was tracking the lives of over 1,000 people born in Dunedin, New Zealand, between 1 April 1972 and 31 March 1973. The people participating in the study were fully committed to it and also received financial support to take part, with those overseeing the project paying for those who had since left Dunedin to come back for various types of tests. Thanks to the explosion of interest in genetics, Moffitt and her fellow investigators easily secured the additional funding to test whether the genetic factors relating to MAO-A production did indeed relate to crime levels.[18]

* Noradrenaline is the UK term for what in the US is known as norepinephrine.

The team split male Dunedin Study participants into groups based on two factors: first, whether they had experienced childhood abuse (a known risk factor for crime), and second, whether their genetic tests indicated they had promoter DNA that was known to result in low levels of the MAO-A enzyme.[19] Their findings confirmed that those subjected to childhood abuse had higher rates of criminality and antisocial behaviour than those who had had abuse-free upbringings. But there were also significant differences between those abuse victims who had 'low promoter' patterns and those with 'high promoter' patterns. Fully 85 per cent of the male abuse victims with low promoter patterns showed routine antisocial behaviour compared to just 45 per cent of male abuse victims with high promoter patterns. Moffitt explains: 'These findings may . . . partly explain why not all victims of maltreatment grow up to victimize others – some genes may actually promote resistance to stress and trauma.'

UNCERTAIN TIES

Such studies taken together feel highly persuasive. But, reading through the detail, we start to notice that their authors provide caveats which go unreported in newspaper write-ups and press notices produced by university communications departments. Describing what his study showed about the links between brain activity and violent behaviour, for example, Professor Adrian Raine took time to emphasize that 'These data do not demonstrate that murderers pleading not guilty by reason of insanity are not responsible for their actions, nor do they demonstrate that PET [brain scans] can be used as a diagnostic technique'[20] – hardly represented by the headline 'Criminal Minds: Adrian Raine thinks brain scans can identify children who may become killers'.[21]

Professor Terrie Moffitt, meanwhile, says her conclusions regarding MAO-A gene expression are only 'suggestive' and emphasizes the importance of nurture in determining future behaviour. 'About half of children who are abused end up with some sort of mental disorder,' explains Moffitt, 'and about half don't. It is a strong environmental risk factor that everyone agrees is causative for children's mental health disorders, but we know there is variation in how children react to it.'[22] She worries too that her sample is not big enough to draw firmer conclusions and wonders why more studies haven't come forward to challenge her findings.

When I meet Professor Moffitt in a café in London, it quickly becomes clear that her greatest enthusiasm is her work examining what can be done to promote improved self-control in children through various interventions. And she never overstates her claims. She suspects there are strong biological influences on children's later behaviour, but does not by any means think this proves that criminal behaviour is genetically determined.[23]

Caution is certainly justified. For these studies don't prove conclusively that our criminal destinies are all in our genes. Media reports of Raine's study tended to emphasize that a high proportion of the violent murderers he examined had differences in certain brain regions. But these same reports failed to mention the fact that there are thousands of people walking this earth today with brain patterns very similar to those of Raine's violent murderers and who behave perfectly normally and have never killed anyone. In other words, people with 'abnormal' brains are often perfectly normal, just as people with apparently 'normal' brains can be both psychologically disturbed and highly criminal. Raine himself has gone some way to proving this point for us. He cites the case of a man who killed sixty-four people over a twelve-year period, for example, and notes that the scans were remarkably similar to those he got when examining his own brain. When asked by a journalist how that discovery felt, he said, 'When you have a brain scan that looks like a serial killer's it does give you pause.'[24]

Not just in crime but in every area, brain scans are extraordinarily unreliable as predictive tools. If we took 10,000 people at random from the general public, for example, we would probably expect there to be around 100 suffering from schizophrenia.[25] According to the latest research, doctors could probably pick up as many as seventy-four of those 100 schizophrenics by scanning the brains of these 10,000 people – which seems quite accurate, at least at first glance. But the problems mount quickly when we consider the number of people who would be diagnosed by brain scans as having schizophrenia when they didn't. Suddenly things become much, much less clear. Out of 10,000 scans, we would wrongly judge a staggering 1,300 people to be suffering from schizophrenia when they were not.[26] Positive 'diagnoses' would therefore only be accurate around 5 per cent of the time.*

Trying to predict serious criminality simply by examining brain scans or patterns of gene expression is even more unproductive. The relationship between brain scans or gene patterns and crime is simply far less clear than it is even in the identification of general health problems. At least 30 per cent of the population carry the 'low pro-moter' version of the MAO-A gene identified as being linked to crime in Moffitt's study, for example, and Moffitt found that there was no correlation between the 'low promoter' version of the gene and crime in the hundreds of men in her study who had not been abused – only in the few dozen who had.

The problem is not simply that these studies can't accurately predict crime, however. Far too often, studies of biological influences on crim-inality assume that crime is one entity – and treat it as a medically definable syndrome. As we've seen, behaviour traits such as impulsive-ness are important in understanding many crimes, but criminal records or arrest rates are not really meaningful measures of person-ality or behaviour traits. A reluctant retail theft to fund a drug habit is a manifestly different type of behaviour from a violent assault in response to a slight. 'Crime' describes an extraordinarily diverse set of acts, carried out by people with very different personalities and differ-ent motivations, acting in radically different immediate contexts.

Media reports, and even academic studies, often forget this. When two people who are biologically similar both commit a crime, for example, we are told we should ask whether their behavioural simi-larities could be related to their biological similarities. Yet a closer look often reveals that their behaviour is really not that similar at all.

---

* These inaccurate diagnoses – known as 'false positives' – are well known in med-ical and other scientific literatures but remain poorly understood by the population at large and even by practitioners. Studies show that doctors, for example, like the rest of us tend to focus on how many of the ill patients such tests pick up and under-estimate the problem of falsely diagnosing people as ill when they are in fact healthy.

Jay Joseph, a Californian psychologist who has written widely on methodological problems in studies linking biology and behaviour, has examined the (extremely rare) investigations which publish detailed notes on all their participants. One such, published in the 1980s, looked at twelve pairs of identical twins who had been separated in their childhood. In his write-up, Niels Juel-Nielsen shared the story of the identical twins Robert and Kaj.[27] Though they were raised separately, Juel-Nielsen assessed both brothers as being 'psychopaths', not based on any independent psychiatric testing but because they 'both lack the check and control of fundamental, uniform impulses'. In Juel-Nielsen's case notes, however, we see that starkly different personalities lie behind the assessment. Robert was a neurotic introvert while Kaj was an outgoing and domineering repeat offender. When they met for the first time, aged forty, Robert was in fact appalled by Kaj's behaviour and described him as 'the most unpleasant person I have ever come across'.[28]

Joseph found another study which provided detailed notes on two identical twins raised together in an abusive and alcoholic family environment in England. Twin A was eventually diagnosed as 'an aggressive psychopath' and according to reports was the dominant twin. He was also convicted of larceny. Notes on the two twins read:

> The patient [twin A] has no friends, and he soon tires of acquaintances whom he makes easily; he is described as being cold-hearted, selfish and unpredictable; he never heeds advice; borrows money, is dishonest, and a shiftless worker; he shows no affection or consideration for anyone – even his four children, for whom he has never accepted responsibility. His brother [twin B] is steady, stable, modest, less quick-tempered and more ambitious. In contrast to his brother's agnosticism, he recently joined the R. C. Church.[29]

What makes the case interesting from our standpoint is the fact that Twin B, despite his respectability and better nature, also had a criminal conviction. Twin A, who was living in a different part of the country, had asked him to pawn stolen jewellery for him, which – unsurprisingly given his general subservience to his twin brother – he did and was convicted for.[30]

USE-DEPENDENT BIOLOGY

Vitally, none of the studies behind the news reports that claim nature determines criminality actually argue that environmental influences don't matter. This is to the academics' credit – because there is a growing body of evidence that suggests our early experiences have both psychological and *physical* effects.

We have known since the 1960s that the brain is highly 'plastic', largely as a result of documented recovery by victims of brain injury. But, since then, discovery after discovery has revealed what we may have intuitively suspected – that our standard brain activity patterns can and do change. Neuronal circuits develop very rapidly through childhood and adolescence and even our adult brains are not 'hard-wired' to act in a particular way. The brain's most significant changes occur through what scientists call 'synaptic pruning', a process whereby 'useful' neural connections are strengthened and less useful connections are selectively removed.

The useful connections are not just those that we use most frequently. A range of studies have shown that the connections linked to certain behaviours appear to be strengthened most when these behaviours are rewarded. Or, put more simply, experience and learning processes are mirrored in the circuitry of our brains. Patterns of activity shift to reflect our behaviour and learning, as indicated in Fig. 12.

Scientists have also been learning that genes are not as immutable as was once assumed. All of our genes are present from birth and remain unchanged throughout our lives. But research now shows that genes can effectively be 'switched on' or 'switched off' depending on a range of factors. The process which shapes how genes are 'expressed' is not predetermined but instead appears to be rather messy and complex. As Professor Sir Michael Rutter, founder of the Social, Genetic and Developmental Psychiatry Unit at the Institute of Psychiatry, King's College London, puts it, gene expression is 'highly dynamic – being influenced by genetic background, chance, and environmental features that span diet, chemicals, and rearing experiences, to mention just a few examples'.[31]

These processes are not well understood. But there are particular

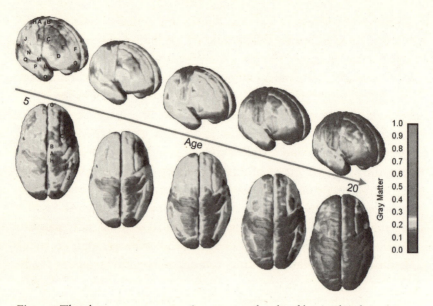

Fig. 12: The slow route to maturity: average levels of brain development for a healthy individual. The Society for Neuroscience explains that 'These images of the human brain show the loss of brain cells between the ages of 5 and 20 (warmer colours indicate more cells, cooler colours indicate less).'[32,33]

types of experience that appear to have noticeable impacts on brain development. After the collapse of the totalitarian Communist regime of Romania's President Nicolae Ceauşescu in 1989, the extreme suffering of orphans raised in Romanian state orphanages was highlighted to the world. Emaciated children were seen tied to beds, lying in their own excrement, HIV was rife, and neglect and abuse were widespread. Many children died. In one institution, at least 137 children, most under three years of age, died within the space of two years.[34] The tragedy prompted an outpouring of Western sympathy and a raft of adoptions by wealthy families, particularly in the UK, France and the US.

After such traumatic experiences, it is perhaps unsurprising that the adoptees did not all adapt smoothly to their new homes. Many had behavioural problems, some long-lasting. Around two thirds of children who had spent at least six months in Romanian state orphanages before being adopted in the UK continued to have problems – ranging from antisocial behaviour to learning difficulties to autistic symptoms at age eleven.[35] And, intriguingly, brain scans on recent adoptees revealed structural differences in the orphans' brains. Abuse and neglect do not always have physical consequences but extreme deprivation might well have biological impacts.

Abuse in the early years of children's lives is particularly damaging because of the importance of early bonding and interaction with a maternal figure. Animals are not humans, but because of this they've been subjected to a far wider set of experiments and testing. And such experiments strongly suggest that early bonding experiences matter enormously. Rats, like humans, can be 'good' or 'bad' parents, with some rat mothers being much more affectionate and protective than others, licking and grooming their pups more and showing different feeding techniques. Their pups end up with lower physiological responses to stress, better memory and learning abilities, and lower levels of gratuitous aggression. What is telling, however, is that these results hold true even when the 'good' rat mothers adopt the pups of 'bad' rat mothers at birth – which rules out straightforward genetic effects.[36] Indeed, good pup-raising practices actually appear to alter gene activity (without, of course, changing the DNA sequence) and result in wider physiological differences. Similar biological benefits to early bonding have been shown in rhesus monkeys and it is likely that they would hold for children if similar experiments were permitted – which we should hope they are not.[37]

Poor early environments can in this way have long-term impacts. As Dr Bruce Perry of the Child Trauma Center in New York puts it, 'The brain continues to be capable of change but it is much easier to organize the brain in healthy ways than it is to take a poorly organized neural system and reorganize it.'[38] But it is important to remember that even extreme abuse does not always lead to physical differences and good care later in life can heal early damage. Most of the Romanian adoptees who moved to Britain from Ceauşescu's brutal orphanages did not exhibit severe antisocial behaviour as adults. And although children who are physically abused prior to age eleven are twice as likely to develop antisocial personality disorders, victims of abuse do not always suffer severe long-term consequences from their ordeals.[39]

TWIN MEANINGS

This reasonable certainty that nurture and experience matter a lot sits in tension with research suggesting that our genetic inheritance is very important too. And this is where we need to look at the research that seeks to disentangle the web of biological and environmental influences on criminal behaviour. How important are our life experiences compared to our biology?

Recent decades have seen hundreds of attempts to answer this question, often using one of three main techniques. The first – generally seen as the most persuasive – is to examine the lives of identical twins who grow up in different families and environments, as in Juel-Nielsen's study above. The idea here is that if such twins, brought up in different environments, have very similar criminal behaviour, then genes are likely to play a major role in determining crime. The second approach – rather more practical due to the shortage of identical twins reared apart – is to look at differences between identical and non-identical twins. Identical twins share almost all their genes, while non-identical twins are no more genetically similar than brothers or sisters. This means that if studies find identical twins to be more similar in their behaviour than non-identical twins, strong genetic influence is likely. The third approach is to look at adopted children to see if their behaviour is more like that of their adoptive parents and siblings (which would suggest environmental influences) or that of their biological parents or siblings growing up elsewhere (which would suggest that genetic predispositions matter).

The results of these studies are intriguing, and underpin many of the headlines emphasizing genetic inheritance in determining crime. It was an adoption study which provoked the *Daily Mail* to highlight that 'New research suggests that criminal behaviour could be "all in the genes"' in 2010.[40] The particular study covered by the *Daily Mail* was based on a large sample of 250 adopted-away children who were first interviewed in US high schools and then re-interviewed regularly over a period of thirteen years. Dr Kevin Beaver of the University of Texas led the study and found that young men and women with a biological parent who had been arrested were up to 4.5 times more likely to be arrested than offspring whose natural parents were law-abiding. Adoptees with jailed biological parents were also more likely to spend time in prison or a young offenders' institution.[41] As Beaver puts it, 'Adoptees who have a biological father or a biological mother who have been arrested previously are significantly more likely to be arrested, sentenced to probation, incarcerated and arrested multiple times.'[42]

Under the byline, 'Life of crime is in the genes, study says', the *Telegraph* reported on a twin study in 2012.[43] Dr J. C. Barnes, a colleague of Dr Beaver at the University of Texas, had analysed data looking at the offending behaviour of 4,000 identical twins, non-identical twins and siblings from the US National Longitudinal Study of Adolescent Health.

Barnes's results confirmed the findings of several similar studies, indicating that identical twins were far more likely to exhibit persistent antisocial behaviour than fraternal twins or siblings. The more serious and persistent the offending, Barnes and his colleagues found, the more genetic factors appeared to matter. As the *Telegraph* reported, 'Up to 70 per cent of our chance of lifelong criminality could be genetic.'[44] Or, as Barnes and his colleagues summarized, 'Genetic factors explained between 56 and 70 per cent of the variance in being classified as a life-course persistent offender across different coding strategies.'[45]

These findings are not anomalies – for the vast majority of studies using twin and adoption methods to understand the impact of genetics on crime argue that crime, and antisocial behaviour generally, is highly 'heritable'. A twin study on psychopathy reports, for example, that its 'results suggest that these traits are equally and substantially heritable with each [of genes and the environment] accounting for roughly half of the total variance in both men and women'.[46] On average, studies since 1975 seem to show, according to Dr Dehryl Mason and Dr Paul Frick, then of the University of Alabama, that 'Approximately 50 per cent of the variance in measures of antisocial behaviour [were] attributable to genetic effects.'[47]

But there is a major problem. For we run the risk of being fooled, as many non-specialist journalists are, by the language used by those aiming to establish conclusively whether nature matters more than nurture. What do you imagine when you hear that genetic factors 'explain' a personality trait? And what does the idea of 'heritability' mean to you? What about behaviour being 'accounted for' by genetic factors?

To me at least, these words have clear implications from their everyday usage. The idea of 'psychopathy' being 'explained', for example, by genetic factors immediately makes me think that genes largely determine whether or not you or I will be (or become) a psychopath. The notion of antisocial behaviour being highly 'heritable', meanwhile, initially implies that it might be likely to pass between generations, from father and mother to child, irrespective of upbringing. The concept of genetic factors 'accounting' for a particular type of criminal behaviour immediately suggests to me that it might be hard to change such behaviours: for example, by adapting the environments in which people grow up and live.

None of these common assumptions is correct, however. The concept of 'heritability' is central to all twin and adoption studies. But it is a highly misleading term. Usually expressed as a percentage, it is the product of a formula. Heritability is usually calculated by measuring:

1. The degree to which people are biologically similar (i.e. their 'relatedness')
2. The degree to which people behave in the same way (i.e. in our example, the extent to which they have the same levels – and sometimes types – of criminal behaviour)

Researchers look at the variations in the behaviour of people with different levels of relatedness who are living in similar environments and use this data to calculate 'heritability'. Let's say we looked at 100 identical and 100 non-identical twins born in Paris, for example. Then let's assume we found the identical twins to be quite similar in their levels of offending. Perhaps, for instance, if one twin had a criminal conviction there was an 80 per cent chance that his or her identical twin sibling did too. Then let's assume we found that non-identical twins were also quite similar, but a bit less so. For example, if one twin had been convicted of a crime there was only a 50 per cent chance that his or her non-identical twin sibling had also committed a crime. Using this hypothetical case, heritability would be calculated by looking at the differences in their levels of behavioural similarity (80 per cent minus 50 per cent = 30 per cent) and then the differences in levels of genetic similarity (100 per cent divided by 50 per cent = 2). Our two numbers 30 per cent and 2 would then be multiplied to get our 'heritability' number, and in this case we might say that crime was 60 per cent 'heritable' – or, to put it another way, 'genetic differences explain 60 per cent of differences in criminal behaviour'.

But what does this number really reveal about whether nature matters more than nurture? For many reasons, not that much. Most obviously, the number says nothing about how likely it is that people's characteristics will be inherited by their children. Oddly, traits that are found using this method to be 0 per cent heritable can be highly genetically influenced. For example, if our study of 100 identical twins and 100 non-identical twins had looked at the number of fingers each twin had, they might easily have found that all twins (both identical and non-identical) had ten fingers (2 x [100 per cent minus 100 per cent] = 0 per cent). Accordingly, heritability of number of fingers would be 0 per cent. Alternatively, traits that are 100 per cent heritable can still be strongly influenced by our environments. Let's say, for example, a US study finds that alcoholism is 90 per cent heritable. Clearly, this does not mean that if you took the offspring of two alcoholic study participants and raised them in a Tibetan monastery without access to alcohol they would end up being alcoholics: they would not. As Professor Terrie Moffitt pointed out in an email to *The New York Times*, 'Knowing something is inherited [in scientific terms] does not IN ANY WAY tell us anything about whether changing the environment will improve it.'[48]

On top of all this, heritability estimates essentially assume that if people who are genetically more similar have more similar offending rates, this is caused by their genetic similarity. There are clearly all sorts of reasons why this might not be the case, even in twin studies. For example, if physical appearance matters in terms of how people are treated and how their transgressions are punished, then identical twins would be treated more similarly than non-identical twins. In this case, then, social attitudes to the way people look will act to make a trait more 'heritable'. Likewise, the very fact that twins are identical may (and again, many argue does) mean that parents and teachers treat these children similarly.

In adoption studies, it is particularly easy to see how these kinds of confusions can lead us to overestimate 'heritability'. Let's say, for example, we conducted an adoption study to find out the heritability of crime (measured by arrest rates) in a country where the vast majority of adoptees were ethnic minorities taken in by white families. Let's say too that this country was operating a system of apartheid in which minorities were barred from access to public services and were disproportionately targeted by the police. This study would most likely find that crime was highly heritable (and tied to race) and that 'genetic factors' mattered for crime rates. In a sense, such statements are accurate but clearly not in the sense that a lay reader would recognize!

What should we now make, then, of the findings of the succession of twin studies looking at 'genetic' influences on crime rates that find crime to be around 50 per cent heritable? Well, clearly less than we might have first thought. For these estimates tell us virtually nothing about the degree to which criminal behaviour is passed down through families and equally little about how possible it is to alter people's levels of criminality by changing the environments they grow up and live in.

It should, in fact, be obvious that social factors must dominate our explanations of crime. Many countries have seen falls in crime of more than 50 per cent in recent decades, and indeed there are tenfold differences in crime rates between many countries – differences that would be hard even for the most committed genetic determinist to explain solely through forms of genetic selection.

ILLUSIONS OF CERTAINTY

Given our uncertainty about the influences of biology on behaviour and our certainty that brain scans and genetic testing provide extremely poor predictors of criminality, it's worrying how often we are persuaded by biological evidence.

Science can blind us – and often does – because we trust doctors and scientists far more than other professional groups.[49] Even the most intelligent non-specialists among us have limited time and capacity to understand the imperfections of complex research methods. Debbie Beaty served on the jury in the trial of a man named Bradley Waldroup, who admitted to 'snapping' and in a fit of rage killing his estranged former wife before also attacking his current wife.[50] When the defence team showed that Waldroup had the version of the MAO-A gene that scientists had demonstrated to be associated with a risk of violence, Debbie was quite persuaded that Waldroup could not be held entirely responsible for his actions. 'Evidently it's just something that doesn't tick right,' she says. 'Some people without this would react totally different than he would.' 'A diagnosis is a diagnosis, it's there,' she says. 'A bad gene is a bad gene.'

We are particularly vulnerable to being overly influenced by the graphical format in which brain-scanning research, for example, is presented. We are easily tempted into seeing visible differences as 'proof'. A red or blue patch here or there can be pointed to as a visible 'cause' of a murderer's actions – and when comparing the 'normal' and 'abnormal' scans shown in court it can be difficult to remember the thousands of people out there with 'abnormal' brain scans who have never committed or will never commit a serious crime. It is also difficult to appreciate that what we are seeing is a 'snapshot' and that the images we see are only of a particular brain at a particular point in time and that an image of the same brain might have looked different five years ago or just the day before, if the subject was performing a different activity.

Judges appear to be little better equipped to resist the allure of biological evidence than the rest of us. In 2011, three researchers from the University of Utah interviewed 181 state judges from nineteen US states.[51] Each judge read a fictional case file of 'Jonathan Donahue', a man convicted of beating a restaurant manager unconscious with a gun butt. The judges were all told that Mr Donahue had been assessed as a psychopath through a standardized interview test. However, half of the judges received only this information, while the other half received further detail. The extra information came in the form of testimony from a 'neurobiologist and renowned expert' who said that the defendant had inherited a gene linked to violent behaviour. The expert's testimony described research very similar to some we have looked at, arguing that this particular gene variant altered the development of the areas of the brain that regulate emotion.

The fact that the offender was a psychopath increased the sentences handed out far above the national average. Judges receiving only the information about the crime and the interview diagnosis of psychopathy recommended sentences of, on average, fourteen years. However, the expert testimony outlining the genetic evidence led to much greater leniency. On average, those who read the genetic evidence recommended sentences of less than thirteen years – an average of one year and one month less than the judges who based their sentences on the crime and psychopathy diagnosis alone.

Other research confirms that we tend to be more lenient when behaviour is seen as being associated with biology. Surprisingly, perhaps, one experiment shows that college students were more forgiving of violence when it was described as linked to a 'chemical imbalance' rather than to 'abusive parents'.[52] This was true even when the biological evidence was only weakly associated with violence. As two of the study authors, John Monterosso of the University of Southern California and Professor Barry Schwartz, explained, 'A brain characteristic that was even weakly associated with violence led people to exonerate the protagonist more than a psychological factor that was strongly associated with violent acts.'[53]

As Monterosso and Schwartz point out, all this suggests that we tend to think about physical causes of behaviour differently from other causes. People, we reason, are not entirely responsible for their actions if there is a physiological factor underpinning their behaviour, but they are responsible when their behaviour is influenced by a psychological factor. When you think about it, this is extremely odd. All psychological states are also biological states and all behaviour is accompanied by some form of brain activity. Given this, what should matter has to be how certain we are that a particular factor causes criminality, not whether or not we can occasionally see some physical indicator of that cause. In other words, if – as it is – being a victim of abuse is a more proven cause of criminality than having a particular variant of a gene, we should – unlike most people serving on our juries – pay far more attention to the abuse than the gene.

This way of thinking helps us to question the extent to which 'new scientific evidence' has added to our understanding of crime. Science has greatly helped us to understand the physical world – for example, by using fingerprinting and DNA testing to uncover who was at a particular crime scene. It has also been useful in understanding the physiological factors that influence mood and decision-making, as we've seen in studies which show that people are more likely to be irritable and aggressive when they are excessively hot. Arguably, we should indeed be trying to learn more about the effects of biological states on decision-making. Recent experiments looking at the impact of diet on prisoner behaviour suggest, for example, that supplementing food with Omega 3 and essential vitamins may reduce violent incidents by a third; it is certainly worth exploring this link through further experiments.[54]

However, the success of science in helping us solve crimes and understand short-term influences on our behaviour has not yet been replicated in our understanding of the origins of criminal behaviour. It's hard to argue that we should object to using biological testing or indicators to understand crime better – we cannot after all rule out more illuminating research in future. But results so far have been disappointing, largely restating in a new language truths we already understood. Did we really need brain-scanning studies, for example, to tell us that extreme abuse and neglect make it more likely that children will develop conduct problems? Should knowing that abuse and neglect in childhood might inflict biological as well as psychological damage really change our attitudes and responses to it?

In many ways, the quest to find the biological indicators and origins of our temperaments resembles the experience of opening a Russian Matryoshka doll. In the nineteenth century, a group of biologists looked at outward appearances in search of answers. Then attention turned to the brain and hormones. Then the world of genes came into view. And now the focus is on epigenetics*. At each stage, biologists promised that we would find new certainties and they invented new languages to explain their endeavours. But at each stage we find that people's environment and experiences interact with their biology in complex ways that are difficult to unravel. When we attempt to disentangle this web, we can say little with absolute certainty – except that our experiences, social contexts and interactions matter and make a great difference to crime rates, and that proclamations that our criminal destinies are fixed at conception should be treated with the utmost scepticism.

* The study of changes in organisms caused by modification of gene expression rather than alteration of the genetic code itself.

Myth 6: Poverty is the real cause of crime

The working-man lived in poverty and want, and saw that others were better off than he. It was not clear to his mind why he, who did more for society than the rich idler, should be the one to suffer under these conditions. Want conquered his inherited respect for the sacredness of property, and he stole . . .

Friedrich Engels[1]

'The common argument that crime is caused by poverty is a kind of slander on the poor'

Henry Mencken[2]

CLOSE RELATIONS

It is September 2013 and the demolition of four fourteen-storey housing blocks that stand at the heart of central Detroit's Brewster-Douglass Housing Project is under way. Huge cutting machines bite chunks out of red-brick walls. Machines spray gallons of water to minimize the dust. And onlookers reminisce about the area. 'You know you had a lot of low incomes, so, you know, we took care of each other,' says Douglas Fuller, a man who lived near the now-razed blocks all his life.[3] News reports remind us of famous Detroiters who grew up in the projects, including Diana Ross.

The overall mood is celebratory, however. The demolition is, according to Detroit's mayor, a former basketball star, Dave Bing, the start of a process of regeneration. The Brewster-Douglass Projects had come to epitomize the city's decline, being seen as one of the poorest and most dangerous neighbourhoods in the city – and indeed the country – from the 1990s. 'This site has long been an eyesore and a breeding ground for crime in our city,' Mayor Bing explains.[4] 'I think's it's time for a change,' Mr Fuller says.[5]

The connection between crime and poverty in the Brewster-Douglass Projects was mirrored in the city as a whole. Three of Detroit's other poorest areas sit atop a 2013 ranking of the most dangerous areas in the US.[6] And while some suburbs are reasonably affluent and safe, overall many people still see Detroit as an exemplar of the symbiotic relationship between crime and poverty. More than a third of Detroit's residents live below the poverty line, making it the poorest major city in the US. Median income in 2013 was a pitiful $25,000 per year and unemployment rates were among the highest of all US cities, around double the national average.[7] Crime, meanwhile, flourishes. Detroiters get frustrated when people point to their city's high crime rates because that can hide the good things it has to offer, but there can be no doubting the facts. From 2008 to 2013, the city was ranked the most violent in the US by *Forbes* magazine, based on FBI crime statistics, and it has repeatedly picked up the dubious title of being the 'US murder capital'.[8] In 2013, rates of lethal violence were ten times the national average.[9]

The relationship between crime and poverty is well known and is central to the Victims and Survivors view, which perceives crime either as a direct response to economic need or a consequence of various forms of inequality. However, we've seen that this relationship is not quite as clear-cut as those who hold this view might expect. Crime generally rose across developed nations from the 1960s to the 1990s even as absolute poverty fell and relative poverty fell or remained constant. Then crime fell rapidly from the 1990s at a time when few developed countries experienced major changes in poverty levels and when inequality was by some measures in fact soaring, particularly in the US and England, where crime rates appear to have dropped particularly dramatically. Among developed countries, higher levels of poverty nationally are not linked to higher national crime rates.

Within cities – and indeed within regions – a relationship between poverty and crime does exist, however. There is more crime in town centres than in residential areas because of the vast numbers of people passing through them and the ample opportunities for retail theft and conflict between night-time revellers. But all the data shows that we feel least safe in the poorest areas of our cities, and if you live in poverty you are certainly more likely to become a victim of crime. Very poor British households (with income levels below £10,000) suffer the highest rates of burglary and, if they own a car, are far more likely to have their vehicles stolen.[10] Residential areas with high crime rates usually have high levels of deprivation too. The New York-based Justice Mapping Center has recently started mapping poverty and crime in different census tracts. In powerful, graphical form it shows areas where more than $1m is being spent annually on incarcerating residents from a single census block. As Eric Cadora, Director of the Justice Mapping Center, points out: 'No one had ever actually sat down and gotten the home street address of everyone going into prison and jail, as well as all the background information about their age and their employment status, etc. And when you have all that data, it tells you a lot about what's going on on the block . . . When we look at the million-dollar blocks that we mapped almost a decade ago, it's a highly concentrated group of public housing and smaller apartment housing all grouped together in a very concentrated manner.'[11]

The link between concentrated poverty and crime is explained in different ways depending on political perspectives. The Victims and Survivors view tends to emphasize the direct impact of unemployment and low incomes. But the idea that poverty breeds crime can also be popular with those on the right of the political spectrum. Poverty per se is not usually the problem, according to the Heroes and Villains view. Rather, the argument is made that individuals and communities come to lose their way, tolerating worklessness first, then vice and criminality. State benefits, rather than enhancing community well-being, are often seen as creating future problems. As David Cameron put it when outlining his government's response to the 2011 London riots, 'One of the biggest parts of this social fight-back is fixing the welfare system. For years we've had a system that encourages the worst in people – that incites laziness, that excuses bad behaviour, that erodes self-discipline, that discourages hard work.'[12]

The effects of poverty are not just felt by the individual. Left-wing commentators will frequently point out, for example, that concentrated poverty leaves entire neighbourhoods without the capacity to help themselves. And those on the right often argue that concentrated worklessness and a shortage of positive role models (including fathers) further encourage the process of moral degeneration.

These arguments about crime and poverty have significant consequences. They inform – and sometimes shape – our national debates about systems of public welfare. They influence our views on how much we should use the tax system to redistribute resources to the poor. And they affect our attempts to ensure that young men don't fall into crime and ex-offenders don't reoffend. So it is vital that we dig deeper to understand the complex relationships between poverty and crime. We need to understand how poverty affects individuals' criminal behaviour. First we shall look at poor, high-crime areas like the Brewster-Douglass Projects and indeed Detroit as a whole.

CHANGING FACES

The Brewster-Douglass Projects were not always the shame of Detroit. Indeed, their completion in 1952 brought delight to the hundreds of working families who took up residence there. As one former police lieutenant put it, 'When I moved to the projects, I felt it was like dying and going to heaven.'[13] The area was seen as a reprieve from Detroit's urban slums, a place of aspiration and optimism. Detroit at the time was thriving, a city of nearly two million people and near-full employment. The 'big three' car companies – Ford, General Motors and Chrysler – were all major employers. Racial segregation was extreme and this was not a city without social problems, but it was arguably less discriminatory than many others and crime was not particularly high. Murder and robbery rates, for example, were seven times lower than they were to be at the end of the century.

In the 1960s and 1970s, however, the city began to change: by then its status as the centre of the global automotive industry was crumbling. And when Detroit's jobs disappeared, so too did hundreds of thousands of its residents. In 1950 Detroit was the fifth-largest city in the US, with nearly two million inhabitants. By 1990 only one million people lived there. And in 2010 the population stood at 713,777, a third of its peak population.

The reasons why people left the city varied, each individual decision being influenced by dozens of factors. Initially, economics was the driving force. As job opportunities disappeared and redundancies threatened, those easily able to relocate and find jobs – or better jobs – outside the city often did so. People with flexible skills, including those in management positions, were among the first to go.

Then, from the early 1960s, the dynamic became more complicated. As the population declined, demand for housing fell and wealthier black families living in Detroit's centre found they were able to relocate to relatively prosperous suburbs, often occupying homes vacated by whites who had left. When they did so, the social and ethnic composition of those neighbourhoods changed. Many whites there became unsettled – uncomfortable living in a multi-ethnic area in an era of racial segregation, or simply concerned by falling house prices. They reacted by moving further out of the city or leaving altogether. Entire neighbourhoods went from almost exclusively white to almost exclusively black within a decade.

Once-desirable majority-black areas such as the Brewster-Douglass Projects experienced knock-on effects. Previously, only working families had been allowed to apply for homes there. But now that more prosperous African-American families could afford a slice of suburban living, demand for Project housing fell and the Detroit Housing Commission could no longer be so selective. Non-working families moved in, including many who were less law-abiding than the previous tenants. This was the time when the Brewster Projects became known as an area of concentrated poverty and high crime rates. As more people moved from the city and the Projects, some apartments were left vacant. They became playgrounds for bored, unsupervised teenagers, bases for drug dealers and their customers, and targets for vandalism and arson.

The steady outflow accelerated still more rapidly from the late 1960s. Racial tension was mounting across the US but the atmosphere in Detroit was particularly explosive, exacerbated by discriminatory practices in the majority-white Detroit Police Department. In 1967, the arrest of eighty-two African-Americans for celebrating the return of two soldiers from Vietnam in an unlicensed drinking venue sparked one of the worst riots in US history. For five days that July, the authorities lost control. There were forty-three deaths (including thirty-three African-Americans); over 2,000 premises were looted or burnt; more than 7,000 arrests were made (mostly of African-Americans); and criminal damage cost the city an estimated $40m–$80m.[14]

Inevitably, the riots had a deep impact on both businesses' and residents' sense of safety. Many of the small businesses affected chose not to reopen or relocated to safer areas, leading to a hollowing-out of Detroit's centre and ever-shrinking tax receipts. 'White flight' took off: 22,000 people had left the city in the year before the riots, 1966.[15] In 1968, the year after the riots, that figure reached 80,000, before falling back to a hefty 40,000 exodus in 1969. In 1970 Detroit still had a small majority of whites, but the exodus continued and by 1980 whites made up just a third of the population.

It was not just the riots' legacy and ongoing economic malaise that led to the continuing exodus, of course. Rapidly rising crime rates also pushed residents away. From the 1960s, gangs became increasingly visible on Detroit's streets, selling drugs, intimidating residents and generating violent conflict. The city had witnessed only one murder in 1960 but by the 1970s there were over a dozen murders each year. In the 1980s and 1990s, around twenty people were murdered annually as the city experienced overall crime rises that were far more dramatic than the averages across the US. When national crime rates fell in the 1990s, Detroit's were slow to drop and remained high. In the 2000s the city's murder rates were five times higher than New York's and its levels of overall crime outstripped those of all other major US cities.

It was whites who left first, but blacks who could afford to move proved just as keen to escape joblessness and crime. Between 2000 and 2010, the city lost a further quarter of a million residents, over three quarters of whom were black.*[16] As more tax-paying residents left, the city's tax base dwindled still further and the council proved incapable of providing good public services, including policing, while also balancing the budget. Detroit's sprawling geography made it expensive to maintain. 'Motor city' had never invested in a tube or tram network, and unoccupied housing became a target for arson as well as an eyesore for neighbours. High demand for public services, incompetence and even outright corruption increased the problems.

In 2013, Detroit was declared bankrupt – a step some hope will enable the city to start rebuilding but others fear will only exacerbate the city's difficulty in attracting and retaining skilled workers and addressing social problems, including crime rates.

Detroit's changes have been unusually dramatic. But they exemplify the general rule that cities and the neighbourhoods within them are rarely static. Even when bricks and mortar stay the same, the people in them change. As Detroit suffered economically, so its social mix transformed. The most affluent and skilled workers and those able to see possibilities beyond their city boundaries generally left the city. And those who stayed throughout this turmoil were people who either had strong attachments and loyalty to their communities or fewer outside options. Included among residents who remained were pensioners, who did not need jobs, and those who had either limited skills to offer employers outside the city or little interest in finding employment. 'The folks with the wherewithal to leave, the folks with the jobs . . . those are the people that have the ability to exercise voting with your feet,' says David Martin, a Professor of Public Policy at Wayne State University in Detroit.[17] Surveys support his claim, with half of Detroit's remaining residents saying they would still consider leaving if they could.[18]

Detroit's story – and the realization that the people who live in a place are not always constant – raises new possibilities. We quickly see, for example, how, rather than poverty causing crime, crime can in a sense lead to poverty by driving out wealthier residents who are able to afford to live in more desirable areas. Those who have fled

---

* The housing crash of 2007 onwards was perhaps the last straw: houses in many areas became virtually unsaleable (three-bedroom homes went for as little as $500).

Detroit certainly cite crime as a major factor, and becoming a victim can be the spark. As one recent resident explains, 'I left Detroit after being the victim of serious crime. All but one of my former neighbours are gone. Almost all of my current neighbours in my suburb left Detroit largely because of violence and crime, many in the last ten years such as myself.'[19]

It's not just in Detroit: across the world, feelings of safety are an important influence on house prices. Problem neighbours are a huge turn-off for prospective buyers and can dramatically devalue a property or make it unsaleable. As one would-be house seller in Scotland explains, for example, 'We are trying to sell our house but are having offers repeatedly withdrawn due to the reputation of our neighbours who rent the property through a private landlord. They are regularly in trouble with the police and are in and out of prison and are well known in the local area. Even the look of their house puts people off – the garden is a mess and the window and door have been smashed quite regularly.'[20]

A range of studies confirm that living near criminals has a real impact on property prices. In the US, 'Megan's Law' dictates that sex offenders must register their addresses, which are made publicly available. Leigh Linden of the University of Texas and Jonah E. Rockoff, who teaches at Columbia University, used this information to show that the arrival of a sex offender reduced the price of neighbouring houses by on average 12 per cent, although house prices over 200 yards away were not affected.[21] People will, unsurprisingly, pay to be away from ex-offenders. Jaren Pope, an Associate Professor at Brigham Young University in Utah, found similar results – but he also discovered that house prices recover once the ex-offender moves away from an area.[22] And in the UK, Dr Steve Gibbons of the London School of Economics conducted a broader study looking not at sex offenders but at overall crime rates. Though it's impossible to separate out the influences on house prices completely, his careful estimates suggested that a reduction in recorded crime of 10 per cent adds around 1.7 per cent to the selling price when compared with the average home in the average neighbourhood.[23]

People will of course tolerate some risks in return for spacious houses, short commutes or good local amenities. The buzz and earnings that accompany big-city life, for example, partly compensate for an increased chance of having your car or bicycle stolen. But the highest-crime residential areas are still often occupied by those with very strong ties to them or little choice as to where they live – usually due to poverty. And while many who move into poor areas will be perfectly law-abiding, there is often a higher chance they'll commit crime – and particularly street crime – than those moving to pricier postcodes. In some cases they'll be problematic tenants whom the council can't afford to house elsewhere, or who have generated so many complaints that their current neighbours need some respite. In others, they might just be people who struggle to hold down regular work because they have some of the behaviour traits that make them more likely to commit crime – as we've seen in Myth 3, impulsiveness, problems with authority and low educational achievement.

MOVING TO OPPORTUNITY

The fact that people are often quite mobile and dislike living in high-crime areas makes it harder to study the effects of poverty and unemployment on crime. Though crime and poverty are bedfellows, it's possible that their relationship is a by-product of patterns of social sorting and selection: poorer people have to live in higher-crime areas while richer ones can leave them. We need to disentangle whether and how financial hardship (or new-found wealth) pushes people into criminality. And we also need to understand what impact living in high-poverty and high-crime areas has on residents. But how do we do this? Surely, after all, people live where they live and there is no way of forcing them to move and then to observe the results?

'So far, since I've been here,' Anique says, 'I've never heard no gunshots, no none of that. That was a big thing that I, I don't know, I didn't realize it, but once you've grown up in a neighbourhood and that's something you heard on a daily basis, you don't know that that's not how it's supposed to be.'[24] Anique has enjoyed life since her move to San Bernardino County, east of Los Angeles. She feels fortunate as she considers the possibility that her daughter Clara might never need to get used to the sound of gunshots that she herself is so familiar with. And she is indeed lucky. Hers is one of a few thousand families across the US that have been helped to move to better neighbourhoods by one of the most ambitious social experiments in history.

The study, named Moving to Opportunity (MTO), is surprisingly little known but it was launched by the US Department of Housing and Urban Development in 1994. The $80m social experiment enrolled nearly 5,000 very low-income families, mostly black and Hispanic, many on welfare, who were living in public housing in inner-city ghettos of Baltimore, Boston, Chicago, Los Angeles and New York City. Families were offered housing subsidies to relocate to wealthier areas, while many of their neighbours (who also took part in the study) were not. Some, of course, refused, preferring to remain close to their current networks of friends and families – but even these families were tracked too. Researchers would interview all the families periodically to see how they were getting on, charting their health, employment, wealth and criminality.

Those leading the project were confident they would see results. But the scheme was not implemented without opposition. In their book on the experiment, Xavier de Souza Briggs, Susan Popkin and John Goering chronicle vigorous resistance which was largely focused around Baltimore, where the Eastern Political Association actively campaigned against the project. In the town of Essex in Baltimore County, their posters read: 'HEAR US SHOUT. People living in drug and crime-infested Lafayette homes and Murphy homes [in Baltimore] could be moving to Essex. The Moving to Opportunity program could affect our neighborhoods, our schools, and the number of families receiving County social services. But this is not a racial issue. It is a matter of safety and quality education for Essex residents.'[25] A local activist against the scheme voiced the other main concern. 'People here moved from Baltimore city, and they worked for that move. Now somebody could move in down the street, not have a job, get a 100-percent rent subsidy, and send their kids to the same school I'm sending my kids to. And that's not fair.'[26] Only behind-the-scenes work by the project's political sponsors in the Clinton administration ensured that the Baltimore-based element of MTO went ahead, albeit in a scaled-back form.

Opposition elsewhere was more muted but, fearful of sparking opposition, MTO was rolled out to the four other target cities with relatively little fanfare. Thousands of families were contacted and, on the whole, responded positively: 5,300 of them applied for the scheme. The main reason for applying was not, as researchers at first expected, the chance to find work. Instead, and unsurprisingly in the light of our Detroit story, four out of five families cited safety as their primary motivation.[27]

Not everyone who applied was successful: only a third (1,820) were chosen for the experimental group. They were given relocation counselling, search assistance and a voucher subsidy, which could be used only if they took up housing in areas where less than 10 per cent of households lived in poverty. Another third remained in public housing and received no additional support (the control group). And the remaining families received a more limited support offer, which comprised standard relocation counselling and a voucher subsidy for use in the private rental market, but no search assistance. The only condition imposed on families lucky enough to receive support was that they had to stay in a low-poverty neighbourhood for at least one year before moving on.

The impact on those who moved was dramatic. Like Anique and Clara, the families involved in MTO were living in some of the very poorest and most dangerous areas in the country, areas not unlike the Brewster-Douglass Projects in 1980s Detroit. A year after the study, the control group (those who hadn't received support) were living in neighbourhoods where around 40 per cent to 80 per cent of households lived in poverty. But they moved to areas that were both richer and much, much safer. Violent crime in destination neighbourhoods was nearly three times lower than the areas families fled from.[28]

Anique was just one of many mothers who enjoyed the benefits. Like 92 per cent of movers, she felt safe in her new neighbourhood during the day. Only 80 per cent of those who stayed put felt safe in the daytime.[29] Safety had knock-on benefits too. Follow-up studies conducted five years after families had taken up the scheme noticed a change in the mothers they were speaking to. On average, mental health improved and levels of psychological distress and depression were down by over one fifth – a reduction comparable to some of the most successful drug-based treatments. One of the reasons for reduced levels of stress was that mothers were less concerned about both their own safety and that of their daughters. Nearly all the women who stayed in high-poverty neighbourhoods referred to how badly men treated women in their communities, with complaints ranging from abusive language to assault. Briana, who like Anique moved out of high-poverty public housing in central LA, explains: 'That's what they're like [in my old area]. They don't like the women my age. They go for the 12-year-olds, the 11-year-olds, and give them drugs, and that's not good . . . I have seen a lot of young girls like that . . . I refuse for my daughter to be like that.'[30]

The mental health benefits of improved security were being felt even ten to fifteen years after the initial moves, even though many participants had by that point been forced to relocate to poorer areas either for personal reasons, to live closer to work or, quite often, because landlords had raised their rents. Physical health was another area of long-term gain, with extreme obesity and diabetes levels down 40–50 per cent among adults who moved. Researchers believe that this was another knock-on benefit of safety: when they are less anxious, people are more likely to take care of their physical health.[31]

In contrast to the benefits in terms of well-being, wealth changed little: parents who moved were as unlikely to be in work as before, and when they did work they were not earning any more than those who stayed in high-poverty neighbourhoods.[32] In many ways, this is unsurprising: the programme did nothing to address skills shortages and other factors that made finding employment difficult for many. But it did suggest that many people overestimate the impact that having working neighbours has on individual motivation for and capacity to retain jobs.

Researchers expected to see improvements in the lives of the children who moved, confidently predicting both short- and long-term effects. Boys, they assumed, would benefit most, particularly by avoiding recruitment into neighbourhood gangs and all the risks that gang membership entails. But they hoped that school outcomes and future employment prospects would improve for the children involved too.

As the results came in, however, there was disappointment. Girls' mental health marginally improved in the first few years following the moves and there was also a very slight fall in 'risky behaviours' such as under-age and unprotected sex.[33] But overall impacts were very small. For boys there was even worse news. In many senses, their outcomes deteriorated. Ten years after their move, boys were 20 per cent more likely to have been excluded from school and also more likely to have been arrested than those who stayed behind. All the children who moved were safer than those who stayed in the most deprived neighbourhoods, but the communities they moved to were not really any safer from them.[34]

This finding was alarming. Researchers could see reasons why better areas might not make a huge amount of difference, but it was very hard to understand why boys might have become worse behaved. As they sought answers, the researchers dug deeper into the information they had collected. The first thing they found was that, while overall arrest rates were higher among boys who moved, arrests for violent crime were lower. They also found that if boys moved back to poorer neighbourhoods, both violent crime and property crime rates reverted to similar levels to those for boys who didn't move.[35] This is interesting. It suggests that where people live doesn't significantly affect willingness to engage in crime, but does influence the types of crime people commit. Boys found greater opportunities for property crime in their new areas but also faced lower risk of violent confrontations.

This idea – that moves affected 'in-the-moment' decisions about which crimes to commit – is consistent with our earlier insights into the importance of the immediate environment for crime rates (Myth 3): neighbourhood wealth can increase crime by providing more tempting targets for burglary and theft. But it may also highlight an interesting way in which housing types affect patterns of crime. Recent research from Pittsburgh appears to demonstrate that high-rise public housing blocks are more likely to be the scene of violent incidents, but they also suffer much lower rates of burglary than low-rise public housing.[36] Presumably it's difficult to make a quick getaway from a burglary on the seventh floor but equally difficult to escape a fight.

We cannot be completely sure why moving into better areas made such little difference to the overall criminality of those who moved. The most likely answer, however, is that neighbourhoods have far less relevance than many argue, and that in-home influences are more important. We have already seen the importance of early-years parenting and education in influencing criminal behaviour (Myths 3 and 5), and researchers found that this applied to the children who moved. Though wealthier, many destination neighbourhoods did not have good schools. When they did, spaces were in short supply. What's more, parents showed less inclination than researchers expected to seek out better-performing schools for their children. This was sometimes due to a preference for stability: many families who moved kept their children in the same schools. But it also appeared to be underpinned by fatalistic attitudes towards children's ability to succeed academically, a tendency to believe their children's educational success would be determined by their aptitude rather than teacher quality, and lower expectations. The main goal for many mothers was to find a school that was safe and 'not too ghetto'.

Researchers also noted that existing family and peer influences remained strong, particularly for boys. Boys were given more freedom than girls by their parents, who worried less about their sons' safety and were more indulgent of risky behaviour, often saying that 'boys will be boys'. As a result, they went back to their former neighbourhoods more frequently than girls to meet up with old friends and made fewer connections in their new areas. Relationships with family members also remained constant, as few movers left their city entirely. And, contrary to many beliefs, this was not always a good thing. Fathers and male relatives were often some of the worst influences in these young people's lives, not least because a large proportion of them had criminal records. Craig, a seventeen-year-old from Los Angeles, described the negative influences in his life, including his violent father and his mother's boyfriends, who he said abused her. He told his interviewer: 'My biggest worry is that I don't get to join the military, and I stay here for the rest of my life . . . My other worry is that when I leave here, I don't want to keep in touch with anybody here. I'm not going to give them my phone number or anything. I'm just going to move away . . . I don't want to be bothered with them . . . the relatives, most of my relatives.'[37]

Moving to Opportunity is, of course, just one study, conducted in five US cities, but its findings hold elsewhere. The effect of neighbourhoods on individual behaviour and achievements is usually relatively small. For example, UK data shows that the type of neighbours a school child lives near has no impact on exam results, their general attitudes towards schooling, or substance use and antisocial behaviour.[38] Similarly, researchers looking into the differences in average wages of different UK cities and neighbourhoods found that well over 80 per cent were associated with the characteristics of people living in those areas, rather than the effect of the areas themselves.[39] The attributes people have been born with or develop from family and other close relationships seem to matter a lot more than the people they live near.

THE ODD EFFECTS OF MONEY

The realization that living in less deprived communities doesn't necessarily improve children's behaviour raises doubts about the efficacy of policies aimed at creating mixed communities in order to reduce crime. There may be other good reasons for social mixing, but subsidizing public housing benefits does not appear to reduce crime and is extremely costly. But what about other policy interventions that seek to reduce crime by targeting poverty more directly? Can we reduce crime by improving employment prospects or by increasing, rescheduling or reallocating state benefits?

In a criminologist's ideal world, there would be programmes that assigned wealth and poverty or jobs and unemployment at random. Unsurprisingly, such experiments have never quite passed muster with politicians, worried about voters' reactions to arbitrary handouts. Lotteries perhaps provide the closest we can get to a type of natural investigation into wealth and crime, but they are few and rarely researched.

These isolated cases do show us, however, that new-found wealth is not always a protective barrier against criminality. Edward Putman was a convicted rapist and many were outraged when he won nearly £5m on the UK national lottery. Surprisingly, he was subsequently jailed not for violence but for fraudulently claiming housing benefit and income support, applying for the undeserved benefits *after* he had won his millions.[40] A Virginia lottery winner, Kay Revell, meanwhile was recently arrested for two counts of drug dealing, despite clearly not needing the money.[41] Some have arguably been pushed closer to crime by lottery winnings. Charles Riddle won $1m in the Michigan Lottery in 1975. His life spiralled out of control before he was sentenced to three years in prison for drug dealing ten years later.[42] Desmond Noonan, part of a family notorious for their involvement in protection rackets, violence and drug distribution, used part of his family's lottery winnings not to go straight but to invest in a wholesale heroin purchase he was later convicted of trafficking.[43]

So there are no simple, automatic connections between poverty and crime. Rather, the relationship between crime and earnings is highly complex and works both ways, with crime often contributing to poverty.[44] Being caught committing crime is, after all, a pretty effective way of losing your job and ruining future employment and income prospects. In most countries, those found guilty of even minor offences need to declare their criminal records to potential employers for five to ten years after their convictions – a fact that creates barriers to employment for thousands of teenagers at the very point in their lives when they most need to build up work experience and skills in order to become attractive to future employers.

Wealth can create criminal opportunities. At the time when people are most flush with cash – pay day – crime peaks across most countries. Violent crime, in particular, spikes wildly, often nearly doubling as wage earners spend their cash on alcohol, drugs and whatever else helps them to celebrate and in turn they encounter various types of social conflict (see Myth 11). And just as pay days affect social routines, so too do wider changes in employment patterns. Rates of burglary rose rapidly from the 1960s, in part because women started to go to work in increasing numbers, leaving homes unsupervised. And wealth – where it is used to buy relatively easy-to-steal but desirable items – can in a sense encourage crime. Burglaries rose as more households became able to afford televisions and video recorders. And they fell in the 1990s when household goods became cheaper and new portable goods (such as phones and laptops) were a more desirable target: one reason for the much slower fall in levels of muggings.

Studies that track people over their lifetimes are a useful way of checking how specific individuals respond to financial need. These confirm that most people don't automatically turn to crime when unemployed. But some people with a previous history of offending do start to commit more crime when they are no longer in work: this could be to make ends meet, because people often lose their jobs when experiencing other stressful events, or possibly because they are spending more time in an unstructured, unsupervised environment.[45] There is another obvious contradiction to the perceived link between poverty and crime. Those who work and earn the *most* in their teens and early twenties are, in fact, more likely to commit crime than their peers.[46] This may be linked to their ability to live a lifestyle with less parental supervision and more risk of getting into trouble – but it's also connected with the fact that teenagers who leave school early are often those who did less well academically or had trouble with school discipline. They may also be striving for greater independence and freedom from home, in some cases because they do not get on with family members. Young people who are paid less well or who don't have jobs often choose to live at home and sacrifice short-term income and accept constraints on their freedom for better future prospects.

Jobs matter, but again not in the obvious way many think. And we see this too with those leaving prison. Research is increasingly pointing to the fact that getting ex-offenders jobs only curtails future offending when the offender is happy with that job and feels it provides satisfaction, status and hope for the future.[47] An income alone is not enough.

You would not think from reading many newspaper reports that the relationship between crime, poverty and unemployment was so partial. In the run-up to reducing unemployment benefits in the UK in 2011 and the extension of a 'Work Programme' to ex-offenders, a series of stories appeared in newspapers sympathetic to the Conservative government. The *Telegraph* headline read: 'Third of unemployed are convicted criminals', while the *Daily Mail* had 'One in three on jobless benefits has got a criminal record: £2bn cost of handouts to underclass is revealed for the first time'.[48, 49] The reports were based on accurate information. They forgot to mention, however, that nearly one in four of the UK's general population has a criminal record according to some estimates – though most have been cautioned or convicted for only a single, and usually minor, offence.[50]

At the same time, the government is also introducing a 'Universal Credit' to 'make work pay'. The policy aims to increase the responsibility and budgeting skills of the unemployed by paying benefits monthly rather than weekly. And it seeks to ensure that work pays by linking the taxation and benefits systems to avoid situations where people do not always earn extra money if they take on more work – a change that sounds simple but requires a multi-billion-pound mega-project to see it implemented. It's a politically popular idea but, even ignoring the fact that the project is already mired in difficulty, there is reason to pause. Again details are important. Very small differences in benefits systems appear to make a difference in crime rates. A US study looked at twelve cities to see how crime rates varied depending on the timing of benefits payments. They found that burglary, theft and robbery rates all went up slightly just before monthly benefits were handed out, suggesting that people running short on money were trying to top up their incomes through crime.[51] But this pattern wasn't seen in cities where benefits were paid weekly – suggesting that the relationship between unemployment and crime was the result of poor planning rather than simple financial need.[52] Financial support at points of transition is also important. Prisons are in theory meant to ensure that prisoners leaving prison quickly receive benefits and housing support, but in practice they often don't.

A THEORY OF RELATIVITY

The complex impact of financial need is likely to be replicated in the area of inequality. As mentioned, crime trends have not mirrored trends in inequality, yet there are still interesting relationships between inequality and crime. In their successful book *The Spirit Level*, Kate Pickett and Richard Wilkinson point out, for example, that US states with higher levels of inequality tend to have higher homicide rates. They claim this is because of the psychological strain that inequality creates for those who are less well-off. I find this partially plausible. Certainly, violence is linked to general strains and frustrations and many fights start in response to perceived slights, which could be interpreted as attempts to gain respect where other sources of social status (such as money) are hard to come by. However, the jury is still out on this connection, largely because relationships between inequality and crime are extraordinarily hard to test.

TURNING TIDES

Before the Brewster-Douglass high rises were demolished, the remaining squatters could look out of their windows and see some of the main attractions of downtown Detroit. Comerica Park, home to the Detroit Tigers Baseball team, was in clear view across the Fisher Freeway, and a few more blocks away are Detroit's opera house and the vast Fillmore entertainment venue.

Today the blocks are gone, but these attractions remain and are symbolic of the fact that Detroit still has something to offer – arguably, more so than before. In 2011, Dan Gilbert, the billionaire founder of Quicken Loans, the biggest online lender in the US, made a series of investments in Detroit's centre. Having been born in the area, Gilbert has embarked on one of the most ambitious attempts single-handedly to regenerate a city ever seen. In a huge gamble, he has spent around a billion dollars on real estate with the aim of turning downtown Detroit into a liveable area with a thriving technology industry. The Madison Theatre Building, purchased and totally refitted in 2011, is now the M@dison Building, housing dozens of tech start-ups, many funded by Gilbert's Detroit Venture Partners. Gilbert has courted other tech companies to encourage them to set up in the area, which is now home to an office for the online giant Twitter. And graduates coming to work in the city can benefit from rent and mortgage subsidies offered by Gilbert's company.

Gilbert is trying to restore the city's fortunes. 'This is not the only solution,' he says to the *New York Times* technology correspondent,

David Segal. 'The education system needs to be addressed. But what we're doing is a big part of the solution. I can't think of a great American city that doesn't have a great downtown.'[53] Wisely, Gilbert is also concentrating on safety. In Chase Tower, another Detroit building, he has set up a command centre where private security guards monitor live CCTV footage from downtown cameras.

Change is already afoot – and the mix of downtown Detroit is changing too. Educated young workers are beginning to arrive and Gilbert hopes many more will come, work, spend their money and pay their taxes. The goal, as in most regeneration schemes, is to create a virtuous circle, attracting to the city those with the most to offer and generating the tax revenues that help improve its infrastructure and public services, including more effective crime reduction. Similar efforts have worked before: for example, in English cities like Manchester (and areas like Salford), proving that Detroit's downward spiral need not necessarily continue.

It will not be easy, but it seems a more sensible approach than many other efforts at regeneration. A few years back I visited Middlesbrough in North Yorkshire and spoke to the mayor, council officials and police about their problems. That city too has been losing residents for decades following job cuts linked to declining activity in the port (Teesport) and in the city's main steel and chemical industries. As in Detroit, empty buildings became a target for crime and vandalism so they have been boarded up and demolished. But in Middlesbrough there are some examples of money being wasted in regeneration efforts. Encouraged by national incentive schemes, the city arguably focused too much on improving its physical appearance rather than on retaining or attracting a skilled workforce.

Officials took me to a recent development of attractive and spacious social housing. Before the houses were built, residents suffered widespread crime and antisocial behaviour, and the feeling was that the shabbiness of the existing housing was partly to blame. Millions of pounds later, however, the problem remains the same, with the same residents causing the same trouble.

This is not, given what we have seen, surprising. The relationship between crime and poverty is complex, and there are few quick fixes for crime. Broad-brush attempts to reduce crime simply by changing the neighbourhoods people live in or their economic conditions often fail because crime is rooted in deep-seated behaviours and not always motivated by money. Money also affects different people in different ways: it can draw them into circumstances where they are more likely to commit crime, but there are also circumstances where extreme need can nudge those on the edge of crime into law-breaking.

We overlook much of this because we see patterns that suggest a close relationship between crime and poverty. We see that poor neighbourhoods often have higher crime rates and that criminals often live in deprived communities and we too readily assume that poverty creates crime. We see that most of the people in prison are poor and too readily assume that their poverty has led them to crime rather than the other way round. Poverty is a factor in crime, but so is wealth. In developed countries at least, crime is seldom motivated by straightforward economic need.

Myth 7: Immigration increases crime rates

Our tolerance is part of what makes Britain, Britain. So conform to it; or don't come here.

Tony Blair, November 2006[1]

THE CRIMES OF OTHERS

Crime and immigration are often paired. They are both sources of great public anxiety, and stories linking crime with immigration are seized upon by those seeking to sell newspapers. Specific incidents of crime committed by immigrants, particularly those residing in a country illegally, receive plenty of attention. 'Drunk illegal immigrant kills couple after sneaking back into country', the *Telegraph* announced.[2] 'Illegal alien to be tried for teen's grisly murder', reported sensationalist US news outlet *The Examiner*, documenting the murder of eighteen-year-old Josh Wilkerson in Texas by Hermilo Moralez, aged nineteen.[3]

Systemic links between crime and immigration are also widely broadcast. 'Immigrant crime soars with foreign prisoners rising', the UK's *Daily Express* informed its readers in 2013.[4] And politicians often link immigration and crime. In 2015, Donald Trump, speaking in hope of becoming the Republican Party's presidential candidate, warned that the undocumented immigrants crossing the Mexican borders were 'people that have lots of problems, and they're bringing those problems [to] us. They're bringing drugs. They're bringing crime. They're rapists. And some, I assume, are good people.'[5]

Links between immigration and organized crime are frequently picked up (see Myth 4), and many argue that fluid borders have created greater opportunities for criminal groups across the world. As the 2013 Europol Threat Assessment warns, 'Diaspora communities offer OCGs [Organized Crime Groups] an established presence in market countries, including legal business structures (LBS), facilities and transportation.'[6]

The issues of crime and immigration are even bound together institutionally. In most countries, responsibility for immigration policy and at least some aspects of crime policy sit within the same government department. The two subjects are therefore often mentioned simultaneously in ministerial statements and official press releases. And the language applied to crime policy, including its focus on threat and protection, typically flows over into immigration. The February 2010 five-year strategy of the Home Office's UK Border Agency was titled 'Protecting our border, protecting the public'.[7] The US Department of Homeland Security, responsible for large parts of immigration and crime policy, has 'a vital mission: to secure the nation from the many threats we face. This requires the dedication of more than 240,000 employees in jobs that range from aviation and border security to emergency response, from cybersecurity analyst to chemical facility inspector. Our duties are wide-ranging, but our goal is clear – keeping America safe.'[8]

The true nature and extent of links between crime and immigration are, nonetheless, widely debated. Few subjects are more politically charged, and the facts presented to us seem to vary wildly according to political leanings or entrenched views. Adding the names of left- or right-leaning newspapers to the search term 'immigration and crime' yields dramatically divergent stories.

A search for 'immigration and crime the *Daily Mail*' (a right-leaning newspaper) generates articles titled: ' "Immigrant crimewave" warning: foreigners were accused of a QUARTER of all crimes in London' (2012); 'Illegal immigrant who married British woman after being charged with crime is allowed to stay in UK for his stepdaughter' (2013); and 'Nearly a fifth of all suspected rapists and murderers arrested last year were immigrants' (2012).[9] The top three results in a search for 'immigration and crime *Guardian*' (a left-leaning newspaper) are 'Migrant Crime wave a myth' (2008); '[Home Secretary] Theresa May rejects "scaremongering" Romanian crime wave claim' (2013) and 'Crime doesn't rise in high immigration areas' (2013).[10]

It's hard to tell which reports to trust. But in recent years, the residents of many countries are becoming more convinced that immigration may be inflating crime levels. The International Social Survey showed that in 1995 only 25 per cent of people agreed with the statement 'Immigrants increase crime rates'. By 2003, 40 per cent agreed. Many answered that they were not sure. But very few regard immigration as good news for crime rates. According to the European Social Survey of 2002 (another big cross-national poll), just 8 per cent thought immigrants 'make a country's crime problems better' while nearly half thought immigration 'made a country's crime problems worse'.[11]

Reading a glut of stories of crimes committed by immigrants – perhaps from a particular country – can certainly increase public concern. But even isolated incidents can shift attitudes when you are unlucky enough to know the victims. As the son of the British victims in the 'Drunk illegal immigrant kills couple' story said: 'While we hold Mereohra responsible for his actions, we feel that our beloved mum and dad would still be alive today if the system had not failed by allowing him to be at liberty in the UK.'[12] The mother of the Texan victim shares the sentiment: 'Josh was murdered through no fault of his own; he went to school one day,' she said. 'If the kid [Moralez] hadn't been here, he'd be alive today.'[13]

Thinking this way in grief and anger is understandable. But if we look beyond such tragic individual cases, is it true that immigrants commit more crime than native citizens? If they do, might immigration control be an effective anti-crime measure? And if not, what contrary lessons are revealed?

TWO WAVES

In 2004, ten countries joined the European Union. Residents of two – Cyprus and Malta – were already members of the Commonwealth and had fewer restrictions on their right to move to the UK. Eight other countries, however, had less easy access to work in EU countries: the Czech Republic, Estonia, Hungary, Latvia, Lithuania, Poland, Slovakia and Slovenia. At the time there were fewer than

200,000 people from these countries in the UK. But many thought that would change slightly once restrictions on these eight 'Accession' countries – known as the 'A8' – were removed. The UK government was expecting to receive around 15,000 extra immigrants per year and planned accordingly. But the estimates were miles off. Within five years, the number of A8 nationals living in the UK had increased by half a million, from around 200,000 to over 700,000.[14] By 2013 the figure stood at around one million, five times the level at the start of the century.[15]

Not all who moved found work or settled quickly. Robert Nowa-kowski had a job as a salesman in Poland but saw the UK as offering more opportunities and new experiences. Yet he was one of many for whom the move proved more difficult and disorientating than expected: 'When I first came here, there was a bad two or three months when I didn't have any friends and I felt really alone. It took some time to learn about job vacancies and where to live.'[16]

News stories started to suggest more widespread problems – and there were concerns about crime. 'Britain's top black police officer: "We are struggling to cope with immigrant crime wave"', the *Daily Mail* warned.[17] Julie Spence, another chief constable, pointed out more difficulties:[18] 'When they [A8 immigrants] arrive they think they can do the same thing as in the country they have come from,' she said. 'There were a lot of people who . . . because they used to carry knives for protection, they think they can carry knives here. We have worked with the communities because they don't necessarily come to commit crime but they need to be told what you can and can't do . . . We can identify a significant rise in drink-driving, which was down to people thinking that what they did where they came from, they could do here.'[19]

Brian Bell and Stephen Machin at the London School of Economics (LSE) became interested. Noting the sparsity of academic research on the subject, they started thinking about how they might test what had really happened to crime as a result of immigration into the UK. Working with another researcher, Francesco Fasani, their approach was to focus on areas that had taken in the most immigrants and see whether crime rates there had risen or fallen compared with other areas. They looked at violent crime and property crime separately in 371 local authorities and tried to spot patterns. Was the arrival of people like Robert Nowakowski leading to an increase in crime?

Many immigrants were, like Robert, young men and therefore more likely to commit more crime (see Myth 2). But, to the surprise of many, the researchers found that areas with higher immigration did not experience more crime. They had roughly the same levels of violent crime as those with lower immigration.[20] And there was in fact *less* property crime in places where there had been a larger A8 influx.[21] This was a striking finding and contradicted warnings from some segments of the media.

The researchers also checked arrest rates for A8 immigrants – admittedly a measure of policing decisions as well as crimes actually committed. They found that they were broadly the same as those for natives, even though the immigrants were on average much poorer.[22] Similarly, they looked at the number of immigrants in prison, testing how many immigrants were convicted and the harshness of their sentences relative to those of natives. The results were the same. 'To the extent that there are more people in prison from A8 countries, this is simply a result of the massive rise in the size of those populations in the UK rather than evidence of increased incarceration rates,' they said.[23] All this suggested that immigration might not only be a solution to a shortage of skills in particular trades or the demand for cheap labour – it might have the beneficial side effect of lowering crime.

This was certainly good news for Britain and for pro-immigration groups. But the researchers were interested in immigration in general, not just from A8 countries. They looked at another wave of immigration to see if the results were similar. From 1990s onwards the UK has accommodated growing numbers of people seeking asylum from war or persecution. Asylum applications have often spiked, most notably between 1998 and 2002 as a result of conflict in Iraq, Afghanistan and Somalia among other places.

Personal accounts highlight similar problems of integration to those of Robert. Jamal Osman is a Somali immigrant who moved to the UK in his early twenties in 1999. By that time, Somalia had endured nearly a decade without a meaningful national government and hundreds of thousands of people had already fled, often to refugee camps in neighbouring countries. 'I came to this country from Somalia in my early twenties with no family and very little English,' Jamal says. 'It took me two years to be comfortable with life in London.'[24]

But the researchers noted some obvious differences between the two immigrant groups. Unlike A8 immigrants, the majority of asylum seekers were women and children.[25] And fewer asylum seekers stayed for long periods: most usually stayed in the UK for significant periods of time to see through the application process, particularly if they lodged appeals, but in total around 70 per cent of the applications were refused or withdrawn. While asylum seekers are awaiting decisions, most receive accommodation and subsistence allowances. And because of this, the LSE researchers could access records that showed reasonably accurately where they had moved to and might settle.

The researchers found that there wasn't any real change in violent crime compared to other areas. But when it came to property crime there was a difference, and this time it was bad news for pro-immigrant groups. Areas with more asylum seekers experienced a slight *increase* in crime. The impact of A8 immigration and that of asylum seekers appeared to be different.

The methods the LSE team had used to identify where asylum seekers settled were not perfect, so they again checked wider crime statistics. And they found that people coming from areas of conflict and persecution were indeed slightly over-represented in data on police arrests and the prison population – being more likely to be imprisoned than both natives and A8 immigrants. This could be attributed to bias in the justice system. But, given the other compatible evidence, the two waves of immigration to Britain do indeed appear to differ in terms of their impact.

The LSE academics thought the reasons for the difference were quite obvious. The asylum seekers were excluded from the labour market, partly because of tight restrictions on employment until residency was granted. And they noted too that allowances for asylum seekers were barely at subsistence level. Single men received £35.52 per week in 2009 compared to £65.45 for those on unemployment benefit. A8 immigrants meanwhile enjoyed good labour market outcomes. By 2009–10, in fact, A8 immigrants were more likely to be employed and less likely to be in receipt of benefits than natives. This is an interesting theory. But Bell and Machin recognize that 'labour market attachment' was not the only difference between the two groups. As they explain, asylum seekers and A8 immigrants 'have very different characteristics and motivations for migration'.[26] A8 immigrants moved primarily to improve their lot financially, drawn to UK wages and employment opportunities, whereas asylum seekers were often driven from their previous lives by war and persecution.

There is another explanation that is intuitively persuasive. Could it be that immigrants bring with them the crime and violence of their home countries? After all, Poland, the main contributor to A8 immigration to Britain, had similar rates of crime to the UK according to mid-2000s cross-national surveys.[27] And while crime rates in many war-torn countries are hard to estimate, there is no doubt that those countries have suffered extreme violence: some, including Somalia, have endured periods of near-complete breakdown in the rule of law.

LAND OF OPPORTUNITY

Ciudad Juárez in Mexico does not enjoy the finest of reputations. One of its most famous buildings is the 'House of Death' on 3633 Calle Parsioneros, which in 2006 was discovered to contain twelve tortured and executed corpses, allegedly victims of Juárez cartel associates. In September 2009, gunmen shot and killed seventeen patients at a drug rehabilitation centre, echoing a similar attack in which twenty were killed in March of the same year.[28] Conflict between the Juárez and Sinaloa cartels is often blamed for the bulk of the trouble, but victims are not limited to those associated with organized crime. Juárez is known as 'the capital of murdered women', after a series of brutal cases in which the bodies of young women were found months after their disappearance, bearing signs of torture, sexual assault and, in some cases, mutilation. In 2009 Ciudad Juárez, with an estimated 2,600 deaths, claimed the dubious title of the world's overall murder capital too, and has since rarely slipped from the top three spots in the rankings.[29]

Mexico's problems are well chronicled and there are serious concerns that violence will flow over into the US. Every few months stories surface which prompt prophecies that the decline has begun. In 2009, Tucson, Arizona experienced a spate of home invasions that were thought to be drug-related, inspiring *The New York Times'* byline 'Mexican Drug Cartel Violence Spills Over, Alarming US'.[30]

Just across the border from Ciudad Juárez, separated only by a narrow river, is another remarkable city, El Paso in Texas. It has one of the highest poverty rates of big US cities, yet is happy and booming. Judging from the large number of immigrants arriving there, low wages are more than compensated for by a growing number of jobs, particularly in government, oil and service sectors, good weather and leisure facilities, and an excellent university. El Paso's population increased from a modest 130,000 in 1950 to over 650,000 at the time of writing (2013), and much of the city's expansion has come from the arrival of aspiring Hispanic immigrants.

An additional attraction is its security. If you'd arrived in El Paso in 2011, you'd have heard a proud claim over the airport's public address system: 'El Paso welcomes you to the safest city in America.'[31]

The claim is justified. In 2009, El Paso reported just twelve murders, a fraction of the 2,600 in neighbouring Juárez. And, with low rates of other crimes, El Paso has since been named America's safest big city three times.

Over a quarter of El Paso's population are foreign-born, mostly from Mexico, and 80 per cent of the city's residents identify themselves as Hispanic or Latino.[32] But Mexicans do not appear to have brought their nation's crime rates with them. El Paso is no anomaly either. Low crime rates are enjoyed by a number of other cities with high levels of Hispanic immigration, including San Diego in California.[33] Indeed, there researchers found (as in the study of A8 immigrants to Britain) that neighbourhoods which received a higher number of immigrants experienced more rapid falls in crime than elsewhere.[34] And, far from the border, a Harvard criminologist, Anthony Sampson, has shown that immigrants into Chicago, residing there both legally and illegally, commit less crime than natives given their relative deprivation. As he writes, 'First-generation immigrants (those born outside the United States) were 45 per cent less likely to commit violence than third-generation Americans, adjusting for individual, family, and neighborhood background.'[35]

These local studies provide the best indications of the overall impact of immigration on US crime rates – largely because national studies are beset by data problems. Prisons do not systematically record the nationality of inmates and, like the data on nationalities of those arrested by the police, often include guesses rather than verified figures.[36] Similar problems are encountered elsewhere. In most of Europe except the UK, the collection and reporting of data based on ethnicity is strictly forbidden (except for that on Roma and Sinti): mindful of the corollary of vigorous ethnic identification in Nazi Germany, only citizenship status is used to measure crime across groups or generations. In some countries, including Sweden, there are even restrictions on reporting countries of birth for those who have acquired Swedish citizenship.

So there are differing views about the validity of generalizations based on nationality or ethnicity. The differences between immigrants from any one country certainly far outweigh the differences between 'the average immigrant' from different nations. Somalis, for example, are over-represented in England's young offender institutions and have some of the worst employment and education outcomes of any group residing in Britain.[37] But criminality is still clearly a minority pursuit and there are plenty of highly successful, law-abiding Somali immigrants: Jamal Osman, having arrived in the country with no family and limited English, is now a successful journalist. Somalis who grew up in a time of conflict share that horrendous experience, but the group is hardly homogeneous. So while some Somali refugees from rural poverty see their UK lives as an improvement, others do not. One Somali mother who fled with her children is grateful for the support she has been given by the UK but still pines for her former life: 'Things are very different and difficult here compared to Somalia. We had an import/export business in Somalia dealing in leather goods from Italy ... We had three houses in

Somalia and our children went to private Italian school, but here we live in a council flat on income support.'[38]

LAND OF OUR FATHERS

Gaps in data make it particularly difficult to examine the extent to which immigrants' children commit crime. But there are interesting trends hidden within the information available in some countries. As we've seen, levels of offending are slightly lower among US economic immigrants than among natives, particularly once socio-economic status is taken into account. But the data on immigrants' children suggests otherwise: the children of Hispanic immigrants in the US, for example, present very similar levels of offending to natives. And, indeed, it's even been shown that the longer first-generation Hispanic immigrants stay in the US, the more similar their offending becomes to that of natives.[39] The same has been found for immigrants to the UK. The LSE academics who looked at A8 immigrants concluded that 'there is little difference between natives and those immigrants who have been in the UK 10 years or more'.[40]

Many regard this as simply a side effect of assimilation. But the patchy European data suggests that some countries at least may be witnessing a different and more worrying phenomenon. In most European countries it appears that second- and third-generation immigrants often, though not always, have significantly higher rates of offending than natives, even when differences in personal and parental wealth are taken into account.[41] This is known as a 'paradox of assimilation'.[42] Second-generation immigrants usually do better than their parents in terms of education and employment but fare far worse with regard to physical and mental health, substance misuse and crime rates.[43]

There are many theories as to why second-generation immigrants experience more difficulties. Many are plausible but all are hard to test. One is that they don't benefit from the same reference points as their parents: they compare their lot with that of others in the country in which they live rather than the country of their parents' birth – which in turn leads to frustrations. Another theory is that second-generation immigrants are caught between two worlds and, consequently, struggle to find their identity. This could plausibly result in problems of adjustment and cause young people to seek other sources of identity – for example, gang membership – or contribute to more general frustrations that end directly or indirectly in crime and violence. A third, related theory points to the difficulties immigrant parents have in ensuring that their children are successful in their new environment. Non-English-speaking parents might, for example, be less well placed to support their children with schoolwork or advise them on the social problems they may face.

A fourth theory is that they are dealt with unfairly. There is certainly good reason to believe that the treatment immigrants receive affects their eventual success. Most European countries appear to have a national, ethnic or religious group that comes in for special criticism in political and media commentary. But 'problem' immigrant groups often differ from country to country. For example, in Germany second-generation Turks are more crime-prone than second-generation Moroccans and are more widely criticized. The opposite is true across the border in the Netherlands, where Moroccans do worse and are more widely attacked in the media.[44]

There is clear evidence of bias in the justice system against ethnic minorities, which one might expect to affect those arriving from non-white countries. For example, blacks in Washington DC are eight times more likely than whites to be arrested for marijuana possession, even though whites are equally likely to smoke it.[45] However, research tends to show that police and legal discrimination is not great enough wholly to account for the over-representation of minority ethnicities and nationalities in our prisons and police cells. These minority groups genuinely do appear to engage in more criminal activity, even if they are additionally disadvantaged by various forms of accidental or deliberate profiling and unfair treatment.

Higher levels of offending might all the same partly result from the frustrations of being discriminated against. There is plenty of evidence that points to the fact that resentment of perceived injustices can make people lash out – with violence or other forms of 'expressive' behaviour, including vandalism and looting. Incidents of perceived or real discrimination have been some of the main triggers for rioting in Western countries over the past century. And myriad smaller incidents may have an equally significant impact, even if they mostly go unreported. Racist taunts at school lead to violent outbursts and, subsequently, suspensions and exclusions, and 'disrespect' on the street can trigger retributive gang violence.[46] Slights and rejection matter. Psychological experiments show that rejection by others often has a powerful effect.[47] In some cases the reaction is positive, encouraging people to work harder to gain social acceptance or win back affection. But for many it is not. Some of those rejected isolate themselves to protect against further psychological pain which they feel ill-equipped to endure. And others lash out, particularly if they perceive their rejection as unfair. Angry reactions can be interpreted as an attempt to intimidate others in order to prevent further abuse, but experiments show that anger is the most common reaction when people have lost all hope of acceptance and feel they won't be able to make their way back into a group.[48]

Repeated rejection has been linked to more damaging coping strategies: self-medication to grapple with social anxiety or depression; withdrawal from socially mixed environments; and rejection of mainstream values or refusal to accept the authority of those whom you see as representative of any unfair treatment received.[49] And all these reactions can in turn increase the likelihood of committing crime. Of course, the greatest risk will be for those less well equipped to resist the temptations of crime (see Myth 3). But it seems plausible that persistent exclusion is a path not just to short-term frustrations and flare-ups but also to questionable choices that can lead to further trouble.

THE MORALITY OF IMMIGRATION

Robert Nowakowski may have had a tricky start to life in England but, like most A8 immigrants, he found work and quickly assimilated. 'I'm working as a night duty receptionist in a big hotel in west London,' he says. 'It's hard work but my life is good.'[50] He has no plans to commit crime: like most Polish immigrants, he has no prior record of criminal or antisocial behaviour, was well looked after by

Fig. 13: 2010 advert, by the Swiss People's Party, depicting 'Ivan S'

his family and well educated in Poland. Some Polish immigrants are no doubt different. But what sets them apart is not strictly their country of origin; it is their prior experiences and differences in personality.

National averages provide an extraordinarily crude guide to whether someone will commit crime. And fortunately most countries, if not everyone within them, recognize this. Some countries still retain extremely basic nationality-based systems for deciding who is allowed to stay within their borders, but increasingly more subtle criteria are at play. Most developed countries now operate 'points-based systems' which determine who can live and work there, depending not so much on nationality as on other grounds: assessing humanitarian suffering, economic potential, ability to fill skills shortages and so on. The systems of filtering they use reveal much about the value that different countries (and political parties) attach to different goals, with some nations giving more weight to humanitarian factors and others favouring economic considerations.

Some politicians and commentators still try to argue that nationality does strongly affect crime, usually adversely. And when they do so, they often draw on isolated cases. Fig. 13 shows a 2010 advertisement by the Swiss People's Party which attempts to persuade voters of the risks of immigration by focusing on a single case of rape committed by an immigrant. That such a stance should determine a party's immigration policy is unsettling, and the implication that immigrants are all rapists preposterously untrue.

Some waves of immigration do present higher rates of crime, others can actually reduce crime; but both pro- and anti-immigration campaigners are guilty of manipulating cases and statistics to bolster arguments that are not based on balanced evidence. Some people think immigration is a bad thing, and seize on examples of immigrant criminality to support their case. Others favour immigration on humanitarian or cultural grounds and do likewise. There are clearly important questions about how we should manage immigration to ensure that immigrant groups – and particularly their children – are not drawn into crime and other social problems. But it is clear that reducing levels of immigration is no panacea for our crime problems.

Myth 8: We need more bobbies on the beat

To ensure the adoration of a theorem for any length of time, faith is not enough; a police force is needed as well.

Albert Camus[1]

THE THIN BLUE LINE

'I got a phone call. I come down here. All the windows were smashed to pieces. All the goods were taken,' the shop owner explained. 'Then we started to clean up here and I heard a big mob around Morgan's [department store], hollering and screaming and window-smashing and everything. So I told the boys "Let's lock the store and get out of here and let them do whatever they want." '[2]

The middle-aged Montreal shop owner saw no point in waiting for the police. After all, he was describing events in Montreal on 7 October 1969, the day that 5,000 of the city's police and fire officers had gone on strike in protest at a lack of progress in pay negotiations. During the daytime, things had been relatively quiet. Bank robberies were estimated to have doubled, but citizens went about their business barely noticing any change in crime levels.[3]

Only after workers had gone home and the shopkeepers locked up did the trouble really start. Two hundred taxi drivers saw the police strike as an opportunity to protest more effectively against a long-held grievance – the fact that the city had granted Murray Hill Limousine Service exclusive rights to pick up passengers from Dorval International (now Montréal-Trudeau) airport.[4] Then others joined the unrest. Reporters spoke of 'left-wing separatists' flowing onto the streets, but there were plenty of rioters without any clear political cause. By the time night fell, windows were being smashed and stores looted. Violence escalated, with two deaths, including the shooting of a police officer, and a number of violent beatings. The small number of officers brought in from Quebec's Provincial Police (Sûreté du Québec) to maintain order were overwhelmed.

Only as events threatened to spiral out of control did the police finally buckle to political pressure and return to work. When they did so, order was quickly restored. Then, as shopkeepers began to clear their empty, glass-strewn shops, the army arrived to support them, standing vigil at Montreal's public buildings. After just sixteen hours, the experience of a police-free city was over.

Similar events have also confirmed the importance of policing. The Boston police strike of 1918 led to widespread rioting. Then a series of actions in the 1970s – in New York, Baltimore, San Francisco, Cleveland and New Orleans – all resulted in spikes in crime, albeit less dramatic ones. And police strikes are not the only proof that police prevent crime. During the Second World War, Denmark endured an uneasy form of occupation by Germany. Fearful that the police were not actively suppressing the Danish Resistance's efforts to undermine their rule, the Nazis interned a large proportion of the Danish police force in concentration camps, leaving the police service decimated. Crime increased noticeably.[5]

Surprisingly, not all police strikes have led to increases in crime. The London strike of 1918, for example, appeared to be a relatively good-natured affair. As vast numbers of police officers crowded into Downing Street to protest against poor pay, there was no discernible increase in disorder elsewhere in the capital. According to *The Times*, the country had seen 'proof' of 'people's ingrained respect for law and order'.[6] Yet a year later that statement was proven overly hasty. In 1919, Liverpool's police officers, who suffered appalling pay and conditions compared to those working in other parts of the country, downed tools. News spread quickly and before long members of the docking communities were looting, openly trying on new clothes in vandalized tailors' shops, and even playing stolen pianos in the street.[7] Fearing Bolshevism when there was probably little reason to, the Prime Minister, Lloyd George, dispatched the army to restore order and the striking police officers were all summarily dismissed.

This episode prompted the British government to put in place arrangements to outlaw strike action by the police which have since been replicated by many other national and regional governments.[8] But periodic and limited actions have continued, with predictable consequences. In 2012, the province of Bahia in Brazil experienced a twelve-day police walkout which led to a short-term doubling of murder rates in the city of Salvador, even though the army provided a degree of security cover.[9]

Police strikes therefore don't always lead to increased crime, but these cases reinforce our already strong association between policing and crime prevention.[10]

When we witness or fall victim to crime, the police are usually the first body we turn to. So for decades one of the most common political responses to crime has been to increase police numbers. As the dust settled after the 2011 London riots, the comment made by the Mayor, Boris Johnson, was predictable: 'What Londoners want to see now is loads of police out there on the streets. That's what's been successful over the last few days. That's the policy people want us to keep up with.'[11] Politicians who follow this logic have overseen significant growth in police numbers in the second half of the twentieth century and the early twenty-first. And we are regularly told of the impact that increased and better policing has had on crime. Sir Hugh Orde, President of the Association of Chief Police Officers, provides a typical police chief's assessment of his time in his previous job. 'In Northern Ireland between 2002 and 2009 (I would choose those years, wouldn't I!), we reduced all crime by 23 per cent.'[12]

Only as budgets tightened have a few governments permitted a quiet reduction in police numbers, much to the outrage of national and local police services. In response to cuts to policing budgets by the Home Secretary, Theresa May, in 2010, the Police Federation of England and Wales paid for a hard-hitting advertising campaign warning of the likely consequences. Its advert shows a little girl cowering in the corner of a room, her hands over her ears, as the shadow of an aggressive man looms over her. 'Consequences of 20% cuts to policing?' the caption warns.

The public are rarely reassured by the idea of fewer police. As Dee Edwards of Mothers Against Murder and Aggression explains, 'The

Fig. 14: Police Federation advert, 2011

kids are telling us they want more police on the streets. If we feel worried as adults, how must the children feel?'[13] Only certain types of policing cut it for the public. We want our police to be visible, not 'stuck behind desks'. We want them to be on hand as soon as possible after a crime. Police must be 'on the beat' to deter would-be wrongdoers and, where this isn't possible, must respond quickly to emergencies, in order to secure the convictions that will avoid future offending, both by the criminal convicted and by others.

The idea that the police are central to crime prevention is a cornerstone of the Heroes and Villains view. In most crime fiction, the police are quite literally the heroes. And it is only their heroism that prevents selfish criminals from preying on the innocent, either because they catch the irredeemably corrupt or because they deter those who will only stop committing crime if they know they'll be caught. Their willingness to put themselves in physical danger keeps us safe and their presence is a reassurance.

Yet while the effect of police strikes shows that the police do indeed perform a vital function in maintaining law and order, do the police really play such a central role in crime reduction? And is it their visibility and the speed of their response that matter most?

OVERWHELMING FORCE

These questions are at once vitally important and far harder to answer than we might think. Looking at policing levels and crime rates in different countries or cities, for example, tells us very little about the impact of policing. If it works, then areas with more police should logically have less crime; but, at the same time, politicians tend to send more officers to high-crime areas to address the problems there. Crime can, in a sense, cause an increase in police numbers.

Because of this, it's very hard to disentangle what is going on. A glance at the numbers shows that areas with higher crime rates tend to have more police officers, but we can't conclude much from that. So hundreds of statistical studies have tried to reach conclusions by looking at changes in police numbers over time and/or by 'controlling' other factors that might influence crime rates. However, such techniques are usually of only limited value, and their inherent problems are exposed by the varied results these studies present. Some conclude that policing reduces crime rates, while a similar number argue that it makes little difference.[14] Some studies even show that increased police presence *increases* crime rates.[15]

The consequences of police strikes shed some light on the question. But the fact that police strikes have sometimes been accompanied by civil unrest does not necessarily mean that more police are always better. After all, there is a big difference between saying that some police are needed to maintain an orderly society and agreeing with the consensus that ever more police are needed to reduce crime levels. Given the sums spent on policing – around £10bn per year in the UK alone – we need to find other ways to determine whether bobbies on the beat really guarantee our safety.

Clarence Kelley was the right man in the right place at the right time. A former FBI agent, the Kansas City Chief of Police was less attached to traditional policing methods than many of his colleagues, but he was by no means an outsider. After ten years in post he had earned the respect of senior colleagues and local politicians, and was trusted with considerable freedom to redeploy police resources. This was also 1972 – a year when crime was rising rapidly across the US and increased police numbers were not stemming the tide. While police chiefs in other US states urged for more of the same, Kelley counselled caution. 'Many of us in the department,' he explains, 'had the feeling we were training, equipping, and deploying men to do a job neither we, nor anyone else, knew much about.'[16]

Kelley asked the Police Foundation, an independent research institute, to help the department ask previously unthinkable questions. Kelley wanted to start at the beginning, examining the effectiveness of patrol. In the 1830s Sir Charles Rowan, the first Commissioner of the London Metropolitan Police, had argued that a constable 'should be able to see every part of his beat at least once in ten minutes or a quarter of an hour'.[17] And as the British model of policing was emulated across the world, patrols became the cornerstone of policing practice worldwide. Chicago's Police Superintendent Orlando Wilson, an influential policing theorist, summarized the received wisdom: 'Patrol is an indispensable service that plays a leading role in the accomplishment of the police purpose. It is the only form of police service that directly attempts to eliminate opportunity for misconduct . . .'[18]

In Kansas, like most other big cities in the US, patrol meant vehicle patrol. Foot patrol was still used, but cities were now designed for cars and vehicle patrolling allowed officers to cover more ground. In the Kansas City Police Department, an estimated 60 per cent of officers' time was spent in marked cars on patrol.

As Kelley's discussions with the Police Foundation progressed, it became clear that asking difficult questions also required difficult decisions. The researchers insisted that the only way to estimate the impact of patrol accurately was to effectively 'switch off' patrols entirely in five of Kansas City's fifteen beat areas. Police would still respond to calls from these 'reactive' areas, but that was about it; they would otherwise stay out of the area unless pursuing active investigations. Several front-line officers were concerned by the potential consequences of not serving these areas, but the experiment's design provided a measure of reassurance: overall levels of policing in the city would remain constant. In fact, patrols more than doubled in five of the other beat areas ('proactive' areas). And in the remaining five areas ('control' areas), historic patrol patterns were maintained.

Kelley was happy to support the researchers' rigour. But if he was to become the first Chief of Police deliberately to do away with police patrols in large tracts of Kansas City, he needed reassurances. Researchers should, he said, conduct their experiment on the effectiveness of vehicle patrol in as scientific a way as possible, but he would have to be able to cancel it if crime reached 'unacceptable limits'.[19]

Concerned that officers would scupper the experiment by providing service to the areas without patrol, it was agreed that observers could periodically monitor police in action to ensure rostered patrol patterns were adhered to. Officers stuck to the plan, however, so the main anxiety became the crime statistics. Kelley and his colleagues were hopeful that they would see improved results in the 'proactive' areas with doubled patrols – but they also watched the data flowing in carefully to ensure the abandoned 'reactive' areas were not going to seed. Months passed without the need to intervene. And even at the scheduled eight-month checkpoint it was decided to continue with the patrol patterns for a further four months. Parts of Kansas therefore went without routine car patrol for a full year, while others enjoyed more than double the usual police presence.

As the data was being analysed, Kelley was offered and took a new job as Director of the FBI, his main task being to restore the agency's reputation in the wake of the Watergate scandal. But his successor in Kansas City, Joseph McNamara, made the decision to see the study through and publish the experiment's evaluation in full. Its conclusions were dry but stark: 'Analysis of the data gathered revealed that the three areas [one with no patrols, one with historic levels of patrolling and one with doubled patrols] experienced no significant differences in the level of crime, citizens' attitudes toward police services, citizens' fear of crime, police response time, or citizens' satisfaction with police response time.'[20] Random patrols in marked cars, which had been absorbing a vast chunk of the department's budget, simply didn't work.

The experiment shocked the policing community but failed fundamentally to shift the political consensus that more police would control rising crime rates across the US. It did, however, lay the ground for further investigation. In 1981, the Police Foundation researchers examined foot patrols in Newark, New Jersey. They

again set up the experiment carefully and even carried out large victimization surveys to ensure that they captured real changes in crime
rates. They found that removing routine foot patrols in the daytime
and early evening was noticed by residents and led to lower resident
satisfaction with the police. There were signs too that fear of crime
was lower in areas where there were more foot patrols. But, as with
car patrols, removing foot patrols from selected beats had no discernible impact on crime. A similar UK study helped to explain why. It
calculated that a police officer patrolling randomly on foot in an
average beat could expect to come within a hundred yards of a burglary in progress just once every eight years.[21] Money was still being
wasted on car patrols, but it seemed that foot patrols were also
expending valuable crime-fighting resources on the benefit of
increased feelings of – rather than real –safety.

Evidence of police effectiveness gradually became even more damn-
ing. One of the main reasons why the police historically favoured
patrolling both by car and on foot was that it was believed to reduce
the time it took for police to arrive at crime scenes: response rates have
long been seen as crucial to deterring and catching criminals. For
many decades, police forces have compared their response times to
those of neighbouring forces and boasted of any improvements. Politicians, meanwhile, have kept an eye out for failings. After average
response times rose in a number of UK police forces in 2013, Britain's
Shadow Home Secretary, Yvette Cooper, attacked: 'These figures
show the service the police provide to the public is being hollowed out.
The police are doing what they can, but the scale and pace of the government's cuts over the last three years is hitting services despite
Theresa May's promises that the frontline would not be hit. People
want to know the police will be there when they need them.'[22]

The problem, however, is that most of the evidence shows that
police response times make no noticeable difference to crime rates –
or even the likelihood of making an arrest. One reason for this is that
the public take so long to report most crimes that the length of time
the police take to react is often not that important. Chief Kelley's
Kansas City experiment found that the average reporting time for
'involvement crimes' like assault, robbery and rape, where victims
interact with perpetrators, was an astonishing forty-one minutes.

They also found that the chances of securing an arrest only improved if police got to the scene within nine minutes of an incident, which was very rarely feasible because of the vast number of occasions when calls took longer than that to come in. These conclusions were later confirmed by a large study by the National Institute of Justice, which involved over 4,000 interviews concerning more than 3,300 crimes.[23] Again, it found that rapid response to crimes did little to affect arrest rates and most victims did not call the police immediately. The fixation on average response times was unjustifiable, particularly when the risk of accidents caused by police cars racing to crime scenes was taken into account. Even the kindest possible interpretation of the evidence pointed to the need carefully to prioritize which incidents merited rapid response. In most cases, the expense was simply not worth it.

That three cornerstones of modern policing – vehicle patrols, foot patrols and rapid response – might have little effect on crime rates is deeply disconcerting. Hundreds of billions of pounds have been spent on police patrols and improving response times over the past century. And it appears that most of this money has been wasted. Perhaps we should pause. Is it possible that the organization that is meant to protect us is actually doing little more than picking up the pieces and providing us with a false sense of security? Riots during strikes suggest we need at least a minimum level of policing to maintain order – but could it be that increased police numbers have little real impact on crime rates?

COUNTER-TERRORISM TACTICS

Three of the bombs exploded simultaneously, before the fourth blew off the top deck of the number 331 bus travelling south from London's King's Cross Station to Russell Square.[24] Fifty-two people were killed, including the four suicide bombers who travelled to London that day, 7 July 2005.

Nothing good came of the tragedy. But it did provide an opportunity to learn more about the impact of policing. After the 7/7 bombings, the Metropolitan Police redeployed officers across the capital.

Operation Theseus, as it was termed, increased the number of hours police officers spent in five central London boroughs by about a third for a period of six weeks after the attack. Policing in other London boroughs was mostly unchanged, however, creating an interesting comparison.

Researchers at the London School of Economics saw their opportunity and started to study whether crime rates had changed as a result of the redeployment of police to central London.[25] The impact of the extra police in London's centre appeared to be instant. In the districts where there was no change in police presence, crime rates remained broadly unaltered. But crime dropped by just over 10 per cent in the areas with increased policing, with the main fall coming in street crimes like robbery, assault and car theft.

There are lots of reasons why a terrorist attack might lead to a reduction in crime in the city centre, irrespective of policing levels. After all, the number of people in these areas also dropped after the terrorist attacks, with fewer visitors to London and commuters also down by over 10 per cent. Yet while passenger numbers only very slowly returned to normal, crime rates immediately normalized once Operation Theseus ended abruptly (though without public announcements) after six weeks. This strongly suggests that the reduction in crime was due to an increased police presence. After taking into account all of the factors, the research team estimated that an increase of 10 per cent in police presence resulted in a 3–4 per cent reduction in crime.

The finding is as confusing as it is intriguing. The Kansas and Newark experiments showed that routine foot and car patrols made little difference to crime, but here we have research appearing to confirm not just that we need some form of police force to prevent widespread disorder but that extra police can reduce crime. It is not an entirely isolated case either. After another terrorist attack, this time on the main Jewish centre in Buenos Aires in 1994, police were positioned to guard potential targets for further anti-Semitic offensives. For the period that extra officers were employed to protect synagogues and other potential targets, vehicle thefts in the block where the additional forces were based and in the next block fell – but there was no discernible effect elsewhere.[26] Both this study and that of London after the 7/7 bombings showed that increasing police in one area rarely leads to more crime elsewhere – a finding that should not be surprising given that the majority of crime is opportunistic or unplanned (see Myths 2 and 3).

This conundrum initially appears hard to explain. But a closer look shows that the findings are not entirely contradictory. The simple truth is that police presence *can* make a difference to crime, but it very much depends on the context in which it is operating. Random patrols in reasonably safe areas, something police still spend a lot of money on, appear unlikely to do much to deter offenders. Meanwhile, police presence at high-crime 'hotspots', of which there are many in urban centres like London and Buenos Aires, can make a real difference to crime rates.

The evidence that so-called 'hotspot' policing works is now compelling. Police in the right place at the right time can prevent violent street crime and thefts – while obviously making no difference at all to crimes such as domestic violence. This is good news, particularly as our ability to police in this way is improving rapidly. Advances in technology and data availability mean it's easier than ever to understand patterns of crime. Mobile phone signals now allow governments (and others) around the world to track patterns of movement and crime information systems are becoming ever more sophisticated. Almost all analysis shows that crime is highly concentrated. In Minneapolis a leading figure in policing research, Professor Larry Sherman, and his colleagues looked at over 300,000 calls to the police from 115,000 distinct 'places' (addresses and intersections). They found that half of the calls came from just 3 per cent of those places.[27] Concentrating resources on these areas makes a difference, but stationing police elsewhere is often prohibitively expensive.

Intelligence about patterns of crime should not be the only factor informing police patrol, however. There are other highly effective ways the police can target crime. Though popular 'gun buy-back' schemes and 'knife amnesties' often fail to get weapons out of the hands of would-be criminals, targeted searches and arrests in gun- or knife-crime hotspots are often more effective. Another Kansas experiment showed that targeted traffic stops and 'field interrogations' in gun crime hotspots during times when most shootings occurred led to an increase of more than two thirds in gun seizures and a halving of gun crime.[28] In a similar area in a different part of town where there was no change in policing activity, there was no change either in the number of guns seized or gun crimes.

Importantly, police officers with powers of arrest aren't needed at all for a vast number of functions that effectively prevent crime. Despite politicians' obsession with the number of uniformed officers, civilian police staff or other public sector workers can often make as big a difference. And they can usually do so more cheaply because (partly due to fear of police strikes) police have managed to negotiate pay deals that are higher than those of most other professions, taking into account their levels of education and training.[29]

Providing home security advice and handing out cheap window locks to burglary victims is a useful, cost-effective way of reducing burglaries, not least because burglars often return after the first break-in. Blocking access to alleyways that provide easy access for burglars can also work. And councils can reduce the risk of assaults and muggings by focusing on street lighting, ensuring good supervision of taxi ranks at closing times, and even providing free transport for night-time revellers. Crimes can be minimized by reducing opportunities to commit crime: by rendering targets less attractive and by making it obvious that offenders stand a good chance of being caught, whether by the police or other capable guardians of public order.

We will explore such approaches further in a subsequent chapter. But one of the obvious advantages of these measures is that, unlike much police work, they are aimed at prevention and avoid the costs of trials and prison accommodation. The disadvantage, however, is that they challenge our deep-rooted convictions about what 'proper' policing is. Politicians repeatedly emphasize 'visibility' and 'action' as the main policing virtues, whereas time spent collecting and analysing data is regarded as a chore to be avoided. Those working in law enforcement who don't have powers of arrest are still regularly described as 'pen pushers' or, in the case of the police community support officers introduced by the Labour government in 2002, 'plastic policemen'. As Oliver Letwin, the Conservative Party's policy supremo, put it when he was Shadow Home Secretary from 2001 to 2003: 'Ladies and gentlemen, we must put the police back on our streets . . . But we have to do more than just provide the extra police officers. We have to make sure that instead of being stuck behind desks, they are put onto the streets and into the neighbourhoods.'[30]

Dangerous police work is seen as particularly valuable – and indeed danger is presented as an essential part of policing. Theresa May's first speech to rank-and-file officers as Home Secretary in 2010 started by listing officers killed in the course of their work, her first line being: 'There is no greater act of humanity than to put your life on the line to protect others.'[31] And as she said to the same audience three years later, 'Being a police officer is a tough, dangerous job. Those of us who work behind desks should never forget that you face the possibility of an encounter with lethal danger every day.'[32] Documentaries, meanwhile, stress the dangerous – and physical – aspects of policing.[33]

This perennial emphasis on danger and action is misleading, however. There is no doubt that aspects of police work are stressful and unpleasant. A thick skin is certainly required in most roles, and police suicide rates rival those of army personnel.[34] But the limited research on the topic shows that policing is in fact markedly safer than many other jobs. Dr Stephen Roberts of the University of Oxford looked at the most dangerous professions in the UK in the 1980s and policing came in at number twenty-four, with deaths at work being ten times less than for fishermen (the most dangerous job) and below farmers, builders and even dustmen![35] In the UK, a check of the police roll of honour and news reports suggests there may even have been years when more people were murdered by off-duty police officers than police officers killed in the line of duty. According to the National Police Officers Roll of Honour, one officer was murdered in 2001 and another was the victim of manslaughter.[36] PC Malcolm Walker was on a routine motorcycle patrol when he stopped a car that proved to be stolen. His vehicle was deliberately rammed by a 23-year-old man who was later convicted of murder. PC Alison Armitage was also run over by a suspect fleeing in a stolen vehicle, her eighteen-year-old killer being subsequently convicted of manslaughter.* The same

---

* Twelve officers were killed in road traffic accidents that year, usually on the way to or from shifts, while another officer died of heart failure at the end of a night shift.

year, however, police constable Karl Bluestone, thirty-six, killed three people, tragically beating his wife and two young sons to death before hanging himself.[37] Policing in the US is slightly more dangerous given high rates of gun ownership and in 2013 there were 111 line-of-duty deaths. But, as in the UK, the biggest cause of death was traffic accidents, which accounted for forty-six cases. Thirty-three officers lost their lives as a result of shooting and eighteen of 'job-related illness'.*[38]

The idea of policing as a dangerous, action-based profession is more than simply misleading: it can lead to extraordinary time-wasting by officers themselves. Senior police chiefs regularly complain, for example, that they find it hard to stop officers from responding en masse to emergency calls rather than attending to other duties as directed. And I have observed this tendency first hand, both during police ride-alongs when I worked in Tony Blair's Strategy Unit and subsequently. I've seen four police cars and a police van (which I was in) arrive for a domestic disturbance. I've seen six detectives arrive, sirens blaring, to eject a sleeping drunk from an office, and several other cases of overkill.

Another fascinating – but near-universal – feature of my police visits was the moment at which an officer would bemoan the fact that it was a 'quiet day'. I have heard this said during every single visit I have been on, though on one occasion, when we spent the day tailing two drug dealers, the apology was more for the fact that it wasn't possible to make an arrest than the lack of appropriately adrenalin-fuelled action. The disappointment officers voice is partly because they suspect that you, like them, want to see 'proper policing' in action, and it is maybe one reason why officers (both accompanied and unaccompanied) race across town to alleviate their boredom.

The emphasis on action also overshadows the importance of good relationships with citizens and communities. Most crimes are solved as a result of victim or witness testimony, not the sophisticated detective

---

* Data on killings by US law enforcement officers is very poor. One estimate shows over 300 killings in 2013 but I know of no reliable data on the proportion of these that are 'justifiable homicides'. There are some indications that murders in the US by police might be about as common as murders of police.

and forensic work we see on television shows. And this applies to 'cold cases' (crimes unsolved for many years) as well as recent crimes. Of recently concluded cold cases in the District of Columbia, 63 per cent were solved following new witness testimony and only 3 per cent involved new DNA evidence.[39] Public co-operation with police investigations is not guaranteed, however; in some circles it is taboo and can lead to reprisals. Distrust between the police and public grows in various ways; it can stem from a simple failure to protect witnesses, but more often it's the result of aggressive policing tactics, particularly those that are perceived as being driven by racial or class profiling.

People who view the police as acting fairly trust them and are, in turn, willing to grant them greater powers. Recognizing this reality, there has been a growing emphasis on 'community policing' across Western countries in recent decades. Evaluation of its effectiveness is made tricky by the fact that the concept of community policing is poorly defined. To some, it simply means more foot patrols – which, as we've seen, are unlikely to make much difference unless they are properly targeted, even though they superficially reassure the public. To others, it means more selective interventions. At the turn of the twenty-first century in London, the Metropolitan Police Service launched Operation Trident to address the problem of black-on-black crime, particularly gun crime involving gangs. The initiative focused heavily on building relationships with those living in the most affected communities and is generally viewed positively, but there has been no formal evaluation of its impact.

The drawback to community policing is, then, identical to that of other policing activities like patrolling. If it's not clear what precisely it is trying to do, its activities are insufficiently targeted and results aren't assessed, then it's quite feasible that community policing will make little difference to the problems being tackled. In order to boost trust of and co-operation with the police, we must analyse why it is that certain communities are hostile to them and test different ways of overcoming the problem. If the purpose of police activity is to improve feelings of safety, for example, targeted techniques are required. And again it may be that other agencies are better placed to achieve results. Feelings of safety are often enhanced less by policing practices than by the 'look and feel' of areas,[40] so better management of litter and graffiti will usually be a cheaper and more effective way of reassuring the public than having visible bobbies on the beat, whether or not that is what people ask for.

POLICE SERVICE

As the dust settled after the Montreal police strike of 1969, the shop-keeper who had abandoned his own property describes the actions of a defiant neighbour to a Canadian Broadcasting Corporation reporter.

'Oh yeah, he held them right off. Nobody came to him . . . He had that gun and nobody come to him.'

The reporter follows up: 'And there's a lesson in there for you too, I think, huh?'

'Oh, I'm not a gun man. Let 'em handle the guns.'[41]

Police strikes do more than illustrate the importance of policing: they reveal its origins. When the police are absent, people quickly reorganize to fulfil essential police functions. Citizens take action to defend property and governments call in other agencies – including the military – to curb unrest. In London's 2011 riots, shopkeepers in Kurdish and Turkish communities in Hackney came out in force to fend off rioters. A coffee shop owner, Yilmaz Karagoz, described the scene: 'There were a lot of them. We came out of our shops but the police asked us to do nothing. But the police did not do anything so, as more came, we chased them off ourselves.' The staff from a local kebab restaurant, armed with knives, played a leading role. 'I don't think they will be coming back,' Karagoz said.[42]

However, not everyone is inclined to take on peacekeeping func-tions. Our Montreal shopkeeper certainly didn't want to – and society is presumably much better off leaving him to run his shop and letting others worry about preventing or curbing riots. His neighbour and our Turkish and Kurdish riot resistance group, meanwhile, may be willing to defend their properties, but without appropriate training they might be more likely to kill an intruder, potentially perpetrating injustice and causing community conflict as well as exposing them-selves to violent reprisals.

In short, the police are our solution to the defence of people and property and administration of justice. As the founder of policing, Sir Robert Peel, put it in 1829, 'The police are the public and the public are the police; the police being only members of the public who are paid to give full time attention to duties which are incumbent on every citizen in the interests of community welfare and existence.'[43]

While the police perform what could be regarded as a *natural* social function, however, we've seen that their effectiveness in reducing crime varies and is often far less than advocates of a Heroes and Villains view suggest. The question of whether there should be more or less police, upon which political debates centre, is much less important than how they are deployed. And received ideas of what 'proper' policing is can, in fact, push the police towards the very activities that we know are ineffective, including random patrols and investment in emergency response. By seeing the police as the organization 'responsible' for reducing crime, we also overlook a far bigger truth: actions by citizens themselves and all manner of government agents can and do affect levels of crime. We need our police to work with these groups, rather than accumulate ever more resources for their own crime 'fight'. Our police services must focus on crime reduction, on prevention rather than cure, using hard data and soft intelligence to find out what works.

Myth 9: Tough sentences are a sure-fire way to deter crime

I know I shall be tax'd with barbarity, when I say, in my opinion, our punishments are too mild. Hanging is the only execution for crimes of the blackest dye for male criminals, which are certainly the greatest number ... in the case of murder, both male and female should be burnt alive.

> Daniel Defoe, *Street Robberies, Considered* (1728)

The degree of civilization in a society can be judged by entering its prisons.

> Fyodor Dostoevsky, *The House of the Dead* (1862)

TIDES OF PUNISHMENT

Bound by his hands and feet, the locksmith is grabbed roughly and attached to an elephant's hind leg by a long cord, which is tied around his waist. As the elephant starts to lumber forwards, his body jerks and bounces against the pavement. His crime is treason. He is believed to have helped four prisoners to escape as part of a plot to oust Gujarat's then ruler, the Guicowar of Baroda.

This is the 1860s and the locksmith is soon to become one of the last men in the region to suffer execution by elephant, a punishment that had been used for centuries throughout South and East Asia. We do not know his exact cause of death. Many sentenced in this way died from a blow to the head as the elephant made its way across the city. But, as the French travel writer and photographer Louis Rousselet described it, some survived to face an even harsher fate. 'After traversing the city, he [the condemned man] is released, and, by a refinement of cruelty, a glass of water is given to him. Then his head is placed upon a stone, and the elephant executioner crushes it beneath his enormous foot.'[1]

Punishment has often been steeped in rich symbolism. Execution by elephant aimed to demonstrate rulers' power through their ability to control the enormous animals. Another brutal penalty, stoning – a sentence still occasionally passed down by tribal courts – demonstrates the social nature of punishment by hiding the executioner among the many. In Europe in the Middle Ages, murderers were offered as slaves to the families of those they had killed: a life for a life.

Yet state punishments, however different in method, all serve two main purposes. They aim to reduce crime by deterring others and discouraging – or entirely preventing – the perpetrator from going on to commit further crimes. And they maintain public support for the rule of law by ensuring that appetites for retribution are satisfied, real or symbolic reparation made, and social disapproval expressed.

Today, many are convinced that modern approaches to punishment fail on both counts. Some hark back nostalgically to the tougher punishments of the past, and there is general agreement that criminals are getting off too lightly: polls in Britain today consistently show that around 80 per cent of people think sentencing is 'too lenient'.[2] Roughly half the population in the UK want the death penalty reintroduced for 'standard murder'.[3] And the majority in Australia, the US and Canada all believe their current systems are too soft. In the US, around two thirds regard sentences for violent crime as too lenient, though there is greater satisfaction with sentences for non-violent offences.[4]

One of the main reasons why people want tougher punishments is the belief that they reduce crime. According to one recent poll, two thirds of the British population agree with the argument that 'The best way to reduce reoffending is to increase the deterrent effect of sentencing – by sending more offenders to prison, making prison life harder, making sentences longer, and making community punishments more demanding.'[5]

Oddly, public criticism that government is too soft on crime ignores the fact that policymakers across the English-speaking world have been increasingly responsive to public dissatisfaction. When crime

L'INDE DES RAJAHS. — Condamné exécuté par un éléphant.
Gravure extraite du *Tour du Monde*. — (Librairie de L. Hachette et Cie.

Fig. 15: Execution by elephant – first published in the 1868 issue of *Le Tour du monde*

first started to rise in the US in the 1960s, few rushed to enact more punitive sentences. But as crime became a more pressing social problem, experts from all fields grew more interested in helping to reduce it. When economists turned their attention to crime, they quickly spotted that – in the US, at least – crime often happened because it 'paid'. In 1968, a seminal work by Gary Becker, the Chicago School economist cited in the introduction to this book, stressed the need to reduce crime by ensuring that the risks and severity of punishment always outweighed its rewards. And in 1975 James Q. Wilson, a Chicago-trained political scientist, published an influential book, *Thinking About Crime*, which emphasized the beneficial effects of keeping criminals behind bars for longer.

Legislators, backed by the public, did not hold back. By the late 1960s, Richard Nixon had launched his 'war on drugs'. In 1976 Gerald Ford broadened this to a more general 'war on crime' as offences continued to rise. Ford introduced stiffer sentences across the board, including tough mandatory minimum terms for gun crimes. But it was under Ronald Reagan and then George Bush that some of the most punitive legislation was introduced: a five-year minimum sentence for first-time offenders possessing 28 or more grams of crack cocaine, for example, alongside greater 'truth in sentencing' measures that meant those convicted served a much higher proportion of their headline sentence rather than being released early for good behaviour. Toughness became a source of political pride. As Reagan boasted, 'Arrests, convictions and prison sentences of sellers and abusers are rising to record levels.'[6]

By 1990 the US prison population had risen fourfold. But finally crime started to fall, and many were sure that the economists had been proven correct. Tough punishments had worked. Rather than pulling back, policymakers therefore sought to push home their advantage. The 1994 Violent Crime Control and Law Enforcement Act introduced capital punishment for an increased number of offences and a Federal 'three strikes and you're out' law, guaranteeing 'mandatory life imprisonment without possibility of parole for Federal offenders with three or more convictions for serious violent felonies or drug trafficking crimes'. Several states established their own even tougher versions of the law for non-Federal crimes. As a result, between 1990 and 2009 the average time served for drug and violent offences rose by a third, and for property crimes by a quarter.[7] And crime continued to fall as the US prison population swelled to around six times its 1960 level.[8]

Across the world, many admired the US success story. Long derided for high crime and gang-related violence in particular, US policy became something to emulate. Among others, Peter Hitchens, an influential British columnist, pushed for action. As he wrote in 2001, 'You might think that our experts would look enviously at America's achievement – serious crime down 16 per cent in four years, violent crime down 20 per cent in the same period. They might be interested to know that it followed the building of nearly 500 new prisons and a general ban on light sentences and early releases.'[9]

In fact, politicians and policymakers had already started to listen. In 1993, the UK's Home Secretary, Michael Howard, famously ushered in a new phase of punitiveness. 'Prison works,' he said. 'It ensures that we are protected from murderers, muggers and rapists – and it makes many who are tempted to commit crime think twice . . . This may mean that more people will go to prison. I do not flinch from that. We shall no longer judge the success of our system of justice by a fall in our prison population.' The prison population rose in step with rising crime from the 1960s to the mid-1990s but then soared. In 1993, ninety people per 100,000 were behind bars; by 2004 the figure was over 140 per 100,000. Shortly after the initial rises, crime in the UK started to fall and kept falling. The number of prisoners stabilized in 2010, but by then crime was half its previous level.[10]

Again influenced by US approaches, Australia and New Zealand also doubled their prison populations between 1992 to 2010, and, after resisting tougher sentences for some time, Canada finally succumbed to a more punitive approach after Stephen Harper was elected Prime Minister in 2006. Two Canadian omnibus crime bills, one passed in 2008 and the other in 2012, introduced a slew of mandatory minimum sentences, provided the option of serving adult sentences on juveniles convicted of serious crimes, eliminated 'conditional sentences' (which allowed some prisoners to serve sentences in the community or under house arrests) for a range of crimes, and gave victims a greater say in an offender's punishment.

Crime has continued to fall across these countries and politicians continue to justify tough sentencing on practical as well as principled grounds. Any attempts at a less punitive approach are usually short-lived. In 2010, the UK's Justice Secretary, Ken Clarke, eager to control the rising costs of imprisonment, took steps to reduce the severity of UK sentencing. But after a bungled interview when Clarke said some rapes were more serious than others, there was outrage and a concerted campaign against him was led by sections of the media who opposed his policy agenda. David Cameron promptly undermined him by binding the government to further increases in sentences for serious offences, and soon after replaced Clarke with Chris Grayling, a law-and-order hardliner. Grayling quickly attacked prison conditions for being too 'comfortable' and went to battle with the European Union over the UK's right to impose 'life means life' sentences for serious and repeat offenders.

Is Grayling focusing on the most effective methods to reduce crime, however? And are the public right to endorse these methods? The logic that people will be less likely to commit crime if they'll face tougher punishment when caught seems self-evident. And the evidence of rising prison populations and falling crime in the US and other English-speaking countries appears to support the link. Indeed, it's quite easy to argue that we should go even further in ensuring that crime doesn't pay – if not by reintroducing execution by elephant, at least by lengthening prison terms and imposing death penalties. Certainly, that is what many who espouse the Heroes and Villains view of crime would propose.

On the other hand, the US now spends over $50bn per year on correction, and across the world a growing proportion of public spending is going towards keeping people behind bars.[11] In some US states more is now spent on prisons than on university education. Perhaps, as many espousing the Victims and Survivors view claim, this money could be better used elsewhere?

RESISTING THE TIDE

Dr Tapio Lappi-Seppälä is a very appropriate representative of the process he describes frequently to curious policymakers and commentators around the world. He is calm and precise, focuses on evidence and recounts Finland's unusual prison experiment in a straightforward and understated manner.[12]

The story he tells me over the phone starts in the 1960s. His native Finland was rapidly recovering from nearly half a century of war and social and political upheaval, but it was still finding its identity. Finland retained close political ties with Russia, partly for pragmatic reasons, but as the country grew in wealth it increasingly sought to emulate its Nordic neighbours, Sweden, Norway and Denmark. Comparisons highlighted many differences, but academics and policymakers became intrigued by one of the starkest contrasts. As Lappi-Seppälä explains, 'When we compared our incarceration rates with those of other Nordic countries we had three to four times the number of prisoners.'[13] Crime rates were broadly comparable to those elsewhere in Scandinavia, so this did not explain the differences. It seemed to be simply the legacy of a series of historical choices that had created a relatively strict penal code.

The debate that ensued would surprise many today. As Lappi-Seppälä explains, Finland's policy elite quickly concluded that 'our position was kind of a disgrace'.[14] Russian levels of incarceration were not something that the country aspired to and the academic and policymaking community quickly agreed that something needed to be done. The problem in Finland was framed as being 'too much prison', whereas the US saw the problem as 'not enough prison'.

The consequences were as dramatic in Finland as they were in the US. While the US was pushing for 'truth in sentencing', introducing mandatory minimum terms and promoting policies such as 'three strikes', Finland embarked on its own radical thirty-year journey. First, the Finns removed from prison almost all those behind bars for defaulting on fines, usually replacing their prison terms with 'suspended sentences' which would only be activated if new and reasonably serious crimes were committed. Then reformers sought to reduce the proportion of prison space taken up by those convicted of theft, drink-driving and other lesser crimes – as well as juvenile offenders. Suspended sentences became the norm for first-time offenders who had been given terms of less than two years in prison. And in the 1990s a further change was enacted with the careful introduction of a new community punishment.

In most countries, new community sentences have usually resulted in tougher penalties overall. Judges like them because they appear to offer offenders the chance to undergo a potentially life-changing experience; but they usually end up using them not instead of prison terms but instead of fines and suspended sentences. The Finnish reforms were carefully designed to ensure they took people out of the prison system, however. A two-step process was introduced whereby the court would give an initial sentence (for which a community order was not a sentencing option) and then, after the initial sentencing decision, assess whether it was appropriate to replace the jail term with a community order.

The final major change was in the use of parole and early release, which Lappi-Seppälä describes as 'one of the most powerful tools in regulating the number of prisoners'.[15] The minimum time before prisoners became eligible for parole fell from four months to just fourteen days and the proportion of headline sentences prisoners were expected to serve fell dramatically.

In terms of reducing numbers in prison, the experiment worked. In 1960 a third of Finnish prison sentences were suspended, rather than served – and by 1990, two thirds were. The number of juveniles in prison fell tenfold. And the likelihood of going to prison when found guilty of theft dropped more than threefold, to a staggeringly low 11 per cent by 1991. In 1971, judges dished out a total of 2,500 years of jail time to those guilty of theft, compared to just 250 years twenty years later. Rates of incarceration in Finland went from being more than three times Swedish and Norwegian levels in 1950 to very similar by the early 1990s.

This reduction is remarkable in itself. But it is even more remarkable when we consider what was happening to crime rates. For no sooner had Finland started to implement its more liberal approach than crime crept gradually upwards, by many measures nearly tripling between 1960 and the late 1980s. Why on earth was there no public backlash?

'Finnish criminal policy is exceptionally expert-oriented,' explains Lappi-Seppälä. 'In a small country like this, reforms have been prepared and conducted by a relatively small group of experts. So far, Finnish politicians have been able to resist the temptation of low-level populism on this issue.'[16] 'Then we have a sensible media. We don't have tabloids!'[17] Lappi-Seppälä argues that the consensual political system, with multi-party politics and numerous coalition governments, also helped reduce the political heat.

But the experience surely provided a clear warning about what can happen if we let sentences become too lenient? At first glance, Finland's falling prison population had cost the country a lot, leading to thousands more crimes each year. Or had it? Probably not. Finland's crime rates rose from the 1960s to the 1990s, but this increase was also experienced by the US despite its soaring prison population, and by other developed countries. Finland's crime trends were also almost

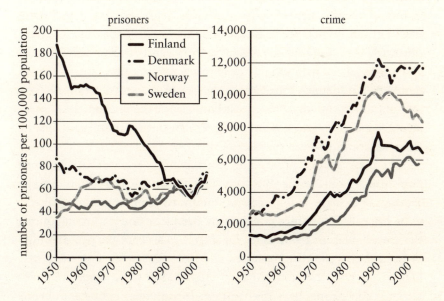

Fig. 16: Prison rates and crime rates: four Scandinavian countries, 1950–2005[18]

Fig. 17: Prison rates and crime rates: Finland and Scotland, 1950–2006[19]

identical to those of its Scandinavian neighbours, despite the country having got much 'softer' on its criminals. Lappi-Seppälä has a good line in graphs which illustrate the apparent irrelevance of severe punishments. Fig. 16 shows the similarity between Finland's crime trends and those of its neighbours, despite its major reduction in prison numbers. And Figure 17 references Scotland, a country similar in size to Finland but one that, like most English-speaking countries, implemented 'tough on crime' sentencing reforms rather than Finnish-style 'decarceration'.

As Lappi-Seppälä points out, 'Perhaps the connection [between punishment and crime rates] is much weaker than one usually assumes.'[20] Looking again internationally, this would certainly appear to be the case. Japan has consistently been assessed as having among the lowest levels of crime in the world, the UK is not particularly high or low relative to other countries and Colombia suffers an extremely high crime rate according to most studies. But these three countries all imprison people at a similar rate. Meanwhile, changes in crime levels do not appear to be linked with changes in the severity of sentencing. Canada was late to embrace punitiveness, yet its crime trends were very similar to those of the US, which experienced an incarceration explosion.[21] Japan was one of the few developed countries to have witnessed a reduction in crime instead of an increase between 1960 and 1990 – but it did so while reducing its prison population by over a third.[22]

Could it be that the lesson many English-speaking countries were learning from the US – that tougher sentencing had helped turn around seemingly incessant rises in crime – was wrong? And why doesn't the logical connection between tougher punishments and fewer crimes always hold up?

THREE MISSHAPEN PARTS OF A PUZZLE

Let's return to the three reasons why tougher sentences should in theory reduce crime. The first is the belief that tough sentences deter those considering crime – by increasing the likely 'costs' of being caught and ensuring that these outweigh the benefits of committing the crime. The second is that tough punishments teach those already convicted the hard lesson that they will pay a high price for future wrongdoing. The third reason is that by keeping criminals locked up they are physically prevented from further offending.

At first glance, it seems obvious that these principles make sense. But the Finnish case suggests we may need to examine each in turn . . .

I. GENERAL DETERRENCE

A double murderer paces across a prison recreation room, facing a group of teenagers sitting in a neat semicircle.

'We got sexual desires too,' the inmate sneers. 'You, tough guy,' he says. 'Take a wild guess. When we got sexual desires, who do you think we get? And don't tell me each other. Who?', the murderer asks, staring intently into the thin face of a dark-haired teenage boy. 'You don't know, hah. Well, I'll tell ya. We get young, dumb mother f**kers just like you.'[23]

The 1978 film *Scared Straight* documents a three-hour visit by young offenders to Rahway State Prison. During the visit, they are subjected to graphic and aggressive accounts of prison life by those serving long-term sentences. Threats flow from the participating inmates as their young visitors sit shoeless on undersized chairs.[24]

The idea of the programme was to turn young troublemakers away from a life of crime. The youngsters were seen as underestimating the hardships of prison, and too thoughtless to consider the consequences of their actions; aware of the harsh reality of prison life, they would, it was assumed, take greater care to avoid it.

The producers were pleased with the results of the programme, not just because of its high viewing figures. From follow-up conversations with those involved in the production they noticed that very few of the young offenders ended up in prison. Their success was publicized and a series of state-funded programmes were designed, based on the *Scared Straight* model. Some were direct copies. In others, teenagers were 'processed' through the prison system and given mock wake-up calls.

These types of programme remain in operation today, and the concept has also evolved into the idea of the 'boot camp', which remains a common prescription for badly behaved teenagers and a stalwart of television documentaries.

But there is a little-known problem with the popularity of 'scared straight' programmes: it's quite likely that they not only don't work, but can be positively harmful. In 2002 a group of researchers examined eleven separate studies which had looked at the difference in offending rates of teenagers who had been 'scared straight' and similar teenagers who hadn't. None of the eleven studies reported a positive impact and some studies showed the intervention to be counterproductive.[25] The researchers were also shocked to discover that when one evaluation showed a particular variant of the 'scared straight' approach to be positively harmful, the evaluation was promptly cancelled but the programme itself allowed to continue.

Of course, it could be said that the programme shouldn't be expected to make much difference. After all, the punishments of those attending did not alter, even if their awareness of prison's hardships might have increased. Perhaps these failures were simply proof that people pay attention only when the actual consequences of wrongdoing change.

California's 'three strikes' law represents a genuine change in the toughness of sentencing and it is unusual in its harshness. Most of the twenty-five or so US states with three-strikes penalties insist that life sentences are applied after three 'serious' offences. But in California, only two offences have to be serious: the third strike can be for any crime at all. News stories report men condemned to 'twenty-five to life' terms after such minor crimes as lying on the theory version of their driving licence test, stealing videotapes and shoplifting under-shirts (i.e. vests in the UK).[26] Introduced in 1994 amid public outrage at the murder of twelve-year-old Polly Klaas, California's law was soon seen by many as a success story. Crime in California plummeted, leading Governor Arnold Schwarzenegger to declare in 2003 that 'It has proven to be an excellent deterrent to violent crime.'[27] The disincentive for those already on two strikes to commit further crime intensified as a result of the law. Suddenly, the consequences of being convicted of a crime became almost unthinkable.

Yet, bizarrely, many people still took the risk – and were duly punished. By 2010, nearly 4,000 people were serving life sentences under 'three strike' provisions, more than half of those having been given their life term after a non-violent offence.[28] The law did have some impact. But a series of studies have been surprised at how little. One, by the economists Eric Helland and Alexander Tabarrok, concludes that people on two strikes were 12.5 per cent less likely to be arrested after the introduction of the 'three strikes' law than before it.[29] Put another way, nearly nine out of ten people on two strikes behaved as they would have done before the change in the law.[30] Another study found that the equivalent of seven out of ten behaved no differently – but suggested that there was some evidence that the seriousness of crimes committed by those eligible for three strikes might have increased.[31] Perhaps, the authors suggest, offenders were of the view that they would 'rather be hanged for a sheep than a lamb', so opted for bigger crimes, or were more likely to commit serious crimes in the hope of evading detection and arrests. This is an intriguing possibility, but the variations in patterns are so small that we can't be sure exactly how much impact 'three strikes' had; we just know that most people ignored the threat.

Why are people paying so little attention to such big changes in punishment levels? A Dutch experiment provides a clue.[32] In the early 1970s, a criminologist, Wouter Buikhuisen, used his powers of persuasion to convince officials in the town of Groningen to help him – and them – understand the impact of tougher enforcement of traffic offences. Police launched a campaign against illegally worn tyres and local newspapers heavily publicized the results of police checks. In nearby Leeuwarden, meanwhile, there was no campaign and no publicity.

The Groningen blitz lasted for two weeks and had a significant impact. Sales of tyres increased and spot checks showed reduced levels of tyre wear and tear. In Leeuwarden, no comparable changes occurred. Interviews with people who had bought new tyres revealed they knew of the impending increase in the likelihood of punishment and this was often what prompted their purchase. But Buikhuisen also interviewed those who were caught despite the high-profile campaign. He discovered that non-compliers were more likely to be younger and less educated, and – unsurprisingly – drove older, more poorly maintained cars. He also found that some of them were unaware of the campaign. Yet his most interesting findings were the attitudes his interviews revealed. Those who ignored warnings were highly fatalistic and said they would continue to drive with worn tyres even during future campaigns.

The experiment reminds us of the lack of forethought and self-preservation involved in many crimes (Myth 3). And it hints at other types of 'irrationality', such as hostile attitudes to rules and regulations. It also shows how non-criminal choices – in this case the forced choice of owning an older car – can have knock-on effects in terms of the risk of law-breaking. But the experiment illustrates too that deterrence works in different ways for different people. This experiment and others suggest that publicizing and enforcing toughened penalties works best on those who already see themselves as people who 'do the right thing'. And compliance usually has as much to do with education as a fear of formal sanctions. In this case, people who bought tyres may simply have been reminded by the campaign that worn tyres were illegal and a potential danger to themselves and others. Meanwhile, people who ignored the likely consequences of their actions during the police campaign in Groningen are not dissimilar to those sentenced under 'three strikes' provisions. They are in a sense deterrence's failures, who for whatever reasons do not calculate the risks and costs of punishment when they commit their crimes or simply ignore them.

This brings us to another important point about the Groningen tyre experiment: it was focused less on toughening penalties than on dramatically increasing people's chances of being caught if they were flouting the law. All the evidence suggests that this is sensible; and indeed those who bought new tyres admitted when interviewed that it was partly the increased likelihood of being caught that prompted them to act, not the severity of the penalty – a response repeatedly endorsed by other experiments. Drink-driving campaigns worked in this way, dramatically upping vehicle stops during high-risk periods and publicizing the results. Other effective police actions (see Myth 8) operate on similar principles. It seems that we don't think too hard about likely penalties unless we realize that there is a pretty good chance of them being applied to us.

The fact that the likelihood of being found out is more important than the toughness of the punishment if caught may be another reason why 'two-strikers' committed further crimes despite the potentially catastrophic consequences. For if they calculated the odds of being caught for each individual crime, they would have reason to hope they would get away with it. In the UK, for example, less than 5 per cent of crimes result in a formal sanction of any sort. More than half of crimes aren't reported, more than half of those are not solved and then many conclude with 'no action'.[33] Prolific criminals know from experience that they have a pretty good chance of getting away with each individual crime, even though they stand a very high chance of being caught in the long run.

All this adds up to a serious blow to the argument that tougher penalties always deter crime. Many people ignore threats of prison, even the prospect of extremely long sentences, while many others will comply with the law even though they would not face serious sanctions. Those who are usually targeted by tough legislation often know that they risk being caught – but take unwise gambles regardless. Perhaps, of course, the comforts of modern prison life hold no fear for them. Perhaps, if punishments were a bit tougher, all this legislation would actually work . . .

2. SPECIFIC DETERRENCE

The windowless cell is eleven feet long and six or seven feet wide and seems designed solely to minimize the risks of prisoners fashioning or hiding weapons. An unforgiving fluorescent light embedded in steel glares down over the smooth silver contours of a conjoined washbasin and seatless toilet. The bed is moulded into the wall – a slab of painted concrete eight inches deep, covered by a dark two-inch-thick mattress that is slightly too small for it. Apart from two towels, a set of clothes, toilet tissue, a handful of books and a few posters the room is bare. This cell has no television, although some inmates do have them if they conform to prison rules.

'Shawn' calls his cell 'the tomb' and spends nearly twenty-three hours a day there. In the other hour or so, he is either showering or exercising alone in an enclosed yard, the length of which he can cover in just six or seven paces. Sunlight only hits the yard floor when the sun is directly overhead. Visits are rare and physical contact is not permitted, except when cuffs are attached for the trips to and from the yard or the shower. At night, Shawn hears the muffled noises from seven similar cells on his corridor, but also shouts and screams from mentally ill or 'acting out' prisoners further afield.[34]

Shawn is just one of over 1,000 inmates living in similar conditions in Pelican Bay Prison's Security Housing Unit (SHU), known as 'the shoe'.[35] Originally these kinds of secure conditions were intended for the 'worst of the worst', those so violent or troubled that they posed a threat to themselves or others. They were also intended as a short-term measure, after which prisoners would quickly be reintegrated into the general prison population.

Across the US, however, 'supermax' facilities with tougher regimes have proliferated, and many contain their own variety of SHUs: Solitary Housing Units, Security Housing Units and Special Housing

Units all operate on the same principle of isolation. These units are intended to serve as a deterrent to further misbehaviour within prison, and advocates argue that such conditions make criminals think twice about committing crime once outside. Many who claim that prisons have become too 'soft' would no doubt approve. As Peter Hitchens complains of the UK system, 'The violent and the dishonest laugh and sneer at a criminal justice system that holds no fear for them.'[36]

Prisoners recognize what the SHUs are for. 'It is punishment,' says one former SHU resident. 'It's meant to break a person.' But prisoner testimony immediately raises questions about the true impact of tougher conditions. Prisoners talk about wanting to avoid isolation in future, but they describe their experiences with worrying undercurrents of anger and frustration.

'Rafael' was held in solitary confinement aged just fifteen. 'I wanted to get out of there,' he says. 'I felt like I wanted to die. I felt like I wanted to hurt somebody. I just wanted. I just, I didn't know how to process what was happening to me without no positive human contact.'[37]

Shawn stands at the door of his cell, talking with determined, wide-eyed conviction. He speaks defiantly of violence towards his captors, the Pelican Bay guards.[38] 'I speared 'em, stabbed 'em, hit 'em, spit on 'em, climbed up on the control booth bars with shit and throwed it all in there and the police shot me with the fire extinguisher. I did it and I'd do it again.'[39] A Pelican Bay warden explains that such 'dirty protest' attacks are common and another SHU inmate, 'Colin', explains how they arise. 'You start talking to yourself,' he says. 'You start doing some embarrassing things like drawing on the walls with various body fluids and erm, and basically provoking others just to have an argument. Er, just dumb stuff, you know.'[40]

A small number of prisoners do, however, find the conditions in SHUs preferable to life in the general population – usually ones who have been the victims of repeated violence. Vicente Garcia explains how he copes with solitary conditions: 'Most people that have been in "the shoe" that can handle it know how to programme. But some people they just don't have that mentality . . . I stay busy. Like, I read a lot . . . I just change my activities, I just, I just maintain it really. Just try to keep myself calm.' But, he continues, 'It does change you. It does make you angry. It's like a dog. You know, you put a dog in a cage and you keep him away from people and you release that dog, he's gonna bite!'[41]

It's hard not to hear this kind of testimony without questioning the effectiveness of such punishment. Though there are only a few studies on the impact of harsher prison conditions on crime and violence, those that exist suggest that within prisons where isolation is common and conditions are more punishing, inmate aggression rises.[42] And though prison violence does not always follow – probably due to the tighter security – it doesn't appear to fall either.[43]

Some US states have recently started to reduce the use of SHUs, largely as a result of pressure from activist groups such as Human Rights Watch and judicial inquiries which have found that conditions fail to meet rules for minimum standards. Mississippi State Penitentiary's SHU was judged to have unacceptable conditions in a judicial review and, despite a spate of violence in 2007, decided to loosen SHU restrictions, allowing more time for socialization and rewards for good behaviour. Violence actually fell and gradually the population in solitary confinement was reduced from 1,000 to 300.[44]

Beyond the prison gates, the evidence certainly doesn't suggest that tough conditions lessen people's likelihood of returning to prison: harsher prison conditions are in fact often found to be associated with higher levels of serious reoffending. In reality, this is mainly because those subjected to more punitive conditions are often more troublesome in the first place. But once that factor is taken into account, there are still no signs that tougher punishments make people less likely to reoffend in future. Indeed, on balance the evidence is that they either make no difference or slightly increase the risk of prompt return to prison.[45]

Similar evidence exists suggesting that *longer* punishments don't help either. It's hard to conduct experiments within the justice system, but some judges do give out significantly longer sentences than others. In many US states, including Pennsylvania, cases are randomly assigned to different judges, which allows researchers to see whether those punished more harshly offend less in future.[46] They do not. Elsewhere, including in the Netherlands, there have been experiments involving the sentencing of offenders either to very short prison

terms or to probation supervision. Again, most of these show no con-
clusive differences in reoffending of those given different sentences,
or suggest that the prison experience even slightly *increases* the likelihood of reoffending.[47]

3. INCAPACITATION

People do unpredictable things in the heat of summer. But few governments have passed legislation as bold as that of Rome in July
2006. At the stroke of a pen, Italy's Collective Pardon Act released
more than 20,000 Italian prisoners. In the space of just a few months,
the country's prison population dropped by a third. The urgent problem of prison overcrowding was solved.

Ex-offenders flooded onto the streets and newspapers reported dramatic consequences. 'Italian prisoners freed in amnesty go on the
rampage', announced the *Telegraph* on 6 August.[48] 'Italy crime spree
blamed on amnesty', reported the *Guardian* in November after a spate
of killings in Naples. Many inmates reoffended almost immediately.[49]
In Sardinia, Massimiliano Formula, thirty-two, and Raimondo Mun-
toni, twenty-eight, were arrested after getting drunk and smashing up
a bar in Nuoro. They then attacked the officers who came to arrest
them. More seriously, a plumber from Udine, Piero Melis, imprisoned
for attacking his wife, Carla, was arrested for trying to strangle her just
six hours after his release.[50]

The act of clemency had had the support of no less a figure than
Pope John Paul II, but its popularity soon waned. Franco Roberti, a
leading light in Naples' fight against the Camorra – the main
Mafia-like grouping in the region – argued the Act had had catastrophic consequences. 'There is an objective fact,' he said, 'that
former prisoners let out because of the pardon have played a role in
almost all the homicides of the past three months.'[51]

Roberti may have been exaggerating, but he had a point. Many
ex-offenders did reoffend quickly and soon ended up back behind
bars. And there was certainly some impact on Italy's crime rate.
However, it was hardly as dramatic as might have been expected.
From 2004 to 2005, the year before the amnesty took effect, total

crime in Italy rose by around 6 per cent, mainly due to increases in theft and other non-violent crime.[52] From 2005 to 2006, a year partly affected by the amnesty, total crime rose only a fraction more – 7 per cent – again due largely to increased acquisitive crime. And the following year, still affected by released prisoners but also characterized by rapidly growing prison numbers, the rise in total crime was 5 per cent. In 2008, crime started to fall again. A general downward trend in murder rates from the late 1990s to the 2010s slowed noticeably in the period from 2006 to 2008. More in-depth statistical studies also appear to confirm that the releases had a clear impact on crime, with those regions that received a greater proportion of pardoned prisoners experiencing on average greater increases in crime.[53]

That releasing crime-prone prisoners should increase crime is not surprising. And there are reasons why this particular approach to reducing prison numbers might have been especially unwise. For example, prisons were even less able to prepare prisoners for release than usual, and ex-offenders flooded out at the same time, making the competition for housing or gainful employment more acute. The period when prisoners are released always holds particular short-term risks too. While in prison, outside relationships often break down and prisoners have no choice but to face up to the fallout when returning home. Whether or not ex-partners have new love interests, there is scope for friction. And there are other tensions: conflicts over unpaid debts, with people involved in the prisoner's conviction, and with new competitors in local illegal trades such as drug trafficking and prostitution, for example.

So the real question is arguably why this mass release of prisoners didn't have an even greater impact on crime rates. There are several likely reasons. First, of course, only a relatively low proportion of people who have committed crimes – or might, in the right circumstances, do so – are locked up at any one time: while prisons do tend to hold the most prolific criminals, they can't contain all society's would-be criminals.

It's also true that not *all* those who are released from prison offend again. Reoffending rates for people who get put in prison are high; but most people do eventually figure out that crime is not the best route to health, wealth and happiness (see Myth 2). This is

particularly true for those affected by California's 'three strikes' legislation, which imprisoned thousands for life at the very point at
which they were, statistically speaking, most likely to reduce their
offending. In November 2012, faced with state bankruptcy partly
because of spiralling prison costs, California revised its 'three strike'
policy and gradually released 1,000 'three-strikers' who had been
convicted of non-violent, non-serious offences. According to the
Stanford Three Strikes Project, only 2 per cent of those released were
convicted of a new crime in the early months of their release.[54] The
reoffending average rate for state prisoners in a comparable (short)
period was eight times higher at 16 per cent.[55]

Perhaps most important, however, is the obvious fact that there is
not an infinite supply of criminal opportunities. There is only so much
demand for illegal commodities like drugs or stolen goods, for instance.
And while clever criminals can create *some* additional demand – for
example, by pushing drugs on new users – there are limits to how far
this can go. Given that much crime is opportunistic (see Myth 3), there
are in fact limits on a wide range of easy criminal opportunities. An
unattended car can only be stolen and burnt out once. Abusive hus-
bands and unfaithful wives can only be murdered once.

These facts help us to understand why keeping more crime-prone
people locked up doesn't always make as much difference to crime as
expected – and why hitting those involved in illegal markets with long
sentences is likely to be particularly counterproductive (see Myth 4). In
these facts, too, we find the seeds of possible reasons why long-term
reduction in prison populations, as in Finland, might have had such
limited fallout in terms of crime rates. We start to see that high rates of
imprisonment can have very negative long-term consequences. Locking up those involved in crime for long periods can, in effect, *increase*
the total number of people who commit crime. When one drug dealer
is imprisoned, he is quickly replaced by another and the pool of criminals (many of whom will eventually be incarcerated) grows. Once these
drug dealers have served their time and been released, they all have
criminal records and disrupted lives. This is not to say that drug dealers should not be punished for law-breaking, but it does suggest that
reducing demand for illegal drugs and easy opportunities for their distribution is likely to yield greater long-term benefits.

In turn, tougher sentencing may 'normalize' prison: once it is no longer reserved for the 'very bad', the stigma of prison lessens and it becomes harder for families and communities to maintain that criminality is abnormal. Net-widening may have wider negative effects too, with more children growing up without fathers, more mothers coping without partners and more parents living without children. If those incarcerated are genuinely volatile and dangerous, then keeping them away from their families is clearly a blessing. But as the more occasional – and less serious – criminals are drawn into the net, benefits become outweighed by disadvantages. In other words, increased use of prison has rapidly diminishing returns once it is no longer reserved for the genuinely dangerous.

This is not to deny that long prison sentences do work in at least one sense. Prison does relatively little to deter others by example, due both to the unthinking nature of much crime and the fact that people pay more attention to the likelihood of capture than their (often unlikely) sentence. Tough punishments do very little to deter those punished from committing crime: indeed painful punishments may even make some people *more* likely to offend in future. But prison does prevent some crime-prone people from committing further crimes in mainstream society, and, where prisons are well managed, limits crimes against fellow inmates.

Those who have hoped that tougher penalties will eliminate wrongdoing have therefore been disappointed – and will continue to be so. The theory that you can have very tough penalties but never need to use them has proven unfounded. Tough sentences tend not to deter much crime because so many crimes are not carefully planned; criminals seem to pay far more attention to their likelihood of being caught than what will happen after that; and prison – while unpleasant – is something that does little to change future behaviour for the better. This creates the conundrum that policymakers must grapple with. When does prison stop being an effective way of containing the most dangerous and start to become an unhelpful drain on resources that drags more and more people into a life of crime, incarcerates many who might soon give up on offending, and exacts wider social costs in terms of lost economic contributions to society and fractured relationships?

This is a question to which we do not yet have precise answers. However, the most careful US studies have estimated that somewhere between only 10 and 27 per cent of the decline in crime in the US was due to its greater use of imprisonment.[56] And this low impact leads most criminologists to conclude that, in the US at least, increasingly tough sentences are no longer cost-effective. I am personally even more sceptical of the benefits of harsher sentences, largely because of the experiences of countries like Finland and Canada, which enjoyed similar falls in crime to the US in the 1990s despite not embracing ever-tougher sentences. More important still, however, my scepticism comes from awareness that the impact even of tough sentences is usually less – and the costs greater – than many other ways of reducing crime. As we shall see, we are much better off spending public money in other ways – on reducing opportunities for crime (see Myth 11), deploying our police carefully (Myth 8) and experimenting with other preventative measures which show that crime can be dramatically reduced through myriad small steps . . .

Myth 10: Leopards can't change their spots

A leopard does not change his spots, or change his feeling
that spots are rather a credit.

Ivy Compton-Burnett[1]

The only thing that one really knows about human nature is
that it changes.

Oscar Wilde[2]

THE MYTH OF PERMANENCE

'My name was Menace and I wanted the world to know it.'[3]

James Horton's deep voice captivates the small conference room he
now addresses. His youth in the 1970s and early 1980s, he explains,
was filled with drugs and anger. He was barely an adult when he
killed a man. Before too long he found himself in prison, awaiting the
gas chamber.

I am only hearing him speak today because of a quirk of the justice
system.

'I had killed a man. But they had locked me up for killing a man I
didn't kill.'

The murder that Horton didn't commit was particularly brutal,
which explained the death sentence. But Horton did not fight the verdict. 'I knew I was a criminal,' he explained. His death penalty was
nonetheless commuted to life without the possibility of parole in
1994. And in 2010 he finally sought legal help to have his conviction
overturned. He was released later that year, on 30 December 2010,
three decades after he entered prison.

Horton expresses remorse, but the audience responds most palpably to his main message, which is one of hope. Many might have joined with judges in calling for his death or life imprisonment on hearing of his past crimes, but not today. Now, this room of policy-makers and criminal justice practitioners appear confident that they are listening to a changed man who no longer poses a danger to society. They lean forward as Horton describes first learning to cope with his anger in prison and now working with Father Greg Boyle, the grey-haired Californian priest with whom he shares a platform.

Horton appears to be one of many whose stories of change disprove the myth of persistent criminality that is so central to the Heroes and Villains account of crime, which we examined in Myth 2. His life – for now at least – exemplifies the wider trend of people moving away from crime as they get older. What intrigues this carefully selected crowd most, however, is whether Horton's experience working with Father Greg Boyle might provide still further lessons. Might his story illuminate the ways in which governments could aid and accelerate the rehabilitation of those who have committed crime? Might his experience reveal the complex processes by which people's criminal tendencies can change?

These questions are of great interest to those assembled because they know that people give up crime slowly. Reoffending rates across the world vary, but around half of those who end up in prison are reconvicted within two years of release in many developed countries.[4] Rates for those convicted in their teens are even worse.[5] Every extra crime committed creates more victims, and every additional jail term or community sentence costs taxpayers money.

FALSE PROMISES

When Chris Grayling became the UK's Justice Secretary in 2012, he faced a difficult task. He needed to cut the costs of the justice system in order to help the government meet ambitious budget targets while improving its performance. Unwilling to lessen the severity of prison terms, he set his sights on the probation service. 'There are some really good examples out there of organisations making good use of the old lags in stopping the new ones,' he said. 'We need more of that for the future.'[6] Grayling was referring specifically to the impressive results reported by a programme run by the charity St Giles Trust, which paired prisoners with ex-offenders who were paid to help inmates with their reintegration into society. The intervention had received positive press coverage. 'Meet me at the prison gates: how mentoring can give hope and help – and save the taxpayer billions,' read one headline in the *Evening Standard*.[7] And the statistics for the so-called 'through the gate' service seemed impressive. The *Evening Standard* story reported: 'A recent analysis found that the St Giles "Through the Gates" scheme resulted in a reoffending rate 40 per cent lower than the national average, with a cost benefit ratio of 1:10 – which means for every £1 invested, £10 was saved down the line in damages, court costs, probation services and so on.'[8]

Grayling embarked on a programme of reforms which he argued would allow schemes like that of the St Giles Trust to spread, as well as ensuring that new initiatives emerged. He would pass control of much of the UK's probation service to private companies and charities, and wherever possible he would pay them only if they improved results. It was an alluring proposition, particularly as Grayling promised to extend support to ex-offenders serving sentences of less than twelve months who had previously received no probation service support. However, it was made less palatable by the threat it posed to the National Probation Service, who argued that the move ignored the fact that they had driven reductions in reoffending across the UK, and that the overall funding for probation would fall considerably.

The 'through the gate' services praised in the *Evening Standard* were being delivered in two much-celebrated pilot schemes in Peterborough and Doncaster prisons, where private companies and charities were working together to deliver new services to prisoners serving less than twelve-month sentences. The arrangements put in place also involved different financing mechanisms, with investors (in this case mostly charitable foundations) only receiving returns if they succeeded in reducing reoffending.[9]

The first year's results were announced in an upbeat government press release: 'Payment by results pilots on track for success'.[10] In Doncaster, the pilot saw 'the rate of offenders being convicted of a further offence at court drop by 5.7 percentage points against the 2009 base-line'.[11] In Peterborough the first results showed 'an 8.4 per cent fall in the number of times offenders are convicted of further offences within a year of release, compared to a national comparison group'.[12] As Grayling put it, 'While the same old approach is having barely any impact on our sky-high reoffending rates, which have hardly changed in a decade, these through-the-gate pilots are getting results.'[13]

This was not the first time new approaches had been heralded, of course. In 2011, after the London riots, Boris Johnson advocated a different 'payment by results' model that offered an alternative solu-tion: 'the Heron wing at Feltham is so important ... We cut reoffending rates in that wing from 80 per cent to 19 per cent. That is a model that I think should be replicated around the country.'[14]

However, all these claims show rhetoric running ahead of reality, and together illustrate just how hard it is to be certain of what govern-ment should do to reduce reoffending. Blatant error was apparent in Johnson's claim. FactCheck, a valuable online resource for truth-seekers, investigated the claims and found that the national reoffending rate for young offenders was nearer 70 per cent and that of Feltham 'at least 40 per cent', according to the BBC.[15] But these cases also reveal more profound difficulties in comparing the results of any scheme with what would have happened without it

We know that people in prison differ widely and, though it's impos-sible to predict accurately in advance who will reoffend, we also know the factors that are associated with a higher chance of reoffending. Probation services across the world invest considerable time and money in assessment systems which help them to understand reoff-ending risks, partly to gauge how much and what type of supervision prisoners should receive during and after release, and partly to iden-tify which interventions prisoners need to help them give up crime. Factors include age (older prisoners are closer to giving up – as seen by high reoffending rates in young-offenders' institutes), crime type (those committing crimes like theft and burglary are most likely to reoffend), sex (men reoffend more than women), and then a wide range of other factors that are referred to as 'offending needs' – includ-ing whether people have drug, alcohol or mental health problems or lack skills or jobs.

section of OASys		percentage of offenders assessed as having a problem	
		community sentences	custodial sentences
1&2*	Offending information*	50%	66%
3	Accommodation	31%	43%
4	Education, Training and Employment (ETE)	53%	65%
5	Financial management and income	22%	29%
6	Relationships	36%	42%
7	Lifestyle and associates	35%	52%
8	Drug misuse	27%	39%
9	Emotional well-being	34%	33%
10	Alcohol misuse	40%	38%
11	Thinking and behaviour	50%	59%
12	Attitudes**	21%	32%
	No. of criminogenic needs	3.99	4.97
	No. of criminogenic needs excluding sections 1&2	3.50	4.31

*Offending information includes the current offence and criminal history

**The percentages with attitudes needs are likely to rise when a amendment is made to the OASys scoring system, effective from early 2005.

Fig. 18: Factors associated with offending in the UK

The case reported by the *Evening Standard* relied on an evaluation that simply matched a group of people receiving 'through the gate' support with national average offending rates, which means they may well have got better results because they were dealing with very different people.[16] Programmes often get good results simply because those who volunteer for support already want to make a change in their lives. Their results were also less certain because relatively few people went through the programme.*

The pilot in Peterborough was planning to get a fairer comparison by helping a large number of people serving sentences of less than twelve months and comparing the results with offenders with similar risk profiles not receiving their support. However, the results of this

* Larger samples generally reduce chance variations in the types of offender being examined.

more careful method of comparison have never been published and the positive interim outcomes reported in the media were based on cruder comparisons between national reoffending trends and those in Peterborough. Then, when Chris Grayling rolled out his national reforms, he effectively destroyed the comparison group before the pilot was complete – as all short-term prisoners would now be given some support.

Further, neither the Doncaster nor the Peterborough pilot was willing to conduct a true randomized trial.* This would have involved asking people to volunteer for support but then turning down, say, one third of them and comparing the results of those helped with those not helped. As is often the case, those involved baulked at the real difficulties of implementing such experiments – charities were highly resistant to the idea of turning people away when they wanted help and prison governors were worried about tensions in prison as a result of perceived unfairness. Arguably, many people also simply don't understand how much difference random selection makes to the reliability of the results. Government meanwhile was clearly reluctant to wait long enough for such a trial to be carried out before acting.

Stories of promising schemes being over-hyped, inadequately evaluated, then acted on before results come through are not uncommon across the world. But they have left us in a situation where we must piece together patchy pieces of evidence and seek out the very rare studies that have been based on pure trials. Chris Grayling's reforms will change the way in which over a half a billion pounds of public money is spent each year, but the truth is that we will have little idea of how much difference they are making. In fact, we do not even know how effective the programmes that apparently inspired the reforms actually are.

---

* The advantages of these trials are not just that they ensure that results are compared between like people. They also take into account the fact that the environments prisoners go back to in various parts of the country can be different – for example, due to variations in local services or police efficiency in apprehending those who do reoffend.

PERSONAL CHANGES

I managed to corner Dylan Dufus and Shabba Thompson on the way to the pub, just after I had seen them standing fifteen feet tall in a film. They had been at the Channel 4 headquarters private screening of the documentary film they co-starred in, *One Mile Away*, taking part in a panel discussion and question-and-answer session which enabled viewers to understand more about how they had engineered a de-escalation of conflict between two rival gangs in neighbouring parts of Birmingham, the Burger Bar Boys and the Johnson Crew. Our conversation unfolded easily – Dufus is a celebrity in his home neighbourhood, having starred in another film, but no prima donna – and I wanted to know more about them and why they'd been able to turn their backs on a life 'on the road', involved in gangs, drug dealing and violence.

The conversation stayed with me, not because it gave me any new insights but because it was the moment I realized that almost everyone I spoke to who had at some point been surrounded by crime eventually talked about how stressful their lives had been. Thompson has been in prison and was shot in 2005. For most of his life, he had to watch which areas of town he ended up in and who he bumped into. There were also worries about the police, as Dufus describes in another interview. 'The paranoia,' he says, 'doesn't just come from the street but from the police ... They approach you when you haven't done anything and they antagonise you until they can drag you back to the station and get your fingerprints and find out where you live. And you're full of testosterone. You're a teenager, you're at that stage where you're liable to explode.'[17] Sometimes pressure comes from the people around those who commit crime: a need to hide behaviour from disapproving mothers, for example. Some young men I've spoken to in prison dismiss all these anxieties – the adrenaline they provide can be thrilling – but eventually the strain usually gets to people.

The process of realizing that crime isn't usually that rewarding is messy, with much debate about which crime-related stresses spark the awareness. But in general people acknowledge that their lifestyle of crime isn't working for them long before they actually start to do anything about it. Take this comment from Tomas, a Swedish man in his late thirties discussing why he turned away from crime in his mid- to late twenties (as so many do). 'My life 12 years ago, I lost my home for the third time, or, maybe it was a little more, 13 years ago, maybe. That was when I started thinking, or I had done that a long time, actually, already when I was 19 I was like "this is not working".'[18] And take this account from another Swedish man interviewed in the same study by Christoffer Carlsson. David is sixty-two, served a six-year prison sentence for murder aged sixteen and spent most of his young and adult life offending – 'committing fraud, burglaries, thefts, selling drugs and using drugs'.[19] 'I remember the last time, crime, drugs and amphetamine, I was so sick of it. But I had no choice, if you could say that. I had nothing to replace it with.'[20]

What triggers a desire for change varies. For Tomas it was a sense of hitting bottom, a common theme in accounts of people who have given up drugs or crime: 'I lost my home, slept on my aunt's couch. And she said, "Hell, you have to do something". And that, I don't know, many people had said that many times, but that sank in. I contacted a Twelve-Step service and started to attend meetings, and . . . did that for a while. It went up and down, but then I had a real relapse, a black-out for a month, I don't remember anything. I did a lot of sick things, just . . . it was just dizzy for a month and a half. And after that, it was as if I just . . . hit bottom. Or, I mean, you could go on forever, but there I, I made a decision. Like, now is enough.'[21]

This example shows that making a decision to change course is not the same as sticking to it. As when people try to give up smoking or to diet, there are always temptations towards worse choices and often people lack the belief that they can change. In some cases, people also suffer from a lack of self-esteem and consider their own lives not worth improving. For those so involved in crime that it has come to define who they are, moving away from it is even harder. As David puts it, 'The thing is, to quit doing this stuff, it's just like becoming somebody else. And becoming somebody else, that doesn't happen overnight.'[22] Another man explains how identity can trump logic when he explains how he ended up in Whitemoor maximum-security prison in the UK after retaliating against someone who stole a chain and threatened him with a knife when he said he wanted it back. 'I went home, and I couldn't sleep. I kept waking up at 2 a.m. saying, "I can't deal with this." My girl was telling me to calm down, let it go. But I kept thinking to myself, "This is going to have to be something big." This isn't going to be just a fist fight. This is going to be big . . . Everybody in the scene knew I was looking for him . . . Then eventually I met him at the pub. I brought this knife and I stabbed him . . . Unless you actually grew up in that situation, you wouldn't understand what I was going through. Common sense is just different in that situation. You just don't have the same common sense. Lying in bed, really, I think about it a lot. "If this . . . If that . . .", but then the "ifs" go away and you just have to say, "This is the real you". I had little choice really. Either you do it, or you do nothing and you get written off the scene altogether. Street-wise, that's suicide – you're back to the bottom of the ladder, you're nobody. Sensible-wise, of course, that's the best thing that could happen to you.'[23]

There are well-known links between a number of life events and successfully giving up – or at least dramatically reducing – crime. As Father Greg Boyle describes his work to the audience of policymakers in London, it's clear that it draws on many of them.

First, employment. In 1992, Father Greg already knew he wanted to conduct fewer funerals of young men. 'In 1988, I buried my first,' he explains. 'I buried my 187th just before flying here.' But that year a wealthy film producer offered to fund Father Greg's plans to help gang members move away from crime. Father Greg used the money to buy a bakery. He called it Homeboy Bakery and employed those former gang members who came to him saying they could not find work elsewhere. When others seeking to leave gangs heard about the programme, more people came to Father Greg for counsel and advice. So he opened Homeboy Tortillas and Homegirl Café. 'Homeboy plumbing was not a success,' he laughs. 'Who knew people weren't that eager to invite ex-gang members into their houses?'[24]

Homeboy Industries is now a social enterprise allowing ex-gang members to work in a wide range of businesses and roles and generating $5m per year but making small losses, largely due to the additional support and fair wages it offers staff. The organization received a further $10m from grants and donations, which is channelled into staff training and various kinds of wider support, including a tattoo-removal centre for those whose past is etched on their skin. Father Greg tells the story of Frank, whose gang markings included a tattoo across his forehead which read 'Fuck the world'. Ex-offenders often describe finding work a life-changing shift – so it is perhaps unsurprising that Homeboy initially developed the motto 'Nothing stops a bullet like a job'.[25]

Second, religion and higher meaning. Several studies show that we should not take claims of prison conversions at face value, as some are ploys to gain social and administrative privileges in prison or to convince parole boards of a change in character.[26] But genuine conversions or simple attachments to religious belief crop up frequently in accounts explaining the path that takes people deeply involved in crime away from it.[27] Father G, as many of his friends call him, brings a clear religious message as he speaks to the gripped room, while never actively pushing membership of a specific church. 'No kinship, no justice. We belong to each other, we are connected,' he says.[28]

Third, relationships. The community that Father Boyle has created within Homeboy Industries emphasizes bonds of friendship and he is clearly a father figure to many. Finding meaningful relationships (in particular, life partners) is a common theme when offenders explain why and when they turned away from crime. Even David, the Swedish man who offended for decades, managed to cut back on drugs and reduce his offending for the right woman. As he put it, 'she made demands, I was on heroin then, too. So she said, it's either me or the drugs. I was madly in love, so I chose her.'[29] A study of offenders in the US, the UK and the Netherlands estimated that men become around a third less likely to be convicted after getting married.[30] And parenting relationships are also associated with moving away from crime, particularly for women. Crime is often seen as incompatible with being a good parent, including by those who regularly get into trouble. As one 26-year-old put it to me on a 2013 visit to a probation service rehabilitation scheme in Shropshire, 'It's just getting silly now. I'm a dad now and I've got to grow up.'[31]

What is most interesting about Father Greg's work is not, however, his focus on employment, religion or relationships – though this is important. Rather, it is that he exudes knowledge gained by experience, including a clear understanding that personal change is not simply about ticking boxes. 'In the early days,' he says in another interview, 'I'd say, "Nothing stops a bullet like a job." When somebody introduces me somewhere and they say that [now], it almost feels creepy . . . But I can see now that, whereas employment and all those things are true [useful], it's kind of superficial. It doesn't get at what this is about. I would find somebody a job, sometimes even a career. But then a monkey wrench would get thrown and something would happen – you know, his lady would leave him or something. Next thing you know, he was back in the neighbourhood and then returned to prison. There was the discovery that no healing had happened. He hadn't gained resilience.

'The difference now with people is the world is going to throw at them what it will but this time they won't be toppled by it. There's that whole process of attachment repair and gaining resilience. The largest task is to re-identify who they are in the world now. You have to move beyond the mind you have. You will say, I used to think courage meant packing a gun. Now, I can see that that has nothing to do with courage.'*32

This recognition that what matters is a shift in mindset and identity is echoed across studies investigating why people commit crime – and it is a reason why we need to be cautious about saying that jobs, marriage, religion or parenthood will stop offending by

---

* Father Greg also shares another insight, which marries with my own views that we tend to misunderstand gangs. 'In the early days I did kind of shuttle diplomacy between gangs – you know, peace treaties, truces, ceasefires, those kinds of things. That was a lesson I learned early on. At Homeboy, we don't work with gangs. We work with gang members. If you work with gangs, you supply oxygen to gangs. You keep them alive because of the attention you pay to them. We're not talking about the Middle East or Northern Ireland, where if you can just sit the sides down, they can discuss issues. I've had people criticize me. They go, "So you're against peacemaking?" And I say: I'm old fashioned. I think peacemaking requires a conflict. And there is no conflict in gang violence. None. Zero. Never. It's not about anything. It's about a lethal absence of hope in young people. Violence becomes a language, the language of the despondent, of the traumatized, of the mentally ill. It's not about, you know, let's sit ourselves down and iron this out; I want my land back, or I want to practice my religion openly. There are no issues to be worked out because it's not about what people think it is. The outsider view always drives the inside of what we do, our policy.'

themselves. They can be helpful in pulling people away from temptations, but few without an underlying motivation to change will stick in work or new relationships for long. Many of the associations between reduced offending and changes in employment or relationships are a result of people choosing and being able to find new roles, and to reshape their identities. This is the reason why in Myth 6 we saw that jobs only make a (moderate) difference to crime when they are considered meaningful and are conducive to improved self-image. And this is why some relationships are clearly more compatible with a law-abiding identity than others. Consider, for example, 'Angie', an ex-offender who has been married twice. In a study by Peggy Giordano and colleagues, Angie describes her first husband as 'a selfish man . . . he would steal the grocery money out of my purse and run out and buy parts for his motorcycle'. But her current husband, a former police officer, 'has a big influence on me, 'cause I'd hate to get into any trouble, and you know he's a very straight and narrow type guy'.[33]

Details are important – and when it comes to helping people give up crime, one of the significant factors is who is offering support. Father Greg is clearly an extraordinary man. Webster, a parolee he employed as a security guard and speaker, explains: 'He loves you. He tells you that he loves you. He tells you he's proud of you. This dude is a remarkable human being.'[34] The sense that he places faith in offenders and builds their belief in their capacity to change is palpable. Who provides support has been shown to matter in a wide range of studies. One, examining parole officers, strongly suggested, for example, that better results are obtained by those who not only support offenders practically but also motivate and instil hope in them, although the authors note that the overall impact of probation supervision is very slight indeed.*[35]

The importance of the internal journey of offenders is clear. But it

---

* The importance of skilled and motivated practitioners is evidenced too in the well-known fact that trials of new support programmes to help people change often perform much better when on a small scale than when rolled out nationally: when doing new things, it is often easier to attract the best staff, and those involved know their efforts are being scrutinized so might put in extra efforts to ensure success.

creates incredible complexity, which generally defies analysis. People are different, and so their responses to different life events and situations vary. Predicting what might encourage an individual to decide to give up crime, or help them do so, is very difficult. For example, for some drug-addicted offenders, the death of a friend is a known trigger point for change but for others it is a cue for a particularly heavy binge. While a call-centre job might be enough of an incentive for one person to reshape his or her life, others might need something more fulfilling, and some people don't need a job at all to go straight. Motherhood, while bringing about change for some, can simply perpetuate a cycle of neglect and behavioural problems. Nicole, a 29-year-old from the US, is like many of the gang members Father Greg works with in that she suffered abuse and neglect in childhood. 'I ran the streets by myself. I was raised up under people, different people's care ... I was raped by just about every man my mother ever had,' she says.[36] Nicole has lived life in and out of prison (her crimes include drug offences, theft and soliciting), but she now has three children. She clearly loves them deeply but provides for them terribly. 'Just the other month, Tommy didn't have no shoes ... slit all the way across the bottom,' she explains in an interview before admitting that when she was given money to buy new ones she spent the money on drugs.[37] She also exposes her children to various risks, including her violent on-off partner. 'He beat me while I was pregnant,' she says. 'Choked me so bad one time that I could not breathe.'[38]

This variation in how events affect people differently amplifies our central problem, however. We know a considerable amount about why, when and how people turn away from crime, but we are not sure exactly which occurrences or which outside supports help them to do so. The fact that different people are likely to benefit from different kinds of support – as recognized in Homeboy Industries' flexible model of wraparound supports – suggests strongly that we need to measure general approaches or 'modes' of helping as well as specific targeted programmes to address problems with literacy, anger management or drug addiction. To make matters even more complex, Father Greg's approach is largely incompatible with any attempts at scientific evaluation. A pending appraisal of Homeboy

Industries shows that 35 per cent of those it supports go on to re-offend compared to a California state average of 65 per cent.[39] But, as in the programmes that triggered Grayling's dramatic changes to the UK probation system, the comparison is flawed. As Father Greg puts it, 'Homeboy Industries is not for those who need help, only those who want it' – and no one is turned away when they want support. Again, we can't measure how people getting support fared compared to others who also wanted to change but who couldn't access Home-boy's services or ethos. Speaking that day, Father Greg did not appear to crave purity of evaluation, however – and indeed he does not help simply because he thinks it works. For him, there is a moral and humane imperative. 'Not everything that works, helps,' he explains, 'but everything that helps, works.'[40]

THE EMERGING SCIENCE OF PERSONAL CHANGE

In Washington State they do justice differently. The Washington State Institute for Public Policy (WSIPP) was established by the State Legislature in 1983 and has since worked tirelessly to ensure that its government's decisions about justice policy are informed by evidence, and that further evidence is developed.[41] WSIPP is relatively small, with a budget of $1.5m, but summarizing the evidence from truly robust trials on recidivism does not take long. In December 2013, it identified just twenty-one cost-effective 'evidence-based' programmes that could be deployed based on US and international research.[*42] Successes included ten different drug treatment approaches, though several other models of drug treatment have not yet been proven

---

* WSIPP defined a programme or practice as 'evidence-based' when it had been 'tested in heterogeneous or intended populations with multiple randomized and/or statistically-controlled evaluations, or one large multiple-site randomized and/or statistically-controlled evaluation, where the weight of the evidence from a system-atic review demonstrates sustained improvements in recidivism or other outcomes of interest. Further, "evidence-based" means a program or practice that can be imple-mented with a set of procedures to allow successful replication in Washington and, when possible, has been determined to be cost beneficial.'

effective.[43] And, intriguingly, two programmes judged effective involved therapeutic interventions to support the desistance of sex offenders, a group that many wrongly believe to be beyond change.[44] Unsurprisingly, other interventions that fared well drew on the understanding we have developed about the need for tailored approaches in supporting offenders to desist. The jargon refers to these approaches as following Canadian 'risk-need-responsivity' principles, while Father Greg might call it 'seeing the person'. The final methods that work involve 'cognitive behavioural therapy' – which can help people change the way they respond to adverse situations – and certain models of supporting education and employment.

If governments used these programmes instead of unproven ones, we might all be safer. But there are still uncertainties about how much difference such programmes would make if they were delivered at true scale. Helping people to change is a messy, complex process and takes time. And the reality is that governments have for many years been as reluctant to invest in programmes that work as in research to determine what the best form of help is.

It is revealing that Chris Grayling's reforms cut overall funding to the probation system in England and Wales, rather than reducing expenditure on prisons. And it is clear that those working in other areas of government are not keen to prioritize helping offenders, even if the benefits of doing so might be greater for society as a whole than helping non-offenders. Ex-offenders often find themselves at the bottom of the list when it comes to receiving housing or employment support, for example – though the UK government and some state governments are slowly changing this.[45] Even in Washington State, what works is rarely what is put into practice. WSIPP's director, Steve Aos, estimates that only about 30 per cent of his institute's advice is taken.[46]

So there are causes for optimism – a slowly growing evidence base, examples of personal transformation that inspire, new institutions to promote evidence-based practice. Yet the reality is that we remain trapped in an unhelpful cycle. Governments are generally unwilling to take the time needed to experiment thoroughly, charities are often reluctant to change their ways to allow proper randomized trials, and most people are instinctively uncomfortable with the idea of prioritizing support for those who have committed crimes. There are enough signs to suggest we should invest in experimentation and in certain measures to reduce reoffending, including drug treatment. But the true question may be one of values. As Father Greg puts it, 'How do we dismantle the barriers that exclude? . . . No us and them, ever again.'[47]

Myth 11: We need radical reforms to reduce crime

It is a capital mistake to theorize before one has data. Insensibly one begins to twist facts to suit theories, instead of theories to suit facts.

Arthur Conan Doyle's Sherlock Holmes[1]

ACTIONS AND REACTIONS

Four girls are celebrating the arrival of 2003 at Uniseven hair salon in Aston, Birmingham. It's 4 a.m. and the party is winding down. The girls stand outside chatting, waiting for a lift home as others move towards their cars.

Nearby, a red Ford Mondeo starts. The men inside it sit tensed behind its tinted windows, adrenalin flowing in response to anger and frustration. Earlier that evening Jermaine Carty, who was said to be at the party, had been at Rosie O'Brien's nightclub in Solihull 'disrespecting' them and their friends, the self-styled Burger Bar Boys. Members of the Johnson Crew, a rival gang believed to have murdered a Burger Bar Boy member the previous year, are also said to be there. The Burger Bar Boys are armed for revenge.

As the Mondeo accelerates, the gang members ready themselves for action. But shooting from a moving target is difficult and the gang's chosen weapon, the MAC-10 machine gun, is known by many as 'spray and pray' because its recoil makes it nearly impossible to fire accurately. As overexcited hands pull the triggers, the bullets spray wildly off target. Neither Carty nor any Johnson Crew members are hit. Instead, the bullets find their own arbitrary victims: four chattering girls. Letisha Shakespeare and Charlene Ellis die almost immediately. Cheryl Shaw and Sophia Ellis, Charlene's sister, are seriously injured.[2]

After the initial outpouring of shock and grief, there was outrage. Britain's media warned that the incident could herald the arrival of US-style gang violence in Britain and demanded action. Under pressure, the Home Secretary, David Blunkett, reacted. Within a week he had announced plans to stiffen penalties for firearms offences, including a mandatory five-year minimum sentence for unlicensed gun possession. 'Introducing a tough minimum sentence for criminals caught with illegal firearms will send a clear message that serious, violent offending will invariably be dealt with in the strongest manner,' he said.[3]

It was another example of a pattern we have already encountered – of responding to public outrage by 'toughening up' the system. California's 'three strikes' law was, as we have seen, triggered by public outrage at the murder of twelve-year-old Polly Klaas; the killing of James Bulger led to a reduction in the age of criminal responsibility in the UK; and the Valachi hearings prompted a range of punitive steps to counter organized crime.

Many factors could contribute to this pattern. Perhaps public and media pressure pins politicians into a corner and they feel they must satisfy the public's thirst for vengeance. Or it could be that politicians and lobby groups use such cases to push existing policy agendas, buying into the philosophy that one should never waste a good crisis. Either way, it's clear that for many decades politicians have felt that visible, dramatic action is the appropriate response to incidents that incite public passion and wider crises of confidence in government's ability to tackle crime.

Tough sentencing and increased police numbers are the most common initiatives, but another perennial favourite has been the visible restructuring of government institutions, in particular the abolition of organizations deemed to be failing and the creation of new ones. In 2010, the Home Secretary, Theresa May, set out her main reforms in a press release entitled 'Radical reforms for police announced'.[4] 'Today,' she said, 'I am starting an ambitious programme of reform for policing in the 21st century. At the strategic level, this includes a new National Crime Agency to strengthen the fight against organised crime and toughen policing at the border. On a local level, it will put local people at the heart of policing by giving them the power to elect Police and Crime Commissioners.'[5] Her colleagues in the Ministry of Justice meanwhile focused their energies on implementing a 'Rehabilitation Revolution', another programme of 'radical reform' involving the outsourcing of probation work to private companies in the hope that they would do a better job than existing staff.

Radical reform appeals to adherents of both narratives of crime that we have explored in this book. The idea of determined criminality that informs the Heroes and Villains view insists that government must pull out all the stops to combat the criminal threat, while the Victims and Survivors approach demands no less radical, though very different, steps to address society's fundamental ills. If you take a look at readers' comments below online articles, you will quickly find a good degree of support for dramatic response to high-profile cases: calls for wider use of the death penalty, the reintroduction of corporal punishment ('the birch') and strict zero tolerance are among the most common remarks in the right-wing press.[6] On the left there are calls for radically tougher sentencing too, but also condemnation of increases in sentencing and institutional reform as mere 'sticking plasters' for deeply entrenched social problems.

But is it really the case that the best reforms are highly visible? We have seen that tougher sentencing often has limited effects on crime, and that the effectiveness of policing depends heavily on the approach used. And we have found good reasons to question the link between crime and factors such as poverty and income inequality. So what is the alternative to the myth-based policymaking that we have found to be so inadequate throughout this book?

THREE MYSTERIES

I want to share with you three cases that simultaneously reveal the shortcomings of our standard responses to crime and indicate that it can be dramatically reduced without vast government expenditure or radical social reform. Each relates to a different type of offence and each confirms what we have already learnt about the real nature of crime.

1. Metal theft

From 2008 to 2011, I spent a few weeks every year working in Pristina, the capital of Kosovo. I was helping to set up a new 'strategic planning office', providing training to the small, talented team whose job it would be to advise the prime minister and his government on how to spend its money wisely. I stayed close to the main government building where I worked, but getting there required a surprising amount of concentration. The wars that had led to the collapse of Yugoslavia and the formation of Kosovo had not helped the condition of the city's already underdeveloped infrastructure. So even in the centre of the capital there were virtually no pavements and my journey involved sharing narrow roads with traffic and trying not to sprain my ankle in a plethora of potholes. The biggest risk, though, was manholes. Often they were missing their covers, which created deep pits that were particularly tricky to spot on dimly lit streets at night.

Unlike the poor condition of the roads and street lighting, the lack of manhole covers could not be explained simply by inadequate resources or neglect. When I spoke to local colleagues, I found out that the city government had replaced the manhole covers many times, but again some of them were promptly stolen. The metal was worth a good deal of money and could easily be melted down for other uses.

I started to pay more attention to the problem of metal theft and found it was not limited to Kosovo. Manhole covers are stolen in many developing – and indeed developed – countries and the mid-2000s had seen a worldwide spike in metal theft, even as overall crime rates fell. The price of metal was rising across the world and criminals were becoming increasingly aware of its value. What sounds like a minor crime was beginning to have dramatic effects. Metal thefts from railways and power plants regularly damaged essential infrastructure. But cultural assets were also targeted. Sculptures worth millions of pounds were being melted down and sold as scrap, either because thieves were unaware of their value or because they were unable to find buyers.

When I was in Kosovo, a UK news story broke about a bronze Henry Moore sculpture that had been stolen from the seventy-two-acre estate of the Henry Moore Foundation in Hertfordshire. As Detective Chief Inspector Jon Humphries of Hertfordshire police reported, 'We have evidence and information suggesting it was cut up on the night, then taken to a location where it was irreparably damaged before it was shipped abroad. In my mind we've managed to kill off the mystery as much as is possible.'[7] It is estimated that the sculpture, worth £3m, may have been sold for as little as £1,500.

Just as governments started to wake up to the metal theft epidemic, something changed. Slowly, the patchy data that existed began to show that metal theft in the UK was no longer rising. Indeed, by 2012 the UK appeared to be experiencing a significant fall, which started when metal prices were dropping but then continued even as metal prices rose again. The data shows that metal theft fell around 40 per cent between March 2012 and March 2013.[8] What had turned the tide so dramatically?

2. Car theft

We shall return to metal theft, but first we will examine an even bigger mystery relating to car theft.

By 1980, most middle-class families in developed nations owned a car.[9] Domestic car sales in countries like the US and the UK were only increasing moderately, usually to people buying second cars or newer models. Car theft was, however, soaring: in many countries the 1980s saw a 50 per cent increase. The proportion of ten- to seventeen-year-olds arrested for motor vehicle theft in the US nearly doubled in the 1980s.[10] And similar patterns were seen in the UK and Australia as joyriding became a rite of passage for some teenagers.[11]

In the 1990s, however, as we have seen, overall crime rates started to fall, including car theft. But something odd seemed to be happening: while property crimes were gradually falling, thefts of vehicles, particularly cars, were plummeting. Data from the US, the UK and Australia shows that vehicle thefts fell by around 60 per cent in the 2000s alone, far more than robbery and burglary. In the UK, vehicle theft went from accounting for around 20 per cent of all recorded crimes in the 1990s to less than 10 per cent by the 2010s.[12]

What caused this dramatic change?

3. Night-time violence

We will return to car theft too. But first we must consider another case: a significant fall in alcohol-related violence.

As Malcolm Gladwell explained in an enjoyable article in *The New Yorker*, violence does not automatically accompany heavy drinking.[13] He tells the story of the anthropologist Dwight Heath, who visited Bolivia in the 1950s to examine the threatened lifestyle of indigenous communities. When he came to document local drinking customs, Heath was immediately struck by the strength of their liquors and the vast quantities they consumed. At big social gatherings it was perfectly normal for people to pass out and fall asleep from overconsumption. Yet despite this, Heath explains, 'There was no social pathology – none. No arguments, no disputes, no sexual aggression, no verbal aggression. There was pleasant conversation or silence.'[14] Heath believed that much of this was due to the social expectations and rituals that surrounded drinking. In this community, drinking was accompanied by a strictly observed etiquette involving a series of toasts, sitting in a circle and the rule of one open bottle at a time. And drunkenness was associated with passive sleepiness rather than aggression.

In the vast majority of countries, however, drinking has rather different rituals. Many people seem to enjoy drinking in public places, mixing with friends but also with strangers. Drinking is viewed as a way of escaping day-to-day responsibilities and forging new relationships, in particular sexual ones.[15] This has led to heightened risks. The biological effects of alcohol, such as poor physical co-ordination, reduced judgement and a focus on the present (which experts have called 'alcohol myopia'), cause problems when combined with these social drinking patterns. People who drink standing up in mixed social groups are more prone to spilling drinks and experiencing misunderstandings as a result: strangers are more likely than friends to perceive a spilt drink as an act of aggression. And the group dynamic means that people worry more about 'losing face' if they do not retaliate, or defend friends and girlfriends. The context of sexual competition also ups the ante.[16]

Most people have seen enough drunken fights – or at least arguments – to understand these dynamics, but here is a young man from Colchester explaining a fairly typical encounter. 'It was just this one bloke, just wanted to take on the world really and when he started coming over to our crowd, I just said, "Look. Enough's enough. Don't come over here and start bringing your trouble over here cos we don't want it." And that's when I blew. Just swinging for the nearest person, which is never a good idea! It's not like I think I'm like big man or anything like that . . . you just do it out of instinct kinda thing . . . Whereas if you were sober you'd have that chance to stop and think.'[17]

These kinds of incidents were on the rise in 1990s Britain. Binge-drinking soared as venues opened later, young people had more money and alcopops such as Bacardi Breezer and Smirnoff Ice were launched. The average weekly alcohol consumption of sixteen- to 24-year-olds increased more than 25 per cent in the 1990s, as did the consequent hospital admissions for alcohol poisoning.[18] Levels of alcohol-related violence rose even when other types of crime started to fall in the late 1990s.

The Welsh capital, Cardiff, was particularly affected. Professor Jonathan Shepherd was working as a surgeon at the University Hospital of Wales there throughout the 1990s and he soon spotted the increasing frequency of extreme violence. 'Weekend after weekend,' he says, 'I was seeing patients who'd been glassed in pubs and clubs, I could spot the telltale signs a mile off.'[19]

Quickly, however, something changed. Professor Shepherd noticed a significant reduction in the number of serious facial injuries he was treating.[20] And the statistics supported his impressions. In the Home Office rankings, Cardiff went from having among the highest rates of 'wounding' incidents in a group of similar UK cities to the fewest.[21] And after 2001 the progress continued. Overall violence-related hospital admissions in Cardiff fell rapidly, the decline again outstripping that of most comparable UK cities.[22] There were improvements nationwide, but Cardiff seemed to be doing particularly well.

What explained the turnaround and Cardiff's notable success?

SECRETS OF SUCCESS

These three mysteries all have distinct explanations which illustrate the complexity of crime and the many factors that affect our behaviour. But they also reveal some general principles. Few are better placed to explain them than Professor Richard Wortley, who is the Director of the Jill Dando Institute of Security and Crime Science at University College London. As he sits opposite me, he tells me about the long journey that took him from working as a prison psychologist in Australia to being the head of an institution that is trying to change the way the UK and, he hopes, other countries tackle crime. Wortley found his first clues by observing prison life.

'I became so very aware that the reason people in front of me were falling apart was not so much who they were but this extraordinary environment.'[23] Wortley felt that it was the day-to-day experiences of prisoners that were contributing both to his heavy caseload of inmates with mental health problems and to high levels of prison violence. As a psychologist, Wortley's job was to diagnose, treat and study inmates' destructive and self-destructive behaviour. But he quickly became frustrated by the standard clinical approaches, which did not appear to be making much difference. 'Maybe it's that I'm not a very good psychologist,' he jokes modestly.

Professor Wortley and his colleagues wondered if there might be another way of dealing with problems of conduct. Instead of focusing on trying to 'treat' individual prisoners, they changed the environment which the inmates encountered on a daily basis. 'It was all about architecture, design and different prison management strategies,' he explains. 'I was just one of the troops and others were leading the effort, but we built a model prison that for a short time at least just had really astounding results. There were low levels of violence. And we had *violent* prisoners in there. It was hugely rewarding,' he reflects, 'much more so than clinical work with offenders.' Many of the improvements came from looking closely at the instances when violence spiked and then making small changes to reduce conflict.

The model spread across Australia, with variable results. But Wortley had already started to wonder if the success he and his colleagues had had in reducing prison violence might have wider implications. If lessening environmental stresses and opportunities for violence worked in prison, where else might this approach be applied? Via a stint teaching psychology, Wortley's focus shifted more and more towards crime, encouraged by Professor Ronald Clarke, theprize-winning British academic we met in the Introduction, and by others who were investigating ways of reducing crime by adjusting the surroundings people found themselves in.

'Those of us who were really interested in the power of the immediate environment formed a pretty tight band . . . we used to meet annually. We still meet annually [but] there's more of us now.' The group has grown because of the ever-increasing evidence base showing that the most effective ways of addressing crime do not involve changing the individual but altering the context in which they operate: by minimizing the number of easy temptations in daily life, crime can be reduced. And results can often be achieved without vast increases in prison populations or police numbers.

Metal theft in the UK started to fall dramatically in 2012 following a number of changes in government policy and local practice. There was no increase in the sanctions for the crime, perhaps sensibly given what we have learnt about the limited impact of sentencing as a deterrent (Myth 9). Instead the focus was not on offenders but on their ability to make money from their crimes: government action made it harder to dispose of stolen metal. One of the most important changes came into effect in 2012. From then on, all scrap metal dealers were required to make payments not 'cash in hand', as had been the norm previously, but by electronic transfer, effectively creating a record of everyone who received money for metal goods – and a way of identifying criminals if it was later discovered that the goods had been stolen. This was reinforced by the parallel requirement for sellers to show identification at the point of sale and for dealers to retain records of transactions for three years and to keep the items they bought in the form in which they were acquired for a minimum of seventy-two hours.[24]

Under a new provision, administered by local authorities, all scrap metal dealers had to be licensed to operate. Firms that did not comply with the new regulations therefore risked a £5,000 fine or the loss of their licence – indeed, some firms were not granted licences in the first place, particularly where owners had been convicted of a relevant offence. In addition, various technologies evolved that help dealers to establish whether metal has been stolen, including the creation of a new forensic product which can be applied to metal and creates a unique, traceable DNA that can also be identified on thieves' hands or clothing.[25]

Given that the vast majority of criminals are not highly determined or professional (see Myths 2 and 3), it stands to reason that making it just slightly harder to gain financially from metal theft contributed to a reduction in the crime. The additional effort of finding new ways to dispose of stolen metal was simply too much for most thieves.

The case is interesting because it shows again how focusing solely on offenders' motivations can mask opportunities to reduce crime by changing the environment in which they operate. Here, business regulation, not criminal law, appears to have been key. Targeting those who unknowingly – or deliberately – facilitate metal theft made sense, and shifted some of the responsibility away from government and onto the industry. And the industry itself willingly complied, because the new regulations simply imposed rules that some of the most successful recyclers had already put into practice and because dodgy dealers were earning the trade a bad name. As Ian Hetherington, Director General of the British Metals Recycling Association, put it, the changes were 'a watershed moment for the industry; it's an opportunity to rid the industry of the "Steptoe and Son" stereotype once and for all'.[26]

The example is also interesting because it shows that certain types of deterrent can be effective. As we explored in Myth 4, businesses are usually run by rational people with a lot to lose from being found guilty of crime; the threat of fines or losses can therefore make them act. Similarly, we've seen that people generally worry more about whether they'll be caught than what the sentence will be if they are (Myth 9). So these changes rightly concentrated on making it more likely that metal thieves would be caught. Even better, they simply stopped criminals from being able to profit from their theft. When asked for identification and bank details, many offenders simply walked away, realizing that metal wasn't really worth stealing after all.

Though we cannot be absolutely certain that metal theft did fall as a result of this strategy – the data is too patchy and there was no controlled experiment – similar initiatives have succeeded elsewhere. The Eau Claire Police Department in Wisconsin required dealers to record sellers' details and built close relations with the industry in order to weed out disreputable operators.[27] They claimed a 50 per cent reduction in metal theft as a result, though again their methods of evaluation were not rigorous.

Sitting opposite me, Richard Wortley uses the term 'crime science' to refer to the movement that recognizes the importance of understanding context and opportunity – known as the 'situational approach'. Details matter, he explains. 'Rather than focusing on underlying social conditions or long-term influences on decision-making, this group focuses on deeply understanding the exact circumstances in which crimes take place and then understanding if and how the temptations of crime can be reduced through small changes.'[28]

What, then, were the circumstances in which car crime happened, and what changed to produce a dramatic improvement in many countries?

We can find a clue by looking at a chart of the most commonly stolen cars today. The National Insurance Crime Bureau releases an annual league table of US vehicle thefts.[29] If you believe that most crime is committed by determined professionals you might expect to find high-value marques like BMW or Mercedes at the top of the list. But the two most-stolen brands in 2013 were in fact the Honda Accord and the Honda Civic. Next come not top-of-the-range sports utility vehicles but Chevrolet and Ford pickups, and in fifth place is the very dated Toyota Camry.[30]

All these cars have two things in common. They were once very popular, meaning there are quite a few of them still around. And they are very old. The oft-stolen Toyota Camry released two models, one in 1990 and one in 1991, and the most-stolen individual model is the 1996 Honda Accord.[31] A similar trend is found in the UK. Again, if you own an old Japanese car, you are the most likely target of theft.[32]

The Mitsubishi Pajero, Nissan Sunny and Nissan Bluebird were the three models with the highest chance of being stolen in 2013.[33]

Old cars all have something in common: poor security. Older models are the most frequently stolen because they are the easiest to steal and the only ones where it is possible to start the engine by 'hot-wiring', the traditional screwdriver-based approach. Cars intended for the Japanese market are particularly vulnerable because they have fewer inbuilt security features, Japanese legislation historically placing fewer security requirements on its cars.

You have to be quite unlucky (or a bit careless) to have your car stolen if you have a recent model: an increasing proportion are stolen either because keys are left in them or because keys have been taken in house burglaries.[34] As Frank Scafidi, spokesman for the National Insurance Crime Bureau, explains, 'There are ways to defeat the high-end security measures, but your average knucklehead doesn't know how to do it.'[35] Few doubt this is one reason for the vast reduction in car theft that has occurred across the world.[36] Interestingly, there is little evidence that car thieves went on to apply their efforts to other vehicles – again suggesting that much crime is highly opportunistic.

While the explanation for falling car crime appears straightforward, the quest for the solution was long and arduous. Richard Wortley is rightly full of praise for Gloria Laycock, his predecessor as Director of the Jill Dando Institute of Security and Crime Science at University College London. Before heading the Institute, Laycock spent thirty years working at the Home Office and observed efforts to curb the growing problem of car crime first hand.[37] In the 1970s, government introduced steering column locks, but these were only for newer cars and could still be bypassed relatively easily. The government also tried using media campaigns to promote awareness of the benefits of steering column locks and other protective measures, most obviously locking car doors and closing windows. Again, these steps had some impact, but not enough. Vehicle theft continued to rise rapidly as car ownership grew and new security measures proved both inconvenient for their users (discouraging their use) and easy for thieves to overcome.

In the 1980s, Laycock's Home Office colleagues therefore decided to act. They commissioned research to find out how cars could be made harder to steal. The report produced was definitive. It concluded: 'Car security could be greatly improved with minimal interference to the design of cars, at relatively little cost, and in a manner that poses no inconvenience to motorists at all.'[38] This was hardly surprising at a time when almost any Ford Cortina could be opened with the same set of Cortina keys.[39] But what was surprising, at least to some of Laycock's colleagues, was just how little action was taken in response to the research. A few companies made minor changes, but ultimately they refused to take the required action. Unlike the scrap metal industry, the car industry couldn't see what was in it for them. If cars were stolen, they didn't suffer financially – on the contrary, they stood to gain by selling more cars to replace the growing number lying burnt out or vandalized across Britain.

Then, in 1991, the UK government launched its first Car Theft Index. This rated cars according to how regularly they were stolen, based on actual theft rates where data was available.[40] The consumer magazine *Which?* took a great interest in publicizing the information, and it received wider press coverage too. As Laycock describes it, 'The security of vehicles became much more of a marketing issue than it had been until then, and the manufacturers began to incorporate more sophisticated security, such as deadlocks and engine immobilisers.'[41] Government had applied its leverage to great effect, and by the late 1990s security was at a level where the industry also acquiesced quietly to a more hardline regulatory approach, when all new cars were required to be fitted with immobilizers.

For Professor Wortley, the fall in car crime is interesting not just in itself but because of its possible role in reducing overall crime rates. 'We all know that crime is going down,' he explains. 'The most dramatic example of that – and some people would argue the thing that's actually driven the rest of it – is the decline in car theft since 1991.'[42] Criminologists have recently argued that by limiting the supply of easily stolen vehicles, car security also reduced other car-related crimes, including some types of burglary and gang-based 'drive-by' shootings. And they have pointed out too that 'joyriding' can be a 'gateway' crime, one that can lead young people towards more serious offences.

These theories are not proven, but they rightly emphasize the importance of understanding the dynamic nature of crime in the real world. When the situations we face every day change, our behaviour changes too – as does criminal behaviour. Car crime today is only easy for those who happen upon old vehicles or have unusual opportunities or expertise. Advances in technology and a government-initiated shift in the attitudes of consumers and car manufacturers have therefore had a dramatic impact across the developed world.

Metal theft, then, was most likely reduced through business regulation and car theft by a combination of technology-enabled change, public information and clever pressure on a recalcitrant car industry. But what of Cardiff's drink problem and the injuries that arose from it?

By the mid-1990s, Professor Jonathan Shepherd was getting increasingly frustrated with the number of serious facial injuries he was treating. But few people were genuinely paying attention to the problem. 'I started to realize,' he reports, 'that even though we were continually seeing the same injuries, they weren't routinely being reported to the police, and so there weren't any trends being correlated, or solutions proposed.'[43]

Shepherd quickly changed this. Working with others in the medical profession, he started to map patterns. One of the most striking findings was that three quarters of the injuries he and other surgeons were treating were caused by a particular type of glass – a straight-sided one-pint glass.[44] Tankards led to far fewer injuries, and toughened plastic glasses were responsible for hardly any. Shepherd also noted that most of the facial injuries he treated occurred when aggressors struck their victims with unbroken glass, which promptly shattered, rather than first breaking the glass and using it as a weapon.[45]

Convinced that the fragility of the glassware most commonly used in Cardiff's pubs and clubs might be part of the problem, Shepherd and his colleagues looked at product design. They carried out a battery of laboratory tests on a wide range of glasses and what they found confirmed his suspicions.[46] While traditional glassware turned into a dangerous stabbing implement when under relatively little strain, tempered glass broke far less frequently and, when it did, crumbled into relatively harmless glass chunks.[47] 'The immediately obvious solution,' Shepherd explains, 'which had an instantaneous benefit, was to put pressure on clubs and city-centre pubs open late to adopt plastic glasses or ones made from toughened glass. Obviously being hit with something hard has its own related issues, but on balance, given the relatively light weight of a glass or bottle, you'll recover far more quickly after being hit by tempered, toughened glass than you would if you were struck by one which shatters and causes severe lacerations.'[48]

As with the car industry, persuading bars and clubs to change their glassware was not straightforward. But in fact, while it is more expensive, tempered glass tends to be much more economical because it lasts much longer. And it has the added benefit of protecting staff against minor (but extremely common) hand injuries.[49] What's more, recent changes in licensing laws allowed local authorities to impose conditions on venue owners – so the use of tempered glass became a condition of licence renewal for those pubs and bars that had a history of violent incidents.[50]

The changes led to a noticeable reduction in serious injuries, not just in Cardiff but across the country as more and more areas gradually adopted Cardiff's approach. Yet Shepherd was not satisfied. 'By the millennium it was obvious that we weren't really making many inroads into actually stopping the crimes themselves . . . Making the environment itself safer was one thing, but we had to get to grips with what actually made people want to fight when they were supposed to be out enjoying themselves.'[51]

Again, knowledge was a crucial agent of change. Hospitals, police and licensees started to share information about where violence was occurring and then agreed strategies. As Shepherd explains: 'The councils now know how to pay more attention to the geography of a town when staggering opening hours and licences, the police know where to concentrate their resources on weekends, CCTVs are better positioned, and paramedics can be on hand to try and reach casualties before their condition worsens.'[52]

The common sense in each of these measures is clear, based as they are on an understanding of the specific circumstances which amplify the risks of violence. Many of Cardiff's fights were happening when clubs ejected their patrons onto the street at the same time, with conflict emerging over such trivial things as getting a taxi when they were in scarce supply. Regulating the flow of people out of establishments therefore made sense. Police presence in hotspots is far more effective than general patrol (see Myth 8). And CCTV does make a difference when it is positioned appropriately, though its benefits may be less in reducing crime than in allowing the authorities to react quickly when crime occurs and to stop incidents from escalating.[53]

Richard Wortley has also been involved in a range of studies on alcohol-related violence. One of these took place in Surfer's Paradise, a tourist town on Australia's Gold Coast. Its permanent population swells with tourists each summer, and alcohol-related disorder increases as a consequence. Several approaches were tried in order to address the problem. These included a reduction in binge-drinking incentives such as happy hours; increased availability of low and non-alcoholic drinks at lower prices, and of food and snacks; staff policies preventing the admission of very drunk people; more varied clientele, not just hard drinkers; smaller glasses and weaker drinks; strategies for dealing with problem customers; and security training.[54] Local premises signed up to a new Code of Practice which detailed their commitment to some of these measures. The results were staggering: physical assaults fell by 52 per cent during the one-year experiment.[55]

As we've already seen, our focus on policing often leads us to forget that there are many guardians of social order. At the simplest level, this includes all of us. Bystanders and friends play a crucial role in determining whether disagreements escalate into violence.[56] But perhaps even more important still are what Wortley and other crime scientists call 'place managers'.

The approach of people working in bars and clubs has a clear effect on alcohol-related violence. Meet Curtis, a 'bouncer' who has worked on the doors of bars and clubs in Colchester, Essex, for over fifteen years.[57] He stands solidly outside the Silk Road during a 7 p.m.– 3 a.m. shift, oozing confidence. A customer complains he has already paid to come in and has a hand stamp to prove it but is rejected for being too drunk; the skinny young man is refusing to move on.

'Go away, you knob,' Curtis tells him.

The young man starts walking away but is muttering curses under his breath. 'Fuck you,' he says.

Curtis retaliates. 'Come here, come here Shirley, Shirley come here. Come here, Come here. Wanker. Come and stand here!'

The young man – whose name is not, of course, Shirley – pauses at a distance but looks as if he is on his way.

'You're a tosser. Walk away, you little bitch,' Curtis continues. 'Walk away, bitch.' Then Curtis immediately contradicts himself. 'Let's do it here,' he says. 'Do it here. Do it here. You're a wanker, mate. You're a wanker, mate.'

Now the younger man is dawdling, feeling increasingly challenged and gesturing at Curtis. Before long he has taken off his top in the street, revealing a thin, pale body half the size of the bulky doorman. He stands tensed. He is threatening to kill Curtis but his face is full of fear.

'Come on, come on, I'll stand here. Come on,' Curtis shouts. 'Your best punch. Come on.'

By this stage Curtis has called his colleague Jamie to the front door. But there is no further escalation. The young man is not quite drunk or stupid enough to take on one doorman, let alone two, and in any case one of his friends is bored. With relative ease, the friend hoists the puny troublemaker over one shoulder and starts walking away down the street. The incident, never truly menacing, has passed.

Curtis is happy for this episode to be filmed by the camera crew of the British television show *Bouncers* and to explain his approach to the film crew afterwards.

'I was trying to reel him in, wa'n I,' he says. 'But he didn't wanna come because if he had I woulda smashed him up. End of.'[58]

A woman's voice asks, 'Would you have been allowed to do that?'

'No,' he says, 'but it woulda just been a single punch. That's it. I wouldn't of kicked him around the street cos you're not allowed to do that. But just one punch and that woulda been it.'

Curtis goes on to explain his philosophy. 'I'm not one of them new doormen that deals with things the PC way. You gotta deal with it the way you see the situation. If someone's intimidating you then you've got to deal with it. It's as simple as that. You know, I've been in the job fifteen years. It's hard to lose that bit o' rough.' Away from the club, in another interview, he expounds further. 'Don't give me grief. Don't give me a hard time. You know. Well if [you say] I'm a twat [I say] you're a twat.'[59]

Curtis is of the 'old school' when it comes to door work. The emphasis for him is on maintaining authority and control. Violence is still a last resort, but not exactly something to be avoided at all costs. However, door work in the UK is gradually changing and fewer and fewer bouncers appear to share Curtis's views. As a recently recruited doorman working in another Colchester bar nearby explains, 'I consider myself to be a doorman, not a bouncer. And you are a gentleman to the extent that you do hold doors open for people, you know. You help them out. If people are drunk you can just help them get home, help them find their friends . . . A bouncer is a brawler, he is a fighter, he doesn't use his communication skills to the best. A doorman, he is a peace-keeper, he is a diplomat.'[60]

It is not hard to see how 'place managers' who see their job as being to reduce tensions and solve problems can contribute to less violence. And tighter regulation of door security firms and employees has helped spur the change. In the 1980s and 1990s, a Labour MP, Ian McCartney, received regular complaints from his Wigan constituents that bouncers were using excessive force and protecting drug dealers and other criminals. He campaigned to ensure that pubs and night-clubs cleaned up their act, earning some vigorous harassment for his trouble. He found a wreath nailed to his front door and was headbut-ted by a disgruntled doorman, Kieron Quinn, in 1996.[61] But the pressure eventually led to a new requirement for all doormen to be licensed by the Security Industry Association, barring those with criminal records and requiring doormen to receive basic training from an accredited provider.[62]

The success of Cardiff and many other cities in tackling alcohol-related violence provides yet another example of the limitations of tough-on-crime approaches. Professor Wortley is enthused as he explains: 'If you want to stop nightclub violence, for argument's sake, almost nothing you do there is to do with deterrence. It's all about stopping people getting angry, intoxicated and frustrated.' Wortley is critical of those who say crime science is just about making it harder to commit crimes. 'Some of the things [that work],' he continues, 'aren't target hardening at all, they're actually things that make places more pleasant. If you want to reduce nightclub violence you don't make it more dungeon-like, you make it less dungeon-like, you make it airy, you make it comfortable, you make it less jostling.'[63] The same is true for reducing violence at sports stadia. Football hooliganism in the UK plummeted in the 1990s for a wide range of reasons. But an important factor was the introduction of all-seater stadia and a concerted effort by clubs to make venues more attractive to children (the fans of the future) and women.[64] This insight might also explain how the custom-designed Norwegian high-security prison, Halden Fengsel, has maintained low levels of violence without any of the usual anti-violence measures used in similar prisons in the US.[65] It contains a blueberry forest within the prison walls, furniture is simply a more basic version of that found in Norwegian homes – no moulded-to-the-wall washbasins or beds here – and inmates (whose rap sheets certainly do not suggest they are less dangerous than those found elsewhere) are given vast freedoms of movement but with clear boundaries and expectations around conduct created by staff.

The precise details of changes that make the difference vary, but these dramatic reductions in crime can provide us with some general rules, some truths to counter crude myths about crime, its causes and what will reduce it . . .

Conclusion

None of the crime reduction success stories in Myth 11 were the result of changes to social structure, perhaps surprisingly for those who lean towards the Victims and Survivors viewpoint. And nor were they attributable to dramatic hikes in prison sentences, the knee-jerk Heroes and Villains response so often deployed by politicians over the past forty years.

Instead, we see a different picture emerging: one in which small changes can make major differences; in which details matter; in which myriad factors can influence the likelihood of crime occurring. In all cases, crime fell when the problem was identified as being crime and not criminals. Some people are of course more likely to commit crime, but the three examples in the previous chapter show how much we are all strongly influenced by our immediate circumstances and the opportunities and stresses they present. The myth of criminal determination (Myth 3) too often obscures this reality, which may even apply to the most apparently predatory crimes.

'When we looked at the patterns of child sex offenders,' Professor Wortley explains, 'they seemed so opportunistic. Just a very simple statistic . . . the average age of the very first offence, the onset offence, was about thirty-two. That struck us as something where these guys have just reached a position where they have easy access to children: their own children, their children's friends, they're school teachers or whatever . . . You've got this delay [in onset of crime compared to other crimes] that I think can only be explained by opportunity . . . We also found high levels of offending versatility among offenders. There's this stereotype out there that these guys are specialists [who only committed sexual crimes]. We found that only 4–5 per cent of our sample were specialists, with more than one conviction for child sexual exploitation and no other offences. Thirty-six per cent had one conviction for child sexual exploitation only. But the majority of them had convictions for all sorts of other offences.'[1]

Defining the problem as crime rather than criminals is only the first step, however. In all cases, the reduction in crime was made possible by a detailed understanding of when, where and why crime occurred, based on careful observation, not preconceptions. The examination of patterns of crime soon reveals possible ways to reduce it – for example, if violent incidents are happening at specific times, dates or locations. Ongoing observation is needed. It is actually quite rare for targeted measures to prevent crime to escalate problems elsewhere, but patterns of social life can change quickly and support for effective practice can fade. One year after the dramatic reduction in crime in Paradise Bay, Wortley's research team went back. They found that few of the measures put in place to control violence were being maintained – so, unsurprisingly, violence had returned to its previous levels.[2]

Having examined and assessed a crime trend, the next step is to ignore the prevailing myth that the criminal justice system alone is responsible for dealing with it: our examples show that local authority officials, doctors, business owners, engineers, private security staff, industry bodies and ordinary citizens all play their part. Often, the police only have a supporting role.

Then comes the need to test new approaches, as illustrated in the three cases in the previous chapter. And if new measures are introduced in a controlled way, we can be even more sure of their effectiveness. For example, numerous experiments have assessed the effectiveness of CCTV by putting cameras in some areas but not in others, and this type of research has helped us to understand where CCTV is most cost-effective; it seems to work particularly well for reducing vehicle crime in car parks, for instance.[3]

These steps may seem simple, yet they are taken far too rarely. Instead we resort to myth-based decision-making, with policy framed for the world portrayed by the media rather than the complex world we actually live in. Never is this truer than in a crisis – because unlike knee-jerk legislation, sensible measures take time to implement.

Professor Wortley thinks the tide may be turning. 'This thinking is now taken up in quite a few police forces,' he says. 'Ten years ago I would have said it was all hopeless and our little meetings we used to go to every year were this kind of self-protection thing – thirty or forty weirdos who thought this way – but it is slowly becoming a more mainstream way of thinking in policy and even in criminology.'[4]

There are other positive signs. In the UK and many other countries, there is a growing set of organizations dedicated to improving the supply of evidence to inform social policy. In recent years, the coalition government set up seven new 'what works' centres to inform policymakers and practitioners of the evidence across a range of areas. The College of Policing, the body that guides practice in the police, houses one of these centres and its Director of Research and Knowledge, Rachel Tuffin, has already succeeded in persuading a range of experts to publish clear, easy-to-understand evidence summaries about good practice around issues such as the use of CCTV, the impact of juvenile-mentoring programmes and neighbourhood watch schemes. Similar resources exist in the US.

Yet the change is gradual. As Wortley puts it, 'Whether it [the crime science approach] translates into policy is a tricky question because it's not very sexy. It's much easier to get up and thump the tub and blame these "evil and horrible offenders". So I think if you're a politician you have to be a bit schizophrenic. You have to know what's really happening and present that to the public in a way that sells. Part of the problem of situational crime prevention,' Wortley continues, 'is it takes the blame out of crime. And people desperately want to hang on to the blame. They want to blame victims and they want to blame offenders. And look, I'm the same. If I see a video of someone committing a crime my immediate reaction is to think, you know, "what a dickhead".' Popular beliefs also constrain investment in evidence. The popularity of 'bobbies on the beat', for example, meant that recent budget reductions in policing led to heavy job losses for data analysts – even though we desperately need better intelligence on patterns of crime to deploy police resources effectively. There are bigger obstacles too, ones deeply embedded in the ways in which government currently operates. In 2007 Lord Sainsbury began the process of setting up a new UK institution, the Institute for

Government, a charity whose goal was to improve the effectiveness of government. I joined when its acting Director, David Halpern, a former University of Cambridge lecturer whom I had worked with in the Prime Minister's Strategy Unit, brought me in on what was meant to be a short-term basis in order to run its first research project. The Institute's remit is so vast and interesting that I've been unable to leave. And many people who have joined have similarly been drawn in by the importance of a subject that could itself fill many books.

Jill Rutter is one of those people – a friend and colleague who joined the Institute in 2010 on a year-long secondment from the Civil Service, where she was Director of Strategy and Sustainable Development at the Department for Environment, Food and Rural Affairs (Defra). She has not returned and has instead used her huge energy to push for better use of evidence in policymaking – and wider reforms to make such changes possible.

'It's not just in crime that there are problems in the way government makes policy. The process is far too closed, with ideas being thought up by clever people in Whitehall based on theories rather than facts. We need to do much more to ensure that ideas are tested with those who will end up implementing them at the front line – in fact anyone who has a stake in decisions – and we need to admit that sometimes, despite our best efforts, things we tried won't work out as intended – and government needs to get better at learning from those failures.'[5]

There are also wider systemic difficulties. Rutter highlights the well-known problem that policymakers change jobs too frequently. Professor Wortley agrees. In four years, he's met five Crime Prevention Ministers. 'Many of them get this stuff . . . but they just don't stick around for long enough.'[6] New ministers, perhaps knowing their time is short, naturally struggle with complex new workloads and resort to conventional responses to crime. But this is not because they are lazy. The job of a politician today is both precarious and hugely demanding, with many ministers lacking backgrounds that prepare them for the reality of running multi-billion-pound government departments and often overwhelmed by diaries full of meetings with eager lobbyists and relentless media pressure to respond to events. Photos of politicians who age rapidly once in power are proof of the demands of the job. 'The only way to cope,' says Rutter, 'is to make sure you prioritize ruthlessly and focus on the few things that will make a big difference.'[7]

This does not excuse the failure to deal effectively with long-term problems such as crime. Sheer self-interest is sometimes involved: politicians are reluctant to defend difficult decisions and, as we've seen, too often play up to rather than challenge myths about crime and its causes. As Rutter says: 'In some ways, government is getting better at developing and using evidence. But there is a long way to go and so often the "big policy announcement" actually ends up being disruptive. Structural changes are a case in point – they usually don't make any difference at the front line and just tie up thousands of hours of time in internal change.'[8]

Improving the way in which government makes decisions about crime is likely to be a slow process. But the endeavour is certainly worthwhile, as the above examples of dramatic crime reduction illustrate. However, there is much to be done: for example, government could work with the mobile phone industry to make a dent in robbery rates, which remain stubbornly high, partly due to industry complacency. Many crimes are facilitated by the Internet, the anonymity of which gives offenders remarkable opportunities. Could these be addressed through new technological security measures? And how might we further tackle crimes of violence by reducing the strains and provocations people encounter in their daily lives?

There is also reason to believe that this approach will gain popularity. As Professor Wortley puts it, 'The evidence wins. I think people are looking around for something new that's gonna work.'[9] He explains his current study in Australia. 'The issue of aboriginal violence and crime is huge in Australia and has been for thirty or forty years. And people have tried all the socially inspired programmes. People have thrown heaps of money at this problem. It's not as though people ignored it at all, it's just what we've done hasn't really worked. Now we're looking at the patterns of crime in this community and particularly sexual abuse in a lot more detail and seeing what difference these kinds of interventions can make.'[10]

Looking at details is one of the keys to crime reduction. After all, we don't always need radical structural reforms or 'big policy announcements' to make progress in tackling crime. And, as I hope this book makes clear, patterns of crime do not always conform to the rules that we expect to apply. Broad social trends influence crime in ways that are complex and hard to predict. We've seen the complex effects of poverty on crime, for example, and observed that improving the general conditions of those living in poverty (as in the Moving to Opportunity scheme) can have less impact than tiny policy tweaks, such as ensuring unemployment benefits are paid weekly rather than monthly. Long-term changes in social attitudes towards crime, meanwhile, *might* have influenced crime rates over the past hundred years but we have no idea how much, and indeed it is hard to find a clear relationship between attitudes to crime and levels of criminal behaviour. Again, we therefore fare best by making carefully selected small changes which can influence behaviour, based on a detailed understanding of the psychological as well as environmental enablers of law-breaking.

Situational crime prevention is rightly evolving, taking on lessons from the emerging science of behavioural economics, whose exponents have now identified a wide range of simple 'nudges' that can encourage people to listen to the 'better angels of their nature'. A recent study found, for example, that people are considerably less likely to understate their income on tax return forms if they have to sign an upfront declaration promising they will provide accurate information (as opposed to signing after they have filled in information). The study reveals again that often those who commit crime (in this case tax fraud) do not necessarily plan to do so but succumb to easy temptations when not reminded of the consequences or immorality of their actions.

Because details are so important, we can rarely guarantee that any new approach to reducing crime will work. All we can do is design interventions that draw on what we have learnt from the decades of careful research shared in this book. This is what Richard Wortley is doing with his next experiment in some of Australia's higher-crime communities, and what many other pioneers are doing in worthy projects that are often hidden from public view. And we can also concentrate our existing government spending on those programmes most likely to succeed, while being constantly willing to experiment with new ways of reducing crime. To date, the most effective approaches to crime prevention have generally focused on reducing easy opportunities for crime and influencing 'in the moment' decisions. But, as we have seen in Myths 3 and 5, early intervention to support children at risk of future offending can be effective, and we have seen that it is possible (though far from easy) to help offenders move away from criminal lifestyles (Myth 10).

There is therefore hope. We have succeeded in stifling car crime, metal theft, alcohol-related violence and football hooliganism. We have learnt vast amounts about what really makes people do bad things, and which environments allow them to. And we know what must be done to have further success. The only obstacle to progress is in our heads; in our unwillingness to relinquish deeply cherished myths; in our reluctance to see the world as it really is.

Acknowledgements

This book took many years to research and write and I could not have done it without the help and support of a vast number of people. First, I want to thank the men and women who have dedicated their lives to furthering our understanding of crime and to reducing it. Many of them you have met in these pages, but many more who have influenced me are hidden in footnotes when they no doubt deserve more limelight.

I want to thank those working in prisons, local authorities and the police service who have helped me to understand the difficult jobs done by those involved in reducing crime and managing its fallout – and those who have helped me access them. There are far too many to name individually but they know who they are. I thank too those in prison and outside it who have spoken to me frankly about their own experiences of crime.

Having criticized many journalistic accounts of crime, I should mention that several journalists have resisted the temptations of myth-based reporting and always provide sound factual stories and nuanced accounts. If I name them, I risk leaving people out but I particularly acknowledge Mark Easton of the BBC, whose knowledge of crime is second to none among UK journalists, and the International Consortium of Investigative Journalists, whose fearless studies of corruption and corporate crime provided the basis for the effective prosecution of companies involved in the global trade in illegal cigarettes. I also thank others who have written accessibly about the realities of crime, including Nick Ross, whose recent book *Crime* also emphasizes the importance of reducing opportunities to commit crime. Earlier attempts at such books had less evidence to draw on, but my work has also been influenced by *A General Theory of Crime*, written by the criminologists Michael Gottfredson and Travis Hirschi.

Then, I want to thank those who have supported my career. I would like to thank Paul Maltby and Stephen Aldridge, who guided my first steps into the world of crime policy at the Prime Minister's Strategy Unit a decade ago. I want to thank my brilliant colleagues at the Institute for Government and specifically Peter Riddell, Andrew Adonis and David Halpern, who were always accommodating when I needed unpaid leave to make progress on my writing. I thank Georgina Capel, my agent, who has been a great source of support and enthusiasm. I thank too everyone at Penguin – Stefan McGrath, Tom Penn and Thi Dinh in particular – for their help and Linden Lawson for her professional and painstaking attention to detail in reviewing my final manuscript. Were it not for her I would have accidentally accused respected legal correspondent and blogger David Allen Green of being the murderer of twelve-year-old Polly Klaas. How I got there from Richard Allen Davis is not entirely clear . . .

Several friends and experts have reviewed drafts informally and I have valued their advice and encouragement: James Backhouse, Tom Chatfield, David Faulkner, Musa Okwonga, Peter Reuter, Pat Mayhew and Russell Webster in particular. All opinions, errors and omissions are, of course, my own.

Most of all, my thanks must, of course, go to my family: my wife, Eliza, who has been an endless source of encouragement and enthusiasm; my father, Tony, who commented invaluably on early drafts and always had time to discuss the trials of writing; my sister, Anna, and my mum, Lyn.

Notes

INTRODUCTION: A WORLD OF FICTIONS

1. George Bernard Shaw, *The Intelligent Woman's Guide to Socialism and Capitalism* (Transaction Publishers, 2005, reprint of 1984 edn), p. 460.
2. P. Mayhew, R. Clarke and D. Elliott, 'Motorcycle Theft, Helmet Legislation and Displacement', *The Howard Journal of Criminal Justice*, vol. 28, 1989, pp. 1–8. doi: 10.1111/j.1468-2311.1989.tb00631.x.
3. Ibid.
4. Ibid.
5. A. Stratton, 'David Cameron on riots: broken society is top of my political agenda', *Guardian*, 15 August 2011: http://www.guardian.co.uk/uk/2011/aug/15/david-cameron-riots-broken-society.
6. A. Sparrow, 'David Cameron aims to extend citizen service scheme in aftermath of riots', *Guardian*, 21 August 2011: http://www.theguardian.com/politics/2011/aug/21/david-cameron-national-citizen-service.
7. Ibid.
8. Diane Abbott, 'A tinder box waiting to explode', *Independent*, 8 August 2011:http://www.independent.co.uk/opinion/commentators/diane-abbott-a-tinder-box-waiting-to-explode-2333574.html.
9. See, for example, K. Hurrell, 'Race Disproportionality in Stops and Searches, 2011–12', Equality and Human Rights Commission 2013: http://www.equalityhumanrights.com/sites/default/files/documents/Briefing_papers/briefing_paper_7_final.pdf. This shows that the Metropolitan Police were seven times more likely to stop and search blacks than whites under 'Section 60' powers (2010–12). Section 60 powers do not require the same grounds of 'reasonable suspicion' as other forms of 'stop and search'. B. Bowling and C. Phillips, 'Disproportionate and Discriminatory: Reviewing the Evidence on Police Stop and Search', *The Modern Law Review*, vol. 70, Issue 6, 2007, find further evidence of racial disparities in the use of various stop-and-search powers.

10. 'Michael Howard: a life in quotes', *Guardian Online*, 26 August 2004: http://www.guardian.co.uk/politics/2004/aug/26/conservatives.uk.

11. H. R.5484 in the Library of Congress: http://thomas.loc.gov/cgi-bin/bdquery/z?do99:HR05484:@@@L&summ2=m&.

12. Barack Obama, *The Audacity of Hope: Thoughts on Reclaiming the American Dream* (Crown, 2006).

13. *Brit Cops: Frontline Crime UK*, episode 7. First aired December 2012.

14. *COPS*, TV show: http://www.youtube.com/watch?v=rJThnnZFoSs.

15. Ibid.

16. S. Venkatesh, *Gang Leader for a Day: A Rogue Sociologist Crosses the Line* (Allen Lane, 2008), p. 16.

17. B. Gorman, '*CSI : Crime Scene Investigation* is the Most Watched Show in the World', in *TV by the Numbers*, 10 June: http://tvbythenumbers.zap2it.com/2010/06/11/csi-crime-scene-investigation-is-the-most-watched-show-in-the-world/53833/.

18. 'Twenty Years of Cuffing Crooks on Camera': http://www.youtube.com/watch?v=EyUPe_Atu98.

19. http://www.broadcastingcable.com/article/159548-Bad_Boys_Big_Money.php.

20. Venkatesh, *Gang Leader for a Day*, pp. 225–6.

21. See, for example, F. Leishman and P. Mason, *Policing and the Media: Facts, Fictions and Factions* (Willan, 2002).

22. See, for example, R. I. Mawby and J. Brown, 'Newspaper Images of the Victim', in *Victimology*, vol. 9, no. 1, 1983, pp. 82–94.

23. N. Yates, *Beyond Evil* (Blake Publishing, 2005).

24. This comparison is noted in C. Greer, 'News Media, Victims and Crime', in P. Davies, P. Francis and C. Greer (eds.), *Victims, Crime and Society* (Sage Publications, 2007).

25. Scripps Howard News Service, 'News coverage ignoring missing minority children', *Gainesville Sun*, 2 December 2005: http://www.gainesville.com/article/20051202/WIRE/212020316.

26. D. Pyrooz, R. Moule and S. Decker, 'The Contribution of Gang Membership to the Victim–Offender Overlap', *Journal of Research in Crime and Delinquency*, vol. 51, no. 3, 2014, pp. 315–48.

27. 'Tough on crime?', *Daily Mirror*, 2 July 2002.

28. P. Williams and J. Dickinson, 'The Relationship between Newspaper Crime Reporting and Fear of Crime', *British Journal of Criminology*, vol. 3, no. 1, 1993, pp. 33–5. The authors estimated that 30 per cent of British newspaper content is dedicated to crime. R. Ericson, P. Baranek and J. Chan, *Representing Order: Crime, Law and Justice in the News*

Media (University of Toronto Press/Open University Press, 1991) high-light their studies in Toronto, finding that 45–75 per cent of quality press and radio news was about various form of deviance.

29. B. Duffy, R. Wake, T. Burrows and P. Bremner, *Closing the Gap: Crime and Public Perceptions*: http://www.ipsos.com/public-affairs/sites/www.ipsos.com.public-affairs/files/documents/closing_the_gaps.pdf.

30. Author interview with Patricia Mayhew, London, 21 July 2015.

31. Mayhew, Clarke and Elliott, 'Motorcycle Theft, Helmet Legislation and Displacement'.

32. Ibid.

33. G. Becker, 'The Economic Way of Looking at Life', *Nobel Lecture*, 9 December 1992: http://www.nobelprize.org/nobel_prizes/economic-sciences/laureates/1992/becker-lecture.pdf.

34. M. Bahrani, 'The economics of crime with Gary Becker', *Chicago Maroon*, 25 May 2012: http://chicagomaroon.com/2012/05/25/the-economics-of-crime-with-gary-becker/.

35. G. Becker, *The Economics of Crime: A Review of Business and Economic Developments* (FBI, 1995).

36. 'London riots: Lidl water thief jailed for six months', *Telegraph Online*, 11 August 2011: http://www.telegraph.co.uk/news/uknews/crime/8695988/London-riots-Lidl-water-thief-jailed-for-six-months.html.

37. S. Giannangelo, *The Psychopathology of Serial Murder: A Theory of Violence* (Praeger Series in Criminology & Crime Control Policy, 1996).

MYTH I: CRIME IS RISING

1. H. L. Mencken, 'The Divine Afflatus', in *Prejudices*, 2nd series (Jonathan Cape, 1921).

2. H. Clifton, 'Rioter profile: the law was obeying us', *Guardian Online*, 9 December 2011: http://www.guardian.co.uk/uk/2011/dec/09/rioter-profile-law-obeying-us.

3. Home Office, *An Overview of Recorded Crimes and Arrests Resulting from Disorder Events in August 2011*: http://www.homeoffice.gov.uk/publications/science-research-statistics/research-statistics/crime-research/overview-disorder-aug2011/overview-disorder-aug2011?view=Binary.

4. Association of British Insurers, press release: 'Londoners are being let down by riot compensation scheme', 10 July 2012: https://www.abi.org.uk/News/News-releases/2012/07/LONDONERS-ARE-BEING-

LET-DOWN-BY-RIOT-COMPENSATION-SCHEME-SAYS-THE-ABI.

5. David Cameron, *Sky News*, 15 August 2011: http://www.youtube.com/watch?v=jcjjzFdU_pA&feature=related.

6. Cited in M. Holehouse, 'UK and London riots: Ed Miliband accuses David Cameron of "shallow and superficial" response', *Telegraph*, 15 August 2011: http://www.telegraph.co.uk/news/politics/ed-miliband/8702037/UK-and-London-riots-Ed-Miliband-accuses-David-Cameron-of-shallow-and-superficial-response.html.

7. R. M., 'Morals: Our Great Moral Decline', *The Economist*, 2 March 2012: http://www.economist.com/blogs/democracyinamerica/2012/03/morals.

8. Gallup, 'Americans' Negativity About U. S. Moral Values Inches Back Up', *Gallup Politics Polls*, 18 May 2012: http://www.gallup.com/poll/154715/americans-negativity-moral-values-inches-back.aspx.

9. Gallup, 'Most Americans Believe Crime in U. S. is Worsening', *Gallup Wellbeing Polls*, 31 October 2011: http://www.gallup.com/poll/150464/americans-believe-crime-worsening.aspx.

10. Data on England and Wales can be found in Home Office, *Crime in England and Wales*, various years. A summary of Australian perceptions can be found in L. Roberts and D. Indermaur, *What Australians Think about Crime and Justice: Results from the 2007 Survey of Social Attitudes*, Australian Institute of Criminology, 2009.

11. M. Howard, 'Full text: Michael Howard's speech on crime', *Guardian*, 10 August 2004: http://www.theguardian.com/politics/2004/aug/10/conservatives.speeches; and Cameron, D., cited in J. Groves, ' "Something deeply wrong in society": David Cameron blames torture case on Broken Britain', *Mail Online*: http://www.dailymail.co.uk/news/article1245171/David-Cameron-charges-Brown-social-recession.html.

12. L. Wood and P. Azadi, 'Riots in Vancouver after Canucks lose Stanley Cup: live blog and photos', 16 June 2011: http://www.vancouverobserver.com/politics/news/2011/06/16/riots-vancouver-after-canucks-lose-stanley-cup-live-blog-and-photos.

13. CBC News, 'Vancouver police arrest more than 100 in riot', 16 June 2011: http://www.cbc.ca/news/canada/british-columbia/story/2011/06/16/bc-riot-thursday.html.

14. Video accompanying above article: http://www.dailymotion.com/video/xjckbz_vancouver-police-arrest-more-than-100-in-riot_news, at 6:48 minutes.

15. M. P. Heron, D. L. Hoyert, S. L. Murphy, J. Q. Xu, K. D. Kochanek and B. Tejada-Vera, 'Deaths: Final data for 2006', in *National Vital Statistics Reports*, vol. 57, no. 14 (National Center for Health Statistics, 2009): http://www.cdc.gov/nchs/data/nvsr/nvsr57/nvsr57_14.pdf. Post-war US measures of homicide rates are considered highly reliable; see, for example, A. Blumstein and J. Wallman (eds.), *The Crime Drop in America* (Cambridge University Press, 2006). Homicide rates in 1945 were 5.7 per 100,000 falling to 4.7 in 1960 before rising and remaining between 8.0 and 10.7 from 1970 to 1995. Rates then fell to 5.6 per 100,000 in 2008 (FBI, 2009). Uniform Crime Reporting by local law enforcement to the FBI started in 1930. The National Center for Health Statistics also provides reliable annual figures.

16. Heron et al., 'Deaths: Final data for 2006'.

17. R. Freeman, 'The Economics of Crime', in O. Ashenfelter and D. Card (eds.), *Handbook of Labor Economics*, vol. 3, 1999.

18. As Moore and Simon report, from 1900 to 2000 in the US there was a sevenfold increase in real terms in Gross Domestic Product. Life expectancy rose from a mere forty-nine years in 1901 to seventy-eight in 2009. American children born in 1900 had only a 40 per cent chance of completing elementary schooling (grade school) compared to 96 per cent in 2000: S. Moore and J. Simon, *It's Getting Better All the Time: 100 Greatest Trends of the Last 100 Years* (Cato Institute, Washington DC, 2000): http://books.google.co.uk/books?id=1ixRxAsdLKwC&printsec=frontcover&source=gbs_navlinks_s#v=onepage&q=&f=false.

19. S. Broadberry and A. Klein, *Aggregate and per Capita GDP in Europe, 1870–2000: Continental, Regional and National Data with Changing Boundaries*, 2011: http://www.cepr.org/meets/wkcn/1/1699/papers/Broadberry_Klein.pdf. CIA, *World Factbook* (2006 data) published in 2009: http://web.archive.org/web/20060706042703/www.cia.gov/cia/publications/factbook/index.html; http://www.parliament.uk/commons/lib/research/rp99/rp99-111.pdf.

20. Home Office, *Crime in England and Wales*, various years. In the 1910s, fewer than 300 people were murdered each year in England and Wales compared to 850 per year by the beginning of the twenty-first century. In 2000–2001 there were 850 recorded murders in England and Wales. Between 2000 and 2004 the murder rate was 1.7 per 100,000 inhabitants.

21. In the 1960s homicide rates across the European countries for which we have data stood at 0.8 per 100,000. By the 1990s the same countries averaged a murder rate of 1.4, low by global or US standards but up by more than half. M. Eisner, 'Modernity Strikes Back? A Historical

Perspective on the Latest Increase in Interpersonal Violence (1960–1990)', *International Journal of Conflict and Violence*, vol. 2 (2), 2008, pp. 288–316: http://www.ijcv.org/docs/2008/eisner.pdf.

Average (unweighted) murder rates per 100,000 of England and Wales, Ireland, Sweden, Norway, Denmark, Belgium, Netherlands, France, Germany, Austria, Italy, Switzerland, Spain, Portugal, Finland (Eisner, 'Modernity Strikes Back').

22. (Rates of 1.8 per 100,000 at 2009.) G. Li, 'Homicide in Canada 2007', Statistics Canada, October 2008. Canada's homicide rate was 1.3 in 1961 but stood at 3 per 100,000 in 1975, before slowly dropping to 1.8 per 100,000 today (Li, 'Homicide in Canada 2007'). Japan is an exception to the overall upward trend in homicide rates across the developed world. There, homicide rates dropped consistently from the 1960s to the 1990s before stabilizing.

23. 22-year-old Jared Loughner shot Giffords in an attack in Tucson, Arizona, that killed five others and injured fourteen in total. Giffords' wounds are described in, for example, A. Jha, 'Gabrielle Giffords shooting: survival factors after gunshot wound to head', *Guardian Online*, 10 January 2011: http://www.theguardian.com/world/2011/jan/10/gabrielle-giffords-shooting-gunshot-wound.

24. A. Harris, S. H. Thomas, G. A. Fisher and D. J. Hirsch, 'Murder and Medicine: The Lethality of a Criminal Assault', *Homicide Studies*, vol. 6, no. 2, 2002, pp. 128–66. In a similar study, the historian Eric Monkkonen found that around two thirds of nineteenth-century murder victims in New York suffered for at least several hours before they died, meaning many would have been saved today: E. Monkkonen, *Murder in New York City* (University of California Press, 2000).

25. Home Office, *Crime in England and Wales*, various years.

26. http://www.nij.gov/nij/journals/254/rape_reporting.html.

27. See, for example, Home Office, 2009; ICVS, 2007; NCVS, 2008.

28. See also *Prison Works* (Wisconsin Policy Research Institute Report, vol. 8, no. 6, 1995): http://www.wpri.org/Reports/Volume8/Vol8no6.pdf, where James Miller, President of the Research Institute, writes: 'Unfortunately, demographics indicate that over the next several years, we are very likely to have a very violent juvenile population expanding in numbers that may lead to a rise in violent crime rates. Unless we have enough prison space to hold these violent offenders, we will be faced with a dilemma.'

29. Cited in F. Zimring, *The Great American Crime Decline* (Oxford University Press, 2008), p. 22.

30. Burglary has fallen by 58 per cent and violence by 49 per cent according to Home Office, 2009.

31. *FBI Uniform Crime Statistics, 2008* (FBI, 2009): http://www.fbi.gov/ ucr/cius2008/data/table_16.html.

32. J. Van Dijk, J. Van Kesteren and P. Smit, *Criminal Victimisation in International Perspective: Key Findings from the 2004/5 ICVS and EU ICS* (WODC, 2007).

33. D. P. Farrington et al. (eds.), *Cross-National Studies in Crime and Justice* (US Bureau of Justice Statistics, 2004).

34. http://www.gallup.com/poll/150464/americans-believe-crime-worsening. aspx.

35. Cabinet Office annual poll in *Crimes in Japan in 2007* (Police Policy Research Centre, National Police Academy, Tokyo, 2008): www.npa. go.jp/english/seisaku5/20081008.pdf.

36. B. Duffy, R. Wake, T. Burrows and P. Bremner, *Closing the Gaps: Crime and Public Perceptions*: http://www.ipsos.com/public-affairs/sites/ www.ipsos.com.public-affairs/files/documents/closing_the_gaps.pdf.

37. Ibid.: http://www.homeoffice.gov.uk/publications/science-research-statistics/research-statistics/crime-research/hosb1811/hosb1811?view= Binary.

38. S. Lichtenstein, P. Slovic, B. Fischhoff, M. Layman and B. Combs, 'Judged Frequency of Lethal Events', *Journal of Experimental Psychology: Human Learning and Memory*, vol. 4, no. 6, November 1978, pp. 551–78.

39. Ibid. Contemporary data suggests that homicide (or rather assault-related death) is about four times less common as a cause of death than diabetes – see J. Q. Xu et al., *National Vital Statistics Reports*, vol. 58, no. 19, 20 May 2010: http://www.cdc.gov/NCHS/data/nvsr/nvsr58/ nvsr58_19.pdf.

40. B. Combs and P. Slovic, 'Causes of Death: Biased Newspaper Coverage and Biased Judgments', *Journalism Quarterly*, vol. 56, no. 4, 1979, pp. 837–43.

41. *Crime in England and Wales 2009/10* (Home Office, 2011).

42. Ibid.

43. S. Sutherland, *Irrationality* (Pinter & Martin, 2009), p. 11.

44. Ibid.

45. Nick Davies' *Flat Earth News* (Vintage, 2009) provides an interesting account of the pressures which modern journalists must resist to produce rigorous copy.

46. Interestingly, there has not been a fall in the number of journalists in most countries. See, for example, Working Party on the Information

Economy, *The Evolution of News and the Internet* (OECD, June 2010): http://www.oecd.org/sti/oecdexaminesthefutureofnewsandtheinternet. htm. However, content demands have increased dramatically.

47. See, for example, H. Kunreuther and M. Pauly, 'Behavioral Economics and Insurance: Principles and Solutions', February 2014 Working Paper: http://opim.wharton.upenn.edu/risk/library/WP201401_HK-MP_BEHAVIORAL-Econ-and-Ins.pdf.

48. Greater Manchester homicide data from *Manchester Evening News*, 'How many more?': http://www.newsmapping.com/manchester.how manymore.html, and population estimate from Office for National Statistics census: http://www.ons.gov.uk/ons/about-ons/what-we-do/FOI/ foi-requests/population/greater-manchester-population-and-religion/ index.html. Baltimore homicide data from http://data.baltimoresun. com/homicides/index.php?range=2009&district=all&zipcode=all&ag e=all&gender=all&race=all&cause=shooting&article=all&show_results= Show+results and population data from http://www.baltometro.org/ content/view/148/210/. Other sources (http://www2.citypaper.com/eat/ story.asp?id=19643) suggest 195 shooting homicides but I have chosen the most recent source.

49. *Crime in England and Wales 2006/7* (Home Office, 2007): http:// webarchive.nationalarchives.gov.uk/20110220105210/rds.homeoffice. gov.uk/rds/pdfs07/hosb1107.pdf.

50. Data from various sources. US 'murder rates' per 100,000 by year from US *Uniform Crime Reports* as prepared by National Archive of Criminal Justice data; Canada 'homicide rates' per 100,000 include Criminal Code offences of murder, manslaughter and infanticide. UK 'homicide rates' per 100,000 1967 to the present based on current (2014) recording practices as calculated by Office for National Statistics. 1961–7 homicide data is based on the following: recorded murders adjusted by the author to reflect new recording practices (estimated 15 per cent of crimes then recorded as murder would not be recorded as murder on current methods of recording – as was the case in 1967–71); population estimates from Office for National Statistics, *Mid-1838 to Mid-2014 Population Estimates for England and Wales*, 2015. Australian 'homicide rates' per 100,000 from 1989 to 2013 from W. Bryant and T. Cussen, *Homicide in Australia: 2010–11 to 2011–12: National Homicide Monitoring Program Report* (Australian Institute of Criminology, 2015). Australian 'homicide rates' from 1973 to 1989 from S. Mukherjee and D. Dagger, *The Size of the Crime Problem in Australia* (Australian Institute of Criminology, 1990).

51. John J. Donohue III and Steven D. Levitt, 'The Impact of Legalized Abortion on Crime', *The Quarterly Journal of Economics*, vol. 116, issue 2, May 2001: http://pricetheory.uchicago.edu/levitt/Papers/DonohueLevittTheImpactOfLegalized2001.pdf.

52. Thomas B. Marvell, 'Prison Population and Crime', paper presented at the DeVoe Moore Center Symposium on the Economics of Crime at Florida State University, 27–9 March 2009.

53. J. Lott, *More Guns, Less Crime* (University of Chicago Press, 2nd edn, 2000).

54. Donohue and Levitt, 'The Impact of Legalized Abortion on Crime'.

55. Bureau of Justice Statistics, *Review of the Private Security Industry: Definitions, Challenges, and Paths Moving Forward*, December 2010, 'More than 1 million private security personnel work directly for U. S. companies (BLS, 2009c). In comparison, as of 2008, more than 883,000 sworn law enforcement officers were employed by federal, state, or local agencies, including municipal police departments, sheriff's departments, and federal law enforcement agencies, as well as other investigative and enforcement agencies and bureaus (BLS, 2009b)': https://www.ncjrs.gov/pdffiles1/bjs/grants/232781.pdf.

56. Russ Roberts in R. Roberts and E. Leamer, 'Leamer on the State of Econometrics', in *Econ Talk Podcast*, 10 May 2010: http://www.econtalk.org/archives/2010/05/leamer_on_the_s.html.

57. T. Rupp, *Meta Analysis of Crime and Deterrence: A Comprehensive Review of the Literature* (2008): http://tuprints.ulb.tu-darmstadt.de/1054/2/rupp_diss.pdf.

58. E. Leamer, 'Let's Take the Con out of Econometrics', *American Economic Review*, vol. 73, no. 1, March 1983, pp. 31–43.

59. Ibid.

60. Ibid.

61. Kimmo Eriksson, 'The Nonsense Math Effect', *Judgment and Decision Making*, vol. 7, no. 6, November 2012: http://journal.sjdm.org/12/12810/jdm12810.pdf.

62. Spurious correlation courtesy of T. Vigen: tylervigen.com/spurious-correlations.

63. Ian Ayres and John J. Donohue III, 'Shooting Down the "More Guns, Less Crime" Hypothesis', *Stanford Law Review*, vol. 55(4), April 2003, p. 1193: doi:10.2139/ssrn.343781.

64. D. Glenn, 'Duelling Economists Reach Settlement in Defamation Lawsuit', *The Chronicle of Higher Education*, 10 August 2007: http://chronicle.com/article/Dueling-Economists-Reach/6720.

65. D. van Mechelen and R. Jethwa, *Recession Crime Wave*, June 2009: http://www.polfed.org/16_Recession_crime_wave_June_09.pdf.

66. D. van Mechelen and R. Jethwa, 'Recession Crime Wave, June 2009': http://www.polfed.org/16_Recession_crime_wave_June_09.pdf. Cartoon by Russ Trindo.

67. R. A. Oppel, 'Steady crime decline baffles experts', *The New York Times*, 23 May 2011: http://www.nytimes.com/2011/05/24/us/24crime.html?_r=0.

MYTH 2: TAKING UP A LIFE OF CRIME

1. Oscar Wilde, *The Picture of Dorian Gray* (Ward, Lock and Co., 1891), chapter 20.

2. R. Alleyne, 'Dwarf burglar: crime is my only career option', *Telegraph*, 25 July 2008: http://www.telegraph.co.uk/news/uknews/2458166/Dwarf-burglar-crime-is-my-only-career-option.html.

3. Ibid.

4. M. Hickley, 'Crime is the "career" of choice in the inner-city', *Mail Online*, 22 December 2006: http://www.dailymail.co.uk/news/article-424444/Crime-career-choice-inner-city.html.

5. J. Lauinger and T. Zambito, 'DNA links 72-year-old career criminal Frank (Frankie Bones) Boehme to 2008 bank break-in', *NY Daily News*, 24 December 2010: http://www.nydailynews.com/news/ny_crime/2010/12/24/2010-12-24_dna_links_a_geezer_to_sloppy_08_hit_on_qns_bank.html; K. Eaves, 'Career criminal back behind bars after burgling house in Eaglescliffe' in the *Evening Gazette*, 10 January 2011: http://www.gazettelive.co.uk/news/teesside-news/2011/01/10/career-criminal-back-behind-bars-after-burgling-house-in-eaglescliffe-84229-27952561/; R. Lamberti, 'New York crime boss arrives in Montreal, bodies begin to fall' in *CNews*, 11 December 2010: http://mafiatoday.com/bonanno-family/new-york-crime-boss-arrives-in-montreal-bodies-begin-to-fall/.

6. This typology is examined in D. Canter and N. Wentink, 'Testing a Typology of Serial Murder: An Empirical Test of the Holmes and Holmes Serial Typology', *Criminal Justice and Behavior*, vol. 31, no. 4, August 2004, pp. 489–515: http://www.ia-ip.org/uploads/library/key%20ip%20publications/Empirical%20Test%20of%20Holmes%20Serial%20Murder%20Typology.pdf.

7. King James Bible, Matthew, 5: 29.

8. R. Merton, *Social Theory and Social Structure* (Free Press, 1968, originally publ. 1949).

9. *1301.0 Year Book Australia, 2009–10*, Australian Bureau of Statistics average weekly earnings statistics 2008: http://www.abs.gov.au/AUSSTATS/abs@.nsf/0/93831E680B4ADFA2CA25773700169C70?opendocument.

10. Males between the ages of fourteen and seventeen are likely to self-report the highest rate of criminal activity, while police arrest and conviction data tend to show the highest rates for those in the mid- to late teens according to S. McVie, 'Patterns of Deviance Underlying the Age–Crime Curve: The Long Term Evidence', *British Society of Criminology*, vol. 7 (2005), and M. Livingston, A. Stewart, T. Allard and J. Ogilvie, 'Understanding Juvenile Offending Trajectories', *The Australia and New Zealand Journal of Criminology*, vol. 41, no. 3, 2008, pp. 345–63.

11. Ibid.

12. Ibid.

13. J. Fox and M. Zawitz, *Homicide Trends in the United States* (Bureau of Justice Statistics, 2003): http://bjs.ojp.usdoj.gov/content/pub/pdf/htius.pdf. In the 1990s, fourteen- to seventeen-year-olds in the US were far *more* likely to commit murder than anyone over the age of twenty-five. See also M. Eisner, 'Modernity Strikes Back? A Historical Perspective on the Latest Increase in Interpersonal Violence (1960–1990)', *International Journal of Conflict and Violence*, vol. 2(2), 2008, pp. 288–316: http://www.ijcv.org/docs/2008/eisner.pdf.

14. H. Petras, P. Nieuwbeerta and A. Piquero, 'Participation and Frequency during Criminal Careers across the Life Span', *Criminology*, 48(2), 2010.

15. N. Britten, 'Britain's oldest career criminal is back in the dock – 10 months after vowing to go straight', *Telegraph*, 27 August 2009.

16. A. Blumstein and P. Cohen, with P. Hsieh, *The Duration of Adult Criminal Careers. Final Report Submitted to National Institute of Justice*, August 1982.

17. Data from Home Office records from 1998. The same data also shows that forty-year-old men were more than five times as likely to receive a caution or conviction as sixty-year-old men.

18. Ibid.

19. Petras, Nieuwbeerta and Piquero, 'Participation and Frequency during Criminal Careers'.

20. See, for example, D. Smith, *Social Inclusion and Early Desistance from Crime* (University of Edinburgh Centre for Law & Society, 2006).

Smith's study of Edinburgh youth showed that when they asked fourteen-year-olds how much trouble they'd been getting into, over half said they had been engaged in four or more delinquent acts in the previous twelve months. But just three years later, aged seventeen, nearly half of those who'd been involved in crime and delinquency had stopped or sharply reduced their offending.

21. Home Office 2000.
22. Data on cautions and convictions from Home Office records 1998. S. Roe and J. Ashe, *Offending, Crime and Justice Survey 2006*, July 2008: http://www.homeoffice.gov.uk/rds/pdfs08/hosb0908.pdf.
23. Cited in H. McNutt, 'Tainted by the James Bulger legacy', *Guardian Online*:http://www.guardian.co.uk/society/2010/mar/03/james-bulger-legacy-disturbed-children.
24. *Daily Mail*, 25 November 1993. The *Telegraph* recalled on the same day that Venables was born on Friday the 13th.
25. D. Nagin and R. E. Tremblay, 'Trajectories of Boys' Physical Aggression, Opposition, and Hyperactivity on the Path to Physically Violent and Non-Violent Juvenile Delinquency', *Child Development*, vol. 70, 1999, pp. 1181–96.
26. Tremblay et al., 199 based on data from the Canadian *Longitudinal Survey of Children and Youth* (NLSCY, 2010).
27. R. Loeber and M. Stouthamer-Loeber, 'Development of Juvenile Aggression and Violence: Some Common Misconceptions and Controversies', *American Psychology*, vol. 53, 1998, pp. 242–59.
28. Saint Augustine, *Confessions*, trans. H. Chadwick (Oxford, 2008), p. 9.
29. Author interview, 5 October 2012.
30. Ibid.
31. UKAID and Penal Reform International, *The Minimum Age of Criminal Responsibility, Justice for Children Briefing No. 4*: http://www.penalreform.org/wp-content/uploads/2013/05/justice-for-children-briefing-4-v6-web_0.pdf.
32. Ibid.
33. ibid.
34. http://www.guardian.co.uk/world/2011/dec/16/barefoot-bandit-sentenced-seven-years.
35. S. Roe and J. Ashe, *Offending, Crime and Justice Survey 2006*, July 2008: http://www.homeoffice.gov.uk/rds/pdfs08/hosb0908.pdf.
36. G. Sereny, *Cries Unheard: The Story of Mary Bell* (Macmillan, 1999).
37. I. Gallagher, 'The social worker who looked after Bulger killer until release gives a first extraordinary account of his "kid gloves" treatment

inside . . .', *Mail Online*, 8 March 2010: http://www.dailymail.co.uk/
news/article-1256109/Robert-Thompson-Social-worker-looked-James-
Bulger-killer-speaks.html#ixzz32ctyXcxD.

38. The Pittsburgh study focused on male youths from disadvantaged backgrounds found a general trajectory of high and increasing aggression
from the ages of 7.5 to 10.5; see A. Piquero, 'Taking Stock of Developmental Trajectories of Criminal Activity', in A. Lieberman (ed.), *The
Long View of Crime: A Synthesis of Longitudinal Research* (Springer,
2008).

39. M. Krohn and T. Thornberry, 'Longitudinal Perspectives on Adolescent Street Gangs', in Lieberman (ed.), *The Long View of Crime*.

MYTH 3: CRIMINALS WILL STOP AT NOTHING

1. Michel de Montaigne, trans. C. Cotton, *The Essays of Montaigne,
Complete* (1877 edition, released by Project Gutenberg, 2006).

2. A. Osborn, 'Thieves pull off biggest gem heist in diamond capital',
Guardian, 19 February 2003: http://www.guardian.co.uk/world/2003/
feb/19/internationalcrime.

3. J. Davis, 'The Untold Story of the World's Biggest Diamond Heist',
Wired Magazine, 3 December 2009: http://www.wired.com/politics/
law/magazine/17-04/ff_diamonds?currentPage=all.

4. Ibid.

5. Associated Press, 27 June 1999: http://www.courtpsychiatrist.com/pdf/
indiana_star.pdf. See also 'Murder suspect fathered child to kill as
revenge', *Daily News, Bowling Green, Kentucky*, 28 June 1999 at
http://news.google.com/newspapers?nid=1696&dat=19990628&id=hf
IaAAAAIBAJ&sjid=4UcEAAAAIBAJ&pg=6743,4084570, and A. E.
Stoner, *Notorious 92: Indiana's Most Heinous Murders in All 92 Coun-
ties* (Rooftop Publishing, 2007).

6. Davis, 'The Untold Story of the World's Biggest Diamond Heist'.

7. National Tea Party, 'Do you think criminals will obey new gun restrictions?': http://nationalteaparty.blogspot.co.uk/2013/01/do-you-think-
criminals-will-obey-new.html.

8. http://www.unicri.it/emerging_crimes/

9. 'Walter Mischel's marshmallow study', in *Mind Changers*, BBC Radio
4, 20 February 2011: http://www.bbc.co.uk/programmes/b00ymjpr.

10. Y. Shoda, W. Mischel and P. Peake, 'Predicting Adolescent Cognitive and
Self-Regulatory Competencies from Preschool Delay of Gratification:
Identifying Diagnostic Conditions', *Developmental Psychology*, vol.

26, no. 6, 1990, pp. 978–86, and A. Bucciol, D. Houser and M. Piovesan, 'Temptation and Productivity: A Field Experiment with Children', *Journal of Economic Behavior and Organization*, vol. 78, nos. 1–2, April 2011, pp. 126–36: http://behaviourlibrary.com/Bucciol%20et%20al%202010.pdf.

11. 'Walter Mischel's marshmallow study', BBC Radio 4.

12. Ibid.

13. A. Caspi, 'The Child is the Father of the Man: Personality Continuities from Childhood to Adulthood', *Journal of Personality and Social Psychology*, vol. 78, 2000, pp. 158–72.

14. D. Farrington and B. Welsh, *Saving Children from a Life of Crime: Early Risk Factors and Effective Interventions* (Oxford University Press, 2008).

15. T. Moffitt, L. Arseneault, D. Belsky, N. Dickson, R. Hancox, H. Harrington, R. Houts, R. Poulton, B. Roberts, S. Ross, M. Sears, W. Murray Thomson and A. Caspi (ed. J. Heckman), 'A Gradient of Childhood Self-Control Predicts Health, Wealth, and Public Safety', *Proceedings of the National Academy of Sciences of the United States of America*, 2010, retrieved at: http://www.pnas.org/content/suppl/2011/01/21/1010076108.DCSupplemental.

16. D. Card and G. Dahl, 'Family Violence and Football: The Effect of Unexpected Emotional Cues on Violent Behavior', in NBER Working Paper no. 15497, November 2009: http://www.colorado.edu/econ/seminars/dahl.pdf.

17. D. Kenrick and S. MacFarlane, 'Ambient Temperature and Horn Honking: A Field Study of the Heat/Aggression Relationship', *Environment and Behavior*, vol. 18, no. 2, March 1986, pp. 179–91.

18. 'Expanded Homicide Data Table 12', in Criminal Justice Information Services Division, *Crime in the United States, 2012*: https://www.fbi.gov/about-us/cjis/ucr/crime-in-the-u.s/2012/crime-in-the-u.s.-2012/offenses-known-to-law-enforcement/expanded-homicide/expanded_homicide_data_table_12_murder_circumstances_2008-2012.xls.

19. E. Anderson, *Code of the Street: Decency, Violence, and the Moral Life of the Inner City* (Norton, 1999).

20. One sniper attack, thirteen 'institutional killings' and 137 'felony type' categorizations not shown. 'Expanded Homicide Data Table 12', in Criminal Justice Information Services Division, *Crime in the United States, 2012*.

21. In England and Wales in 2013, the murder 'detection' rate was 90 per cent, according to K. Smith et al., *Crimes Detected in England and*

Wales 2012/13 (Home Office, 2013). The 2013 murder clearance rate in Germany was 95.8 per cent and the 2014 clearance rate 96.5 per cent, according to *Police Crime Statistics, Federal Republic of Germany, Report 2014* (abridged; Bundeskriminalamt, 2014).

22. There may be rational good reasons why people commit crimes closer to home. For example, offenders may have difficulty with transporting stolen goods or (as with most young offenders) not be able to drive to alternative locations with more attractive targets. However, short travel distances do suggest that criminals are not seeking to maximize gains efficiently.

23. P. Wiles and A. Costello, *The Road to Nowhere: The Evidence for Travelling Criminals*, Home Office Research Study 207, 2000: www. homeoffice.gov.uk.

24. I. Hearnden and C. Magill, *Decision-Making by House Burglars: Offenders' Perspectives* (Home Office, 2004).

25. M. Arnosky, 'Former FBI agent talks art theft at Michener': http:// www.philly.com/community/pa/bucks/102795839.html?c=r. Thomas Crowne is the fictional star of two films who lives a glamorous lifestyle while engaging in ever more audacious schemes to steal art treasures.

26. S. Venkatesh, *Gang Leader for a Day* (Allen Lane, 2008).

27. M. Charest, 'Peut on se fier aux délinquants pour estimer leurs gains criminels?', *Criminologie*, vol. 37, no. 2, 2004, pp. 63–87. These figures are based on the median earnings, calculated through confidential interviews which asked offenders to detail their offences and earnings for each offence. C$ to GB£ exchange rate of 0.449 is from 15 June 2000, which coincides with the mid-year of the study.

28. P. Carrington, A. Matarazzo and P. deSouza, 'Court Careers of a Canadian Birth Cohort' (Ministry of Industry, Canada, 2005). According to this study, even counting burglary and theft as one type of offence, only 19.9 per cent of Canadians with more than one conviction could be counted as property crime 'specialists', i.e. only convicted for property crimes. Likewise, each time an offender was sent to court he or she would become less likely to show only one substantive type of offence – those referred thirteen or more times had only a tiny (5 per cent) chance of being specialized in one type of offence (usually this broad 'property crime' tag).

29. In the 1980s, Professor David Farrington of Cambridge University developed a more analytical approach to understanding criminal specialization – using the 'forward specialization coefficient'. He identified considerable variation by offence type, with greater specialization

in offences such as burglary and vehicle theft, and less for vandalism, weapons and trespass – but confirmed the general principle that specialization was an exception rather than a rule.

30. UK and Montreal data from Wiles and Costello, *The Road to Nowhere*. Melbourne data from *Retail Theft in Western Australia*, Special Burglary Series no. 1 (Crime Research Centre, University of Western Australia, 2007). This study also found that over a third of burglaries were less than two thirds of a mile away from offenders' homes.

31. Wiles and Costello, *The Road to Nowhere*.

32. Ibid.

33. *Homicide in Canada, 2013* (Statistics Canada, 2014): http://www.statcan.gc.ca/pub/85-002-x/2014001/article/14108-eng.htm.

34. See data tables for *Crime Statistics, Focus on Violent Crime and Sexual Offences, 2013/14* (Office for National Statistics, 2015): http://www.ons.gov.uk/ons/publications/re-reference-tables.html?edition=tcm%3A77-376027.

35. 33.5 per cent of completed US burglaries between 2004 and 2007 were by people known to the victims (10.6 per cent by 'intimates/former intimates') according to S. Catalano, *Victimization during Household Burglary, Bureau of Justice Statistics Special Report* (US Bureau of Justice Statistics, September 2010): http://www.bjs.gov/content/pub/pdf/vdhb.pdf. The true proportion of burglaries committed by those known to victims may be far higher as only 24 per cent of burglaries were confirmed to have been committed by strangers, with 42 per cent of offenders 'unknown'.

36. Copeland, 2002.

37. See, for example, Australian Institute of Criminology, *Crime in Australia: Facts and Figures 2008* (Australian Government, 2009).

38. See, for example, A. Walker, J. Flatley, C. Kershaw and D. Moon, *Crime in England and Wales: Findings from the British Crime Survey and police recorded crime* (Home Office, July 2009); J. Fox and M. Zawitz, *Homicide Trends in the United States* (Bureau of Justice Statistics, January 2007): http://bjs.ojp.usdoj.gov/content/pub/pdf/htius.pdf.

39. The link between drug use and crime is somewhat confirmed by a study looking at Harlem heroin users between 1980 and 1982. There, daily heroin users reported the highest crime rates, with 209 non-drug crimes per year compared to 162 among regular users and 116 among irregular users. See B. Johnson et al., *Taking Care of Business – The Economics of Crime by Heroin Abusers* (National Development and Research Institute, 1985).

40. I. Dobinson and P. Ward, *Drugs and Crime* (NSW Bureau of Crime Statistics and Research, 1985). Darke, Kaye and Finlay-Jones found that 77 per cent of their sample of 400 methadone clients from New South Wales had committed criminal acts before they first used heroin: S. Darke, S. Kaye and R. Finlay-Jones, 'Drug Use and Injection Risk-Taking among Prison Methadone Maintenance Patients', *Addiction*, vol. 93, no. 8, 1 August 1998.

41. J. Davis, 'The Untold Story of the World's Biggest Diamond Heist', *Wired Magazine*, 3 December 2009: http://www.wired.com/politics/law/magazine/17-04/ff_diamonds?currentPage=all.

42. Associated Press, 27 June 1999: http://www.courtpsychiatrist.com/pdf/indiana_star.pdf. See also 'Murder suspect fathered child to kill as revenge', *Daily News, Bowling Green, Kentucky*, 28 June 1999.

43. J. Guinn, *Go Down Together* (Simon & Schuster, 2009).

44. D. Matera, *John Dillinger: The Life and Death of America's First Celebrity Criminal* (Carroll and Graf, 2004).

45. Cited in A. Rosenthal, 'Taking message on road, Bush pushes crime bill', *The New York Times*, 24 January 1990: http://www.nytimes.com/1990/01/24/us/taking-message-on-road-bush-pushes-crime-bill.html.

MYTH 4: ORGANIZED CRIME IS BIG, BAD AND BOOMING

1. John Steinbeck, *The Short Reign of Pippin IV: A Fabrication* (Viking Press, 1957).

2. 'Joe (Joe Cargo) Valachi' – National Crime Syndicate and Joseph 'the Rat' Valachi, 6 December 2004: https://www.youtube.com/watch?v=24M4lcAnKko.

3. Ibid.

4. 'The Conglomerate of Crime', *Time* magazine cover story, Friday, 22 August 1969: http://www.time.com/time/magazine/article/0,9171,213662,00.html. P. Maas, *The Valachi Papers* (Putnam, 1969) – Attorney General Robert Kennedy (Chapter 2, p. 36).

5. Statement by Attorney General Robert F. Kennedy to the Permanent Subcommittee on Investigations of the Senate Government Operations Committee, 25 September 1963: http://www.justice.gov/ag/rfkspeeches/1963/09-25-1963.pdf.

6. Ibid.

7. Ibid.

8. Ibid.

9. FBI, National Gang Threat Assessment, 2009: http://www.fbi.gov/stats-services/publications/national-gang-threat-assessment-2009-pdf.

10. Presidential Decision Directives 42: International Organized Crime.

11. B. Obama, 'Foreword', *Strategy to Combat Transnational Organised Crime*, 19 July 2011: https://www.whitehouse.gov/sites/default/files/Strategy_to_Combat_Transnational_Organized_Crime_July_2011.pdf

12. J. Lawler, CEO keynote address, International Serious and Organized Crime Conference, 30 July 2013: http://www.crimecommission.gov.au/media/ceo-keynote-address-international-serious-organized-crime-conference.

13. https://www.unodc.org/unodc/en/frontpage/2012/July/new-unodc-campaign-highlights-transnational-organized-crime-as-an-us-870-billion-a-year-business.html

14. C. Veillette et al., 'Plan Colombia: A Progress Report' (Congressional Research Service, the Library of Congress, 2005): http://www.fas.org/sgp/crs/row/RL32774.pdf.

15. P. Reuter, interviews with author, 5 and 12 September 2013.

16. P. Reuter, 'The Organization of Illegal Markets: An Economic Analysis', National Institute of Justice (University Press of the Pacific, 2004, repr. from 1985 edn).

17. Ibid.

18. E. Kleemans, 'Crossing Borders: Organized Crime in the Netherlands', in C. Fijnaut and L. Paoli (eds.), *Organized Crime in Europe* (Springer, 2005).

19. S. Zhang and K. Chin, 'Enter the Dragon: Inside Chinese Human Smuggling Organizations', *Criminology*, vol. 40, 2002, pp. 737–68, and V. Hysi, *Organized Crime in Albania: The Ugly Side of Capitalism and Democracy* (Springer, 2005).

20. Author interview with David Sweanor, 30 September 2013.

21. J. Collin, E. LeGresley, R. MacKenzie, S. Lawrence and K. Lee, 'Complicity in Contraband: Cigarette Smuggling in Asia', *Tobacco Control*, vol. 13, 2004, p. 111: http://cgch.lshtm.ac.uk/Complicity%20in%20contraband%20BAT%20and%20cigarette%20smuggling%20in%20Asia.pdf.

22. K. Dunt, BAT letter to Eduardo Grant, Noblexa-Picardo, 24 June 1992. British American Tobacco. Bates No. 301674939/4940. Cited in Collin et al., 'Complicity in Contraband'.

23. See, for example, Bangladesh and Burma documentation cited in Collin et al., 'Complicity in Contraband'.

24. 'Tobacco's Other Secret', CBC News: http://www.cbsnews.com/2100-500164_162-150825.html.

25. Ibid.

26. Ibid.

27. Ibid.

28. R. Blackwell, 'Tobacco giants to pay $550-million settlement', *The Globe and Mail*, 13 April 2010: http://www.theglobeandmail.com/news/national/tobacco-giants-to-pay-550-million-settlement/article4314713/.

29. M. W. Guevara, 'The World's Most Widely Smuggled Legal Substance', in *Tobacco Underground* (International Consortium of Investigative Journalists, 2008): http://www.icij.org/project/tobacco-underground/worlds-most-widely-smuggled-legal-substance.

30. HM Revenue & Customs figures cited in Cancer Research UK, 'The Facts about the Illicit Tobacco Market': http://www.cancerresearchuk.org/prod_consump/groups/cr_common/@nre/@pol/documents/general content/cr_095817.pdf.

31. Evidence to the Kefauver Committee noted the extensive involvement of police and local government officials in corruption relating to illegal gambling in Miami – and indeed tolerance of gambling (then illegal) was an open secret in that city. Further evidence is cited in R. Munting, *An Economic and Social History of Gambling in Britain and the USA* (Manchester University Press, 1996), pp. 204–6.

32. Cited in P. Van Duyne, 'Crime and Commercial Activity: An Introduction to Two Half-Brothers', in P. Van Duyne, K. Von Lampe, M. Van Dijck and J. Newell (eds.), *The Organized Crime Economy: Managing Crime Markets in Europe* (Wolf Legal Publishers, 2005).

33. L. Paoli, 'Organized Crime in Italy: Mafia and Illegal Markets – Exception and Normality', in Fijnaut and Paoli (eds.) *Organised Crime in Europe*, p. 287.

34. Paoli, 'Organized Crime in Italy: Mafia and Illegal Markets', in Fijnaut and Paoli (eds.), *Organized Crime in Europe*.

35. Kleemans, 'Crossing Borders'.

36. Unknown reporter, 'Canadian naval drug bust worth $150M happened "peacefully"', *CBC News*, 1 April 2013: http://www.cbc.ca/news/world/canadian-naval-drug-bust-worth-150m-happened-peacefully-1.1396477; H. Gye, 'Now even drug barons are going green as police raid solar-powered cannabis factory growing £500,000 worth of plants', *Daily Mail*, 1 February 2013: http://www.dailymail.co.uk/news/article-2271751/Now-drug-barons-going-green-police-raid-solar-powered-cannabis-factory-growing-500-000-worth-plants html#ixzz2dHPw6mpK.

37. *Extending Our Reach: A Comprehensive Approach to Tackling Serious Organized Crime* (Home Office/Cabinet Office, 2009).

38. W. Bender and staff writer, 'Law enforcement likes getting really high off drug busts', *Enquirer*, 27 July 2012: http://articles.philly.com/2012-07-27/news/32890201_1_drug-laws-drug-busts-ethan-nadelmann.

39. Ibid.

40. R. L. Miller, *Drug Warriors and Their Prey: From Police Power to Police State* (Praeger, 1996).

41. Ibid.

42. P. Reuter and J. Caulkins, 'An Assessment of Drug Incarceration and Foreign Interventions' for evidence session with US Domestic Policy Subcommittee, Oversight and Reform Committee, 19 May 2009.

43. Biography Channel, *Frank Lucas – Mini-bio*: http://www.youtube.com/watch?v=SL78pouE_Hk.

44. Ibid.

45. M. Jacobson, 'The Return of Superfly', *New York Magazine*, 14 July 2000: http://nymag.com/nymag/features/3649/.

46. Ibid.

47. http://planetill.com/2009/09/ron-chepesiuk-dispelling-the-myth-of-the-american-gangster/

48. http://www.naijarules.com/xf/index.php?threads/is-american-gangster-really-all-that-true.26185/.

49. http://wn.com/frank_lucas.

50. R. Chepesiuk and A. Gonzalez, 'Frank Lucas and "American Gangster" – the Myth and the Reality', December 2007: http://www.americanmafia.com/Feature_Articles_406.html.

51. Jacobson, 'The Return of Superfly'.

52. Robert Lacey, *Little Man: Meyer Lansky and the Gangster Life* (Little, Brown, 1991).

53. Statement by Attorney General Robert F. Kennedy to the Permanent Subcommittee on Investigations of the Senate Government Operations Committee, 25 September 1963: http://www.justice.gov/ag/rfkspeeches/1963/09-25-1963.pdf.

54. http://en.wikipedia.org/wiki/Vito_genovese.

55. Reuter, interviews with author, 5 and 12 September 2013.

56. P. Reuter and V. Greenfield, 'Measuring Global Drug Markets: How good are the numbers and why should we care about them?': http://www.stopthewarondrugs.org/wp-content/uploads/2013/05/Reuter-P.-Greenfield-V.-2001-Measuring-Global-Drug-Markets-How-good-are-the-numbers-and-why-should-we-care-about-them.pdf.

57. F. Varese, 'General Introduction: What is Organized Crime?', in Varese (ed.), *Organized Crime: Critical Concepts in Criminology* (Routledge, 2010).

58. Ibid.

59. https://www.unodc.org/unodc/en/organized-crime/.

60. Royal Canadian Mounted Police, ' "What's the Link?" with Organized Crime', retrieved 22 September 2013: http://www.rcmp-grc.gc.ca/occo/index-eng.htm.

61. For a summary of literature on gang desistence, including the importance of creating pulls to attract individuals out of gangs, see M. Young et al., 'Getting Out of Gangs, Staying Out of Gangs: Gang Intervention and Desistence Strategies', *National Gang Center Bulletin*, no. 8, January 2013: https://www.nationalgangcenter.gov/Content/Documents/Getting-Out-Staying-Out.pdf.

62. US Supreme Court Calero-Toledo v. Pearson Yacht Leasing Co., 416 US 663 (1974), appeal from the United States District Court for the District of Puerto Rico, No. 73-157. Argued 7 January 1974. Decided 15 May 1974: http://caselaw.lp.findlaw.com/cgi-bin/getcase.pl?court=us&vol=416&invol=663.

63. S., Stilman, 'Taken', *The New Yorker*, 12 August 2013: http://www.newyorker.com/reporting/2013/08/12/130812fa_fact_stillman?currentPage=1.

64. Ibid.

65. For example, 94 per cent of the financial assets of Dutch criminals subjected to asset seizure since 1994 were located in Dutch bank accounts. Cited in P. Van Duyne, 'Organized Crime (Threat) as a Policy Challenge: A Tautology', *Journal of Criminal Justice and Security*, year 12, no. 4.

66. Joseph 'the Rat' Valachi, 6 December 2004: https://www.youtube.com/watch?v=24M4lcAnKko.

67. This episode is also described in S. Raab, *Five Families* (Robson, 2006), p. 136.

68. *The Snitch System* (Northwestern University School of Law Center on Wrongful Convictions, 2004): http://www.law.northwestern.edu/legal-clinic/wrongfulconvictions/documents/SnitchSystemBooklet.pdf.

69. G. Gudjonsson and J. Pearse, 'Suspect Interviews and False Confessions', *Current Directions in Psychological Science*, vol. 20, no. 1, February 2011, pp. 33–7.

70. Mobsters – Joseph 'Joe Cargo' Valachi: http://www.dailymotion.com/video/x1ageel_mobsters-joseph-joe-cargo-valachi-the-rat_shortfilms.

71. Reuter, interviews with author, 5 and 12 September 2013.

MYTH 5: BIOLOGY DETERMINES CRIMINALITY

1. Arthur Conan Doyle, 'The Final Problem', in *The Memoirs of Sherlock Holmes* (John Murray, 1893).

2. 'Confession', in the *Philadelphia Inquirer*, 12 April 1896, cited in K. Ramsland, *Inside the Minds of Serial Killers: Why They Kill* (Praeger, 2006).

3. 'East Side man charged with killing his wife', *The New York Times*, 8 January 1991, retrieved 10 August 2010 at: http://www.nytimes.com/1991/01/08/nyregion/east-side-man-charged-with-killing-his-wife.html?scp=2&sq=herbert+weinstein+window&st=nyt.

4. J. Rosen, 'The brain on the stand', *The New York Times*, 11 March 2007.

5. N. Rafter, *The Criminal Brain: Understanding Biological Theories of Crime* (New York University Press, 2008).

6. A. Flowers, *Bound to Die: The Shocking True Story of Bobby Joe Long, America's Most Savage Serial Killer* (Pinnacle, 1995).

7. J. M. Harlow, 'Recovery from the Passage of an Iron Bar through the Head', *Publications of the Massachusetts Medical Society*, vol. 2, 1868, pp. 327–47 (also in booklet form published in Boston in 1869 by D. H. Clapp); reproduced in M. Macmillan, *An Odd Kind of Fame: Stories of Phineas Gage* (MIT Press, 2000).

8. 'Is a life of crime hereditary? New research suggests that criminal behaviour could be "all in the genes"', *Mail Online*, 25 November 2010: http://www.dailymail.co.uk/sciencetech/article-1332927/New-research-suggests-criminal-behaviour-genes.html#ixzz2OYwW8QnB.

9. P. Cohen, 'Genetic basis for crime: a new look', *The New York Times*, 19 June 2011: http://www.nytimes.com/2011/06/20/arts/genetics-and-crime-at-institute-of-justice-conference.html?pagewanted=all&_r=0.

10. M. Marchant, 'Should We Screen Kids' Brains and Genes to ID Future Criminals?', *Slate*, 17 October 2012: http://www.slate.com/articles/technology/future_tense/2012/10/should_kids_brains_and_genes_be_screened_to_detect_future_criminals.html.

11. Ibid.

12. 'Lighter Sentence for Murderer with "Bad Genes"', *Nature*, 30 October 2009: http://www.nature.com/news/2009/091030/full/news.2009.1050.html.

13. Cited in J. Joseph, *The Gene Illusion: Genetic Research in Psychiatry and Psychology* (Algora Publishing, 2004).

14. Death Penalty Information Center, *Facts about the Death Penalty*, 22 June 2010: http://www.deathpenaltyinfo.org/FactSheet.pdf.

15. A. Raine, 'Murderous Minds: Can We See the Mark of Cain?', *Cerebrum*, 1 April 1999, recovered 10 August 2010 at: http://www.dana.org/news/cerebrum/detail.aspx?id=3066.

16. Ibid.

17. Ibid.

18. Author interview with Terrie Moffitt, London, 3 July 2012.

19. A. Caspi, J. McClay, T. E. Moffitt, J. Mill, J. Martin, I. Craig, A. Taylor and R. Poulton, 'Role of Genotype in the Cycle of Violence in Maltreated Children', *Science*, vol. 297, August 2002; A. Raine, M. Buchsbaum and L. LaCasse, 'Brain Abnormalities in Murderers Indicated by Positron Emission Tomography', *Biological Psychiatry*, vol. 42, 1997, pp. 495–508: http://wardakhan.org/notes/Original%20Studies/Physiological%20Psychology/Adrian-Raine-%20Monte-Buchsbaum-and-Lori-LaCasse.pdf.

20. Raine, Buchsbaum and LaCasse, 'Brain Abnormalities in Murderers Indicated by Positron Emission Tomography'.

21. J. Fischman, 'Criminal Minds: Adrian Raine Thinks Brain Scans Can Identify Children Who May Become Killers', *The Chronicle of Higher Education*, 12 June 2011: http://chronicle.com/article/Can-This-Man-Predict-Whether/127792/.

22. Author interview with Terrie Moffitt, London, 3 July 2012.

23. Ibid.

24. T. Adams, 'How to spot a murderer's brain', *Observer*, 12 May 2013: http://www.theguardian.com/science/2013/may/12/how-to-spot-a-murderers-brain.

25. This is based on National Institute of Mental Health estimates (and E. M. Goldner, L. Hsu, P. Waraich and J. M. Somers, 'Prevalence and Incidence Studies of Schizophrenic Disorders: A Systematic Review of the Literature', *Canadian Journal of Psychiatry*, 2002).

26. This calculation assumes that 1 per cent of the population will suffer from schizophrenia (Goldner et al., 'Prevalence and Incidence Studies of Schizophrenic Disorders'), that testing will pick up 73.9 per cent of those suffering ('sensitivity statistic' from C. Davatzikos et al., 'Whole-Brain Morphometric Study of Schizophrenia Reveals a Spatially Complex Set of Focal Abnormalities', *JAMA Archives of General Psychiatry*, vol. 62, 2005, pp. 1218–27), and will correctly assess those not suffering as not suffering in 87.3 per cent of cases (specificity statistic of 87.3 per cent – from same source). If 10,000 people are tested using these values, 74 of the 100 schizophrenics in the sample will be correctly diagnosed, 26 will be falsely given the all-clear, and a staggering 1,257 will be falsely diagnosed as having the disease. This means that only 74 out of the total 1,331 positive diagnoses (5 per cent) would be accurate: http://www.rad.upenn.edu/sbia/papers/2005-schizophrenia.pdf.

27. J. Joseph, 'Separated Twins and the Genetics of Personality Differences: A Critique', *The American Journal of Psychology*, vol. 114, no. 1, spring 2001, pp. 1–30.

28. Ibid.

29. J. Joseph, 'Is Crime in the Genes? A Critical Review of Twin and Adoption Studies of Criminality and Antisocial Behavior', *Journal of Mind and Behavior*, vol. 22, 2001, pp. 179–218.

30. Ibid.

31. M. Rutter, 'Gene–Environment Interdependence', *European Journal of Developmental Psychology*, vol. 9, issue 4, 2012: http://thebrainand themind.co.uk/Build/Assets/readings/Rutter%20review%20paper%20 gxE%202012.pdf.

32. See Society for Neuroscience, 'Teen Brain Vulnerability Exposed', 31 December 2011, at BrainFacts.org: http://www.brainfacts.org/ across-the-lifespan/youth-and-aging/articles/2011/teen-brain-vulnerability- exposed/.

33. Image adapted from N. Gogtay et al., 'Dynamic Mapping of Human Cortical Development during Childhood through Early Adulthood', *PNAS*, vol. 101, no. 21, 2004, pp. 8174–79, fig. 3. copyright © National Academy of Sciences, USA, 2004.

34. C. Roger, 'What became of Romania's neglected orphans?', BBC News online: http://news.bbc.co.uk/1/hi/world/europe/8425001.stm.

35. J. Kreppner, M. Rutter, C. Beckett, J. Castle, E. Colvert, C. Groothues, A. Hawkins, T. O'Connor, S. Stevens and E. Sonuga-Barke, 'Normality and Impairment Following Profound Early Institutional Deprivation: A Longitudinal Follow-Up into Early Adolescence', *Developmental Psychology*, vol. 43, no. 4, 2007.

36. I. Weaver et al., 'Epigenetic Programming by Maternal Behavior', *Nature Neuroscience*, vol. 7, 2004, pp. 847–54.

37. G. Kraemer, 'Psychobiology of Early Social Attachment in Rhesus Monkeys: Clinical Implications', *Annals of the New York Academy of Sciences*, vol. 807, 1997, pp. 401–18.

38. B. Perry, 'Childhood Experience and the Expression of Genetic Potential: What Childhood Neglect Tells Us about Nature and Nurture', *Brain and Mind*, vol. 3, 2002, pp. 79–100.

39. M. Maxfield and C. Widom, 'The Cycle of Violence Revisited 6 Years Later', *JAMA Pediatrics*, vol. 150, no. 4, 1996; J. E. Lansford, K. A. Dodge, G. S. Pettit, J. E. Bates, J. Crozier and J. Kaplow, '12-Year Prospective Study of the Long-term Effects of Early Child Physical Maltreatment on Psychological, Behavioral, and Academic Problems in Adolescence', *JAMA Pediatrics*, vol. 156, no. 8, 2002; J. Ludwig and J. Kling, 'Is Crime Contagious', NBER Working Paper no. 12409, August 2006.

40. 'Is a life of crime hereditary?', *Mail Online*, 25 November 2010: http://www.dailymail.co.uk/sciencetech/article-1332927/New-research-suggests-criminal-behaviour-genes.html#ixzz2OYwW8QnB.

41. K. M. Beaver, 'Genetic Influences on being Processed through the Criminal Justice System: Results from a Sample of Adoptees', *Biological Psychiatry*, vol. 69, issue 3, February 2011, pp. 282–7. doi: 10.1016/j.biopsych.2010.09.007. Epub 2010 Nov 10.

42. 'Is a life of crime hereditary?', *Mail Online*, 25 November 2010.

43. 'Life of crime is in the genes, study claims', *Telegraph*, 26 January 2012: http://www.telegraph.co.uk/science/science-news/9040997/Life-of-crime-is-in-the-genes-study-claims.html.

44. Ibid.

45. J. C. Barnes, K. M. Beaver and B. B. Boutwell, 'Examining the Genetic Underpinnings to Moffitt's Developmental Taxonomy: A Behavioural Genetic Analysis', *Criminology*, vol. 49, issue 4, 2011, pp. 923–54. doi: 10.1111/j.1745-9125.2011.00243.x.

46. D. Blonigen, 'Psychopathic Personality Traits: Heritability and Genetic Overlap with Internalizing and Externalizing Psychopathology', in *Psychological Medicine*, vol. 35, issue 5, May 2005, pp. 637–48: http://www.ncbi.nlm.nih.gov/pmc/articles/PMC2242349/.

47. D. Mason and P. Frick, 'The Heritability of Antisocial Behavior: A Meta-Analysis of Twin and Adoption Studies', *Journal of Psychopathology and Behavioral Assessment*, vol. 16, 1994, pp. 301–23.

48. P. Cohen, 'Genetic basis for crime: a new look', *The New York Times*, 19 June 2011: http://www.nytimes.com/2011/06/20/arts/genetics-and-crime-at-institute-of-justice-conference.html?pagewanted=all&_r=0#h [BapFes,2].

49. On average 88 per cent of people trusted doctors to tell the truth between 1983 and 2011, 77 per cent trusted professors, 61 per cent scientists, 28 per cent business leaders and just 18 per cent trusted politicians. Ipsos MORI, Trust in the Professions poll, 2011: http://www.ipsos-mori.com/researchpublications/researcharchive/2818/Doctors-are-most-trusted-profession-politicians-least-trusted.aspx.

50. B. Hadley, 'Can genes make you murder?', in National Public Radio (NPR) online series *Inside the Criminal Brain*, 1 July 2010: http://www.npr.org/templates/story/story.php?storyId=128043329.

51. L. Aspinwall, T. Brown and J. Tabery, 'The Double-Edged Sword: Does Biomechanism Increase or Decrease Judges' Sentencing of Psychopaths?', *Science*, vol. 337, no. 6096, 17 August 2012.

52. J. Monterosso, E. Royzman and B. Schwartz, 'Explaining Away Responsibility: Effects of Scientific Explanation on Perceived Culpability', *Ethics and Behavior*, vol. 15, issue 2, 2005: http://www.tandfonline. com/doi/abs/10.1207/s15327019eb1502_4#preview.

53. J. Monterosso and B. Schwartz, 'Did your brain make you do it?', *The New York Times Sunday Review*, 27 July 2012: http://www.nytimes. com/2012/07/29/opinion/sunday/neuroscience-and-moral-responsibility.html?_r=1.

54. See, for example, C. Gesch et al., 'Influence of Supplementary Vitamins, Minerals and Essential Fatty Acids on the Antisocial Behaviour of Young Adult Prisoners: Randomised Placebo Controlled Trial', *The British Journal of Psychiatry*, vol. 181, 2002, pp. 22–8. See also a replication of the Gesch study in the Netherlands: 'Effects of Nutritional Supplements on Aggression, Rule-Breaking, and Psychopathology among Young Adult Prisoners', *Aggressive Behavior*, vol. 36, issue 2, 2010 and a later replication by Gesch and colleagues.

MYTH 6: POVERTY IS THE REAL CAUSE OF CRIME

1. Friedrich Engels, *The Condition of the Working Class in England* (*Die Lage der arbeitenden Klasse in England*, 1845; 1st English translation 1887).

2. H. L. (Henry Lewis) Mencken (1880–1956), *Minority Report: H. L. Mencken's Notebooks* (Knopf, 1956), extract 273, p. 190.

3. 'Former Brewster-Douglass Housing Project demolition under way', WXYZ-TV Detroit, Channel 7, 4 September 2013: http://www.youtube. com/watch?v=Plp9GeHjUP4.

4. K. Abbey-Lambertz, 'Demolition begins on Detroit's Brewster-Douglass Projects, first black U.S. housing development', *Huffington Post*, 4 September 2013: http://www.huffingtonpost.com/2013/09/04/brewster-douglass-projects-demolition-detroit_n_3865482.html.

5. 'Former Brewster-Douglass Housing Project demolition under way', WXYZ-TV Detroit, Channel 7, 4 September 2013: http://www.you tube.com/watch?v=Plp9GeHjUP4.

6. K. Abbey-Lambertz, 'Most dangerous neighbourhoods: Detroit home to 3 most violent areas in America', *Huffington Post*, 5 February 2013: http://www.huffingtonpost.com/2013/05/02/most-dangerous-neighborhoods-america-detroit_n_3187931.html.

7. Detroit's unemployment rate has fluctuated considerably in recent years and varies depending on which areas are included as being

within the city. The Bureau of Labor Statistics estimated that in 2010 Detroit had the highest unemployment rate of all large metropolitan areas at 24.8 per cent (nearly four times the national average): see http://www.bls.gov/lau/lacilg10.htm. However, 2015 figures reveal falling unemployment in recent years, with an unemployment rate of around 50 per cent above the national average – see, for example, Bureau of Labor Statistics, *Detroit Area Economic Summary*, September 2015: http://www.bls.gov/regions/midwest/summary/blssummary_detroit.pdf.

8. See D. Fisher, 'Detroit Again Tops List of Most Dangerous Cities, As Crime Rate Dips', *Forbes*, 22 October 2013: http://www.forbes.com/sites/danielfisher/2013/10/22/detroit-again-tops-list-of-most-dangerous-cities-but-crime-rate-dips/ for 2008–2013 reference.

9. Detroit's murder rate in 2013 was 45 per 100,000 compared to a national average rate of 4.5 per 100,000. See FBI, *Crime in the United States, Murder*, 2014: https://www.fbi.gov/about-us/cjis/ucr/crime-in-the-u.s/2013/crime-in-the-u.s.-2013/violent-crime/murder-topic-page/murdermain_final.pdf.

10. Home Office, *Crime in England and Wales*, various years.

11. D. Orsen, '"Million-Dollar Blocks" Map Incarceration's Costs', in *NPR's Cities Project*, 2 October 2012: http://www.npr.org/2012/10/02/162149431/million-dollar-blocks-map-incarcerations-costs.

12. 'PM's speech on the fightback after the riots', 15 August 2011: https://www.gov.uk/government/speeches/pms-speech-on-the-fightback-after-the-riots.

13. 'Detroit journal; when life in the Projects was good', *The New York Times* archives, 31 July 1991: http://www.nytimes.com/1991/07/31/us/detroit-journal-when-life-in-the-projects-was-good.html.

14. Michigan State Insurance Commission estimate of December 1967, quoted in the National Advisory Commission on Civil Disorders, also known as Kerner Report, 9 February 1968. Archived from the original on 5 June 2011, retrieved 24 April 2011.

15. Coleman Young, *Hard Stuff: The Autobiography of Mayor Coleman Young* (Viking, 1994).

16. K. Linebaugh, 'Detroit's Population Crashes', *The Wall Street Journal*, 23 March 2011: http://online.wsj.com/news/articles/SB10001424052748704461304576216850733151470.

17. A. Kellogg, 'Black Flight Hits Detroit', *The Wall Street Journal*, 5 June 2010: http://online.wsj.com/news/articles/SB10001424052748704292004575230532248715858.

18. C. MacDonald, 'Poll: crime drives Detroiters out; 40% expect to leave within 5 years', *Detroit News*, 9 October 2012: http://www.detroit-news.com/article/20121009/METRO01/210090369.

19. This quote was taken from an internet discussion forum on Detroit that has subsequently been closed. It was just one of dozens of similar comments – crime and jobs were the two main reasons cited for leaving the city.

20. Scottish Law Online Discussion Forum: http://www.scottishlaw.org.uk/cgi-bin/yabb2/YaBB.pl?num=1207578092/1.

21. L. Linden and J. E. Rockoff, 'Estimates of the Impact of Crime Risk on Property Values from Megan's Laws', *American Economic Review*, vol. 98, no. 3, June 2008, pp. 1103–27: http://www0.gsb.columbia.edu/faculty/jrockoff/aer.98.3.pdf.

22. J. Pope, 'Fear of Crime and Housing Prices: Household Reactions to Sex Offender Registries', *Journal of Urban Economics*, 2008: https://economics.byu.edu/Documents/Jaren%20Pope/pope_fear_of_crime_JUE2.pdf.

23. S. Gibbons, 'The Costs of Urban Property Crime', *The Economic Journal*, vol. 114, issue 499, 2004, pp. F441–F463. doi: 10.1111/j.1468-0297.2004.00254.x. Earlier version at: http://cep.lse.ac.uk/pubs/download/dp0574.pdf.

24. X. De Souza Briggs, S. Popkin and J. Goering, *Moving to Opportunity: The Story of an American Experiment to Fight Ghetto Poverty* (Oxford University Press, 2004).

25. Ibid.

26. Ibid.

27. Ibid.

28. J. Ludwig, G. Duncan, L. Gennetian, L. Katz, R. Kessler, J. Kling and L. Sanbonmatsu, 'Long-Term Neighborhood Effects on Low-Income Families: Evidence from Moving to Opportunity', *American Economic Review: Papers and Proceedings*, vol. 103, no. 3, May 2013, pp. 226–31.

29. Ibid.

30. De Souza Briggs, Popkin and Goering, *Moving to Opportunity*.

31. Ludwig et al., 'Long-Term Neighborhood Effects on Low-Income Families'.

32. Ibid.

33. M. Sciandra, L. Sanbonmatsu, G. J. Duncan, L. A. Gennetian, L. F. Katz, R. C. Kessler, J. R. Kling and J. Ludwig, 'Long-Term Effects of the Moving to Opportunity Residential Mobility Experiment on Crime and Delinquency', *Journal of Experimental Criminology*, vol. 9, issue 4, September 2013, pp. 451–89.

34. Ibid.

35. Ibid.

36. T. Ireland, T. Thornberry and R. Loeber, 'Violence among Adolescents Living in Public Housing: A Two-Site Analysis', *Criminology and Public Policy*, issue 1, 2003, pp. 3–38.

37. De Souza Briggs, Popkin and Goering, *Moving to Opportunity*.

38. S. Gibbons, O. Silva and F. Weinhardt, 'Do Neighbours Affect Teenage Outcomes? Evidence from Neighbourhood Changes in England', Spatial Economics Research Centre, London, discussion paper, 2010.

39. H. G. Overman and S. Gibbons, 'In Unequal Britain Who You are is Much More Important Than Where You Live in Determining Earnings', British Politics and Policy at LSE (11 November 2011). For a good summary of the primacy of individual characteristics rather than neighbourhood effects being important see P. Cheshire, S. Gibbons and I. Gordon, 'Policies for "Mixed Communities": A Critical Evaluation', Spatial Economics Research Centre, 2008: http://www.spatialeconomics. ac.uk/textonly/SERC/publications/download/sercpp002.pdf.

40. J. Fahey, 'Benefit fraud Lottery winner Edward Putman jailed', *Independent*, 24 July 2012: http://www.independent.co.uk/news/uk/crime/ benefit-fraud-lottery-winner-edward-putman-jailed-7972974.html.

41. 'Virginia lottery winner arrested on narcotics charges', *Portsmouth News and Weather*:http://www.wvec.com/my-city/portsmouth/Virginia- lottery-winner-arrested-on-narcotics-charges-211448881.html.

42. 'Lucky Loser ends up behind bars following $1 million lottery win in Euromillions: Whatever happened to . . . ? Stories of lottery winners from around the world': http://www.euro-millions.org/america/554/.

43. J. Narain, ' "Celebrity" crime family who won £1m EuroMillions jack- pot in trouble AGAIN after gangster's son used cash to bankroll heroin deal', *Daily Mail Online*, 19 September 2013: http://www.dailymail. co.uk/news/article-2424988/Desmond-Noonan-jailed-heroin-deal- lottery-winnings.html.

44. C. Uggen and S. Wakefield, 'What Have We Learned from Longitu- dinal Studies of Work and Crime?', in A. Lieberman (ed.), *The Long View of Crime: A Synthesis of Longitudinal Research* (Springer, 2008).

45. D. Farrington and B. Welsh, *Saving Children from a Life of Crime: Early Risk Factors and Effective Interventions* (Oxford University Press, 2008).

46. J. Staff, D. Osgood, J. Schulenberg, J. Bachman and E. Messersmith, 'Explaining the Relationship between Employment and Juvenile Delin- quency', *Criminology*, vol. 48, issue 4, 2010.

47. Uggen and Wakefield, 'What Have We Learned from Longitudinal Studies of Work and Crime?'

48. http://www.telegraph.co.uk/news/uknews/crime/8979769/Third-of-unemployed-are-convicted-criminals.html

49. http://www.dailymail.co.uk/news/article-2079176/One-jobless-benefits-got-criminal-record.html#ixzz2lpgjolqo.

50. There is some robust research which estimates that nearly a quarter of the UK population born in 1953 had received a caution or conviction (33 per cent of males and 9 per cent of females) – mostly for only one offence. See J. Prime, S. White, S. Liriano and K. Patel, *Criminal Careers of Those Born between 1953 and 1978*, Home Office Statistical Bulletin, April 2001: http://webarchive.nationalarchives.gov.uk/20110218135832/http:/rds.homeoffice.gov.uk/rds/pdfs/hosb401.pdf.

51. C. Foley, 'Welfare Payments & Crime', NBER Working Paper no. 14074, issued June 2008, NBER Program(s).

52. Ibid.

53. D. Segal, 'A missionary's quest to remake Motor City', *The New York Times*, 13 April 2013: http://www.nytimes.com/2013/04/14/business/dan-gilberts-quest-to-remake-downtown-detroit.html?pagewanted=1&_r=2&adxnnl=1&adxnnlx=1388174409-6VDXQeiori4pErR%20Y%20driw.

MYTH 7: IMMIGRATION INCREASES CRIME RATES

1. Tony Blair, cited in 'Blair toughens stance on religious tolerance and cultural assimilation – Europe – International Herald Tribune', *The New York Times Online*, 8 November 2006: http://www.nytimes.com/2006/12/08/world/europe/08iht-blair.3836374.html?_r=0.

2. T. Whitehead, 'Drunk illegal immigrant kills couple after sneaking back into country', *Telegraph*, 19 December 2013: http://www.telegraph.co.uk/news/uknews/immigration/9290571/Drunk-illegal-immigrant-kills-couple-after-sneaking-back-into-country.html.

3. D. Gibson, 'Illegal alien to be tried for teen's grisly murder two years after being charged' in *The Examiner*, 10 August 2012: http://www.examiner.com/article/illegal-alien-to-be-tried-for-teen-s-grisly-murder-two-years-after-being-charged.

4. M. Giannangeli, 'Immigrant crime soars with foreign prisoners rising', *Daily Express Online*, 17 February 2013: http://www.express.co.uk/news/uk/378232/Immigrant-crime-soars-with-foreign-prisoners-rising.

5. Trump is cited in various reports including I. Hod, 'Donald Trump vs. Rupert Murdoch's immigrant crime rate claims: why biggest victim is the truth', *The Wrap*, 14 July 2015: http://www.thewrap.com/

donald-trump-vs-rupert-murdochs-immigrant-crime-rate-claims-why-biggest-victim-is-the-truth/#sthash.AYzCVLeR.dpuf. On 26 February 2015, speaking at a House Rules Committee hearing, the Republican Senator Pete Sessions said: 'Every day, all along border states, maybe other places, there are murders by people who have been arrested coming into this country, who have been released by the Obama administration, I believe in violation of the law, who are murdering Americans all over our cities': https://www.youtube.com/watch?v=Xjs6F722ToQ#t=23m28s; and J. Farah, 'Illegal Aliens Murder 12 Americans Daily', *WorldNetDaily*, 28 November 2006: http://www.wnd.com/2006/11/39031/.

6. *Europol SOCTA 2013: European Serious and Organised Crime Threat Assessment*: https://www.europol.europa.eu/sites/default/files/publications/socta2013.pdf.

7. Home Office, *Protecting Our Border, Protecting the Public: The UK Border Agency's Five Year Strategy for Enforcing our Immigration Rules and Addressing Immigration and Cross Border Crime*, February 2010.

8. https://www.dhs.gov/about-dhs, retrieved 20 December 2013.

9. Search conducted November 2013.

10. Ibid.

11. European Social Survey data (all years) is available at http://www.europeansocialsurvey.org/data/round-index.html.

12. J. Doyle and C. Brooke, 'Drunken illegal immigrant who sneaked back into Britain after being deported used car "as a weapon" and killed "honest" pensioner couple in 100mph smash', *Daily Mail Online*, 25 May 2012: http://www.dailymail.co.uk/news/article-2149952/Eduard-Mereohra-Drunken-illegal-immigrant-killed-pensioner-couple-100mph-smash.html#ixzz20O2lqJOq.

13. T. Hesson, 'Is fear of immigrant criminals overblown?', at Fusion online: http://fusion.net/justice/story/fact-check-fear-immigrant-criminals-overblown-15409.

14. E. Gillingham, *Understanding A8 Migration to the UK since Accession*, Office for National Statistics, 2010.

15. C. Vargas-Silva, *Briefing: Migration Flows of A8 and Other EU Migrants to and from the UK*: http://www.migrationobservatory.ox.ac.uk/sites/files/migobs/Migration%20Flows%20of%20A8%20and%20other%20EU%20Migrants%20to%20and%20from%20the%20UK.pdf.

16. 'Immigration: migrants in their own words', *Telegraph*, 3 April 2008: http://www.telegraph.co.uk/news/features/3636123/Immigration-migrants-in-their-own-words.html.

17. 'Britain's top black police officer: "We are struggling to cope with immigrant crime wave"': http://www.dailymail.co.uk/news/article-510685/

Britains-black-police-officer-We-struggling-cope-immigrant-crime-wave. html#ixzz2orNFS4ot.

18. 'Police chief fears migrant impact', BBC News online, 19 September 2007: http://news.bbc.co.uk/1/hi/7001768.stm.

19. F. Attewill, 'Increased immigration boosts knife crime and drink-driving, police chief says', *Guardian*, 19 September 2007: http://www.theguardian. com/uk/2007/sep/19/immigration.immigrationandpublicservices.

20. B. Bell, F. Fasani and S. Machin, 'Crime and Immigration: Evidence from Large Immigrant Waves', LSE Centre for Economic Performance Discussion Paper series CDP no. 12/10, 2010: http://www.cream-migration.org/publ_uploads/CDP_12_10.pdf.

21. Ibid.

22. Ibid.

23. Ibid.

24. J. Osman, 'Immigration nation: one man's journey from Somalia', Channel 4 News, 25 April 2013: http://www.channel4.com/news/ the-dreams-of-immigrants-and-the-harsh-reality.

25. H. Harris, *The Somali Community in the UK: What We Know and How We Know It*, King's College London, June 2004: http://www.icar. org.uk/somalicommunityreport.pdf.

26. Bell, Fasani and Machin, 'Crime and Immigration'.

27. J. Van Dijk, J. Van Kesteren and P. Smit, *Criminal Victimisation in International Perspective: Key Findings from 2004/5* (Boom Legal Publishers, 2007).

28. '17 patients killed in shooting at Mexican drug rehab center', CNN, 3 September 2009: http://edition.cnn.com/2009/WORLD/americas/09 /03/mexico.killings/.

29. L. Carlson, 'Murder Capital of the World', in *Foreign Policy in Focus*, Institute for Policy Studies, February 2010: http://www.fpif.org/articles/ murder_capital_of_the_world.

30. R. Archibold, 'Mexican drug cartel violence spills over, alarming U.S.', *The New York Times*, 22 March 2009: http://www.nytimes. com/2009/03/23/us/23border.html?pagewanted=all&_r=0.

31. Washington Office on Latin America, *An Uneasy Coexistence: Security and Migration along the El Paso–Ciudad Juárez Border*: http:// www.wola.org/commentary/an_uneasy_coexistence.

32. State and County quick facts: El Paso County, Texas, US Census Bureau: http://quickfacts.census.gov/qfd/states/48/48141.html, retrieved 30 December 2013.

33. J. Stowell, S. Messner, K. McGeever and L. Raffalovich, 'Immigration and the Recent Violent Crime Drop in the United States: A Pooled,

Cross-Sectional Time-Series Analysis of Metropolitan Areas', *Criminology*, vol. 47, issue 3, 2009.

34. R. Martinez, J. Stowell and M. Lee, 'Immigration and Crime in an Era of Transformation: a Longitudinal Analysis of Homicides in San Diego Neighborhoods, 1980–2000', *Criminology*, vol. 48, issue 3, 2010.

35. A. Sampson, 'Rethinking Crime and Immigration', *Contexts* feature: http://contexts.org/articles/winter-2008/sampson/#study.

36. According to one study – K. Butcher, 'Why are Immigrants' Incarceration Rates So Low?' (2007) – immigrants had an institutionalization rate 30 per cent lower than that of natives in 1980, 49 per cent in 1990, and 20 per cent in 2000. But such wild fluctuations do not appear highly plausible.

37. Cited in Harris, *The Somali Community in the UK*.

38. Ibid.

39. L. Berdadi and M. Bucerius, 'Immigrants and Their Children', in M. Tonry (ed.), *Oxford Handbook of Ethnicity, Crime and Immigration* (Oxford University Press, 2013).

40. B. Bell, and S. Machin, *The Impact of Migration on Crime and Victimisation: A Report for the Migration Advisory Committee*, December 2011: http://www.ukba.homeoffice.gov.uk/sitecontent/documents/aboutus/workingwithus/mac/27-analysis-migration/02-research-projects/lse-consulting?view=Binary.

41. Berdadi and Bucerius, 'Immigrants and Their Children'.

42. R. Rumbaut and W. Ewing, 'The Myth of Immigrant Criminality and the Paradox of Assimilation: Incarceration Rates among Native and Foreign-Born Men', American Immigration Law Foundation, 2007: http://www.immigrationpolicy.org/sites/default/files/docs/Imm%20Criminality%20(IPC).pdf.

43. Ibid.

44. Berdadi and Bucerius, 'Immigrants and Their Children'.

45. 'Crime stats show D. C. leads nation in per capita marijuana arrests', *Washington City Paper*, 13 October 2010 : http://www.washingtoncitypaper.com/articles/39580/dc-leads-nation-in-per-capita-marijuana-arrests-crime-stats.

46. See, for example, B. Clarkson, 'A blow against racism: student strikes back after being hit, taunted – and finds himself charged with assault', Sun News Canada, 28 April 2009: http://www.torontosun.com/news/canada/2009/04/28/9272411-sun.html.

47. For a good summary of the evidence on the responses to rejection see L. Richman and M. Leary, 'Reactions to Discrimination, Stigmatization, Ostracism, and Other Forms of Interpersonal Rejection: A Multimotive

Model', *Psychological Review*, vol. 116, no. 2, April 2009, pp. 365–83: http://www.ncbi.nlm.nih.gov/pmc/articles/PMC2763620/.

48. Ibid.
49. Ibid.
50. 'Immigration: migrants in their own words', *Telegraph*, 3 April 2008: http://www.telegraph.co.uk/news/features/3636123/Immigration-migrants-in-their-own-words.html.

MYTH 8: WE NEED MORE BOBBIES ON THE BEAT

1. Albert Camus, *The Rebel* (*L'Homme révolté*, 1951).
2. '1969: Montreal's night of terror', Canadian Broadcasting Corporation Television News Special, 8 October 1969: http://www.cbc.ca/archives/categories/politics/civil-unrest/general-27/montreals-night-of-terror.html.
3. G. Marx, 'Issueless Riots', in J. Short and M. Wolfgang, *Collective Violence* (Transaction Publishers, 1972); '1969: Montreal's night of terror', Canadian Broadcasting Corporation Television News Special.
4. Ibid.
5. S. Hurwitz and K. Christiansen, *Criminology* (George Allen and Unwin, 2nd edn, 1983), pp. 177–8.
6. Cited in R. Reiner, 'Fewer police does not mean Christmas for criminals', *Guardian*, 10 March 2011: http://www.theguardian.com/commentisfree/2011/mar/10/police-crime-disorder-cuts.
7. Ibid.
8. 'Things we forgot to remember: police strike', BBC Radio 4, 20 November 2011: http://www.bbc.co.uk/programmes/b017c8h0.
9. 'Brazilian police end strike in Bahia, but Rio walkout continues', *Guardian*, 12 February 2012: http://www.theguardian.com/world/2012/feb/12/brazilian-police-strike-bahia-rio.
10. See E. Pfuhl, 'Police Strikes and Conventional Crime', *Criminology*, vol. 21, issue 3, November 1983, pp. 489–504. This reports that municipal police strikes had a limited impact on reported rates of burglary, robbery, larceny and auto theft in the eleven US cities.
11. 'Now Boris Johnson says we need MORE police as cuts row intensifies', *Daily Mail*, 15 August 2011: http://www.dailymail.co.uk/news/article-2025883/London-riots-Boris-Johnson-says-need-MORE-police-cuts-row-intensifies.html#ixzz2pc1W71GJ.
12. H. Orde, speech at the CFA annual lecture 2012: http://www.acpo.police.uk/ContentPages/Speeches/201205SirHughOrdeCFAannuallecture.aspx.

13. Cited in 'Do we need more police back on our streets', *Daily Express*, 5 July 2008: http://www.express.co.uk/comment/haveyoursay/51215/ Do-we-need-more-police-back-on-our-streets.

14. T. Rupp, *Meta Analysis of Crime and Deterrence: A Comprehensive Review of the Literature*, 2008: http://tuprints.ulb.tu-darmstadt. de/1054/2/rupp_diss.pdf.

15. Ibid.

16. G. Kelling, T. Pate, D. Dieckman and C. Brown, *The Kansas City Preventative Patrol Experiment: A Summary Report*, Police Foundation, 1974: https://www.ncjrs.gov/pdffiles1/Digitization/42537NCJRS.pdf.

17. Cited in M. Easton., *Britain etc.* (Simon & Schuster, 2012).

18. Kelling et al., *The Kansas City Preventative Patrol Experiment*.

19. Ibid.

20. Ibid.

21. R. V. Clarke and M. Hough, *Crime and Police Effectiveness*, Home Office Research Study no. 79 (HMSO, 1984).

22. D. Boffey and M. McClenaghan, 'Police take longer to respond to 999 calls as spending cuts bite', *Observer*, 14 July 2013: http://www. theguardian.com/uk-news/2013/jul/14/police-longer-999-callout-times.

23. L. Sherman and J. Eck, 'Policing for Crime Prevention', in L. Sherman et al. (eds.), *Evidence-Based Crime Prevention* (Routledge, rev. edn, 2002).

24. '7 July bombings: what happened', BBC News online: http://news.bbc. co.uk/1/shared/spl/hi/uk/05/london_blasts/what_happened/html/ russell_sq.stm.

25. M. Draca, S. Machin and R. Witt, 'Panic on the Streets of London: Police, Crime, and the July 2005 Terror Attacks', *American Economic Review*, vol. 101, no. 5, August 2011, pp. 2157–81.

26. R. De Tella and E. Schargrodsky, 'Do Police Reduce Crime? Estimates Using the Allocation of Police Forces after a Terrorist Attack', *American Economic Review*, vol. 94, no. 1, March 2004, pp. 115–33.

27. L. Sherman, P. Gartin and M. Buerger, 'Hot Spots of Predatory Crime: Routine Activities and the Criminology of Place', *Criminology*, vol. 27, pp. 27–56.

28. L. Sherman, J. Shaw and D. Rogan, *The Kansas City Gun Experiment. Research in Brief*: https://www.ncjrs.gov/pdffiles/kang.pdf.

29. T. Gash, 'Modernising the Police Workforce', Institute for Public Policy Research, 2008.

30. 'Full text: Oliver Letwin's speech: Speech by the shadow home secretary, Oliver Letwin, to the Conservative party conference 2003', *Guardian*, 7 October 2003: http://www.theguardian.com/politics/2003/oct/07/ conservatives2003.conservatives4.

31. T. May, Home Secretary's speech to the Police Federation on 19 May 2010 in Bournemouth, Home Office, 2010: https://www.gov.uk/government/speeches/police-reform-theresa-mays-speech-to-the-police-federation.

32. T. May, Speech to the Police Federation Annual Conference 2013, Home Office, 2013: https://www.gov.uk/government/speeches/home-secretary-speech-to-police-federation-annual-conference-2013.

33. See, for example, A. Doyle, ' "Cops": Television Policing as Policing Reality', in M. Fishman and G. Cavendar (eds.), *Entertaining Crime: Television Reality Programs* (Walter de Gruyter, 1988).

34. 'The Badge of Life: A Study of Police Suicides, 2008–2012': http://www.policesuicidestudy.com/.

35. S. Roberts, 'Hazardous Occupations in Great Britain', *The Lancet*, vol. 360, issue 9332, August 2002, pp. 543–4.

36. See National Police Officers Roll of Honour Research Project at: http://www.policerollofhonour.org.uk/national_roll/2001/NPORH_2001.htm.

37. 'Suicide policeman kills wife and sons', *Telegraph*, 29 August 2001: http://www.telegraph.co.uk/news/1338846/Suicide-policeman-kills-wife-and-sons.html.

38. National Law Enforcement Memorial Fund, *Research Bulletin: Law Enforcement Officer Deaths: Preliminary 2013*: http://www.nleomf.org/assets/pdfs/reports/2013-End-of-Year-Preliminary-Report.pdf.
Note that this data is the most recent estimate and tallies well with more rigorous statistical investigations in Uniform Crime Reports (2010): http://www.fbi.gov/about-us/cjis/ucr/leoka/leoka-2010/summaryleoka2010.pdf.

39. R. C. Davis, C. J. Jensen, L. Burgette and K. Burnett, 'Working Smarter on Cold Cases: Identifying Factors Associated with Successful Cold Case Investigations', *Journal of Forensic Sciences*, vol. 59, 2014, pp. 375–82.

40. See an overview in M. Innes, *Signal Crimes: Social Reactions to Crime and Disorder*, Chapter 6 (Oxford University Press, 2014).

41. '1969: Montreal's night of terror', Canadian Broadcasting Corporation Television News Special.

42. P. Beaumont, J. Coleman and P. Lewis, 'London riots: "People are fighting back. It's their neighbourhoods at stake" ', *Guardian*, 10 August 2011: http://www.theguardian.com/uk/2011/aug/09/london-riots-fighting-neighbourhoods.

43. R. Peel, 'Bill for Improving the Police in and near the Metropolis, 1829', cited in C. Reith, *A New Study of Police History* (Oliver and Boyd, 1956).

MYTH 9: TOUGH SENTENCES ARE A SURE-FIRE WAY TO DETER CRIME

1. L. Rousselet, *India and Its Native Princes* (first pub. London, 1875; repr. New Delhi, 2005), p. 113.
2. M. Ashcroft, *Public Opinion and the Criminal Justice Debate*, 2011: http://www.lordashcroft.com/pdf/03042011_crime_punishment_and_the_people.pdf.
3. Ibid.
4. Princeton Survey Research Associates International, 'The NCSC Sentencing Attitudes Survey: A Report on the Findings', *Indiana Law Journal*, vol. 82, issue 5 (special issue), article 14: http://www.repository. law.indiana.edu/cgi/viewcontent.cgi?article=1534&context=ilj.
5. Ashcroft, *Public Opinion and the Criminal Justice Debate*.
6. 'Remarks on Signing the Anti-Drug Abuse Act of 1988', 18 November 1988: http://www.reagan.utexas.edu/archives/speeches/1988/111888c. htm.
7. Pew Center, *Time Served: The High Cost, Low Return of Longer Prison Terms*: http://www.pewstates.org/uploadedFiles/PCS_Assets/ 2012/Pew_Time_Served_report.pdf.
8. Bureau of Justice Statistics, *National Prisoner Statistics and Survey of Jails*: http://www.bjs.gov/index.cfm?ty=pbdetail&iid=4843.
9. P. Hitchens, 'What happened to punishment?', *Daily Mail*, 18 February 2001: http://www.dailymail.co.uk/columnists/article-124919/What-happened-punishment.html.
10. International Centre for Prison Studies, *World Prison Brief: England and Wales*: http://www.prisonstudies.org/country/united-kingdom-england-wales.
11. Pew Center, *Time Served*.
12. See, for example, 'Tapio Lappi-Seppälä speech to The Jesuit Center for Faith and Justice', Ireland, 2012: http://www.youtube.com/watch?v= W-aoRI8uatQ.
13. Author interview with Tapio Lappi-Seppälä, 1 April 2014.
14. Ibid.
15. 'Tapio Lappi-Seppälä speech to The Jesuit Center for Faith and Justice'.
16. W. Hodge, 'Finnish prisons: no gates or armed guards', *The New York Times*, 2 January 2003: http://www.nytimes.com/2003/01/02/ international/europe/02FINL.html.
17. 'Tapio Lappi-Seppälä speech to The Jesuit Center for Faith and Justice'.

18. Taken from Tapio Lappi-Seppälä, speech to the Jesuit Center for Faith and Justice, Ireland, 2012. For the Nordics, the crime data is 'crimes against criminal codes excluding traffic offences (for those Nordic countries that had traffic offences in their criminal codes)'. Prisoner numbers are the annual average number of prisoners held in penal. Data is compiled from H. von Hofer, T. Lappi-Seppälä and L. Westfelt, *Nordic Criminal Statistics 1950–2010: Summary of a Report*, 8th revised edition, Stockholms universitet, Kriminologiska institutionen, 2012.

19. Taken from Tapio Lappi-Seppälä, speech to the Jesuit Center for Faith and Justice', Ireland, 2012. For Scotland, crimes are 'crimes', not 'offences' (which are treated summarily). Data is from Scottish official statistics and draws on the work of Alec Spencer in A. Spencer, *Rethinking Imprisonment in Scotland: The Dilemma for Prison Reform and the Challenges Beyond*, 2007: http://www.gov.scot/resource/doc/1102/0056826.pdf.

20. Author interview with Tapio Lappi-Seppälä, 1 April 2014.

21. C. Webster and A. Doob, 'Punitive Trends and Stable Imprisonment Rates in Canada', in M. Tonry (ed.), *Crime, Punishment and Politics* (University of Chicago Press, 2007).

22. D. Johnson, 'Crime and Punishment in Contemporary Japan', in Tonry (ed.), *Crime, Punishment and Politics*.

23. *Scared Straight*, 1978. Documentary film directed by Arnold Shapiro. Extract at: http://www.youtube.com/watch?v=AKzcvmM47TY.

24. Ibid.

25. A. Petrosino, C. Turpin-Petrosino and J. Buehler, ' "Scared Straight" and Other Juvenile Awareness Programs for Preventing Juvenile Delinquency', *Cochrane Database of Systematic Reviews* 2002, issue 2, art. no. CD002796. doi: 10.1002/14651858.CD002796. Updated in 2004 and available at: file:///C:/Users/gasht/Downloads/Scared%20Straight_R.pdf.

26. A. Coleman, 'Three strikes may be out', *Pasadena Weekly*: http://da.lacounty.gov/pdf/3strikesPasadenaWeekly.pdf.

27. A. Schwarzenegger, 2003 gubernatorial campaign website, JoinArnold.com, 29 August 2003.

28. E. Bazelon, 'Arguing three strikes', *The New York Times*, 21 May 2010: http://www.nytimes.com/2010/05/23/magazine/23strikes-t.html?pagewanted=all.

29. E. Helland and A. Tabarrok, 'Does Three Strikes Deter? A Non-Parametric Estimation': http://www.threestrikes.org/ThreeStrikesA-Taba.pdf.

30. Ibid.

31. 'I'd Rather be Hanged for a Sheep than a Lamb: The Unintended Consequences of California's Three Strikes Law', American Law and Economics Association Annual Meeting, New York University (May 2005), Harvard University (October 2007), APPAM Annual Meeting (November 2007), Harvard Law School (2008), Yale Law School (May 2008).

32. Study by Buikhuisen, 1974, cited by D. Beyleveld, 'Deterrence Research as a Basis for Deterrence Policies', *Howard Journal of Criminal Justice*, vol. 18, issue 3, 1979.

33. Digest 4, 'Attrition through the Criminal Justice System', Home Office, 1999.

34. Description of footage of the prison taken from G. Mitchell, producer, 'Gangland', episode 1 of the television series *Lockdown* (also known as *America's Hardest Prisons*), National Geographic Channel, 2007, and from J. West, producer, *No Way Out*, a documentary for *Mother Jones*, 18 October 2012: http://www.motherjones.com/politics/2012/10/video-shane-bauer-solitary.

35. California Department of Corrections and Rehabilitation, Pelican Bay State Prison: http://www.cdcr.ca.gov/Facilities_Locator/PBSP.html.

36. Hitchens, 'What happened to punishment?'.

37. Human Rights Watch, 'US: Teens in Solitary Confinement', 28 November 2012: https://www.youtube.com/watch?v=i7hynBLs1fU.

38. Mitchell, producer, 'Gangland'.

39. Ibid.

40. Ibid.

41. See testimony of Vicente Garcia in A. Leithead, 'Are California's prison isolation units torture?', *BBC News Los Angeles*, 11 December 2013: http://www.bbc.co.uk/news/world-us-canada-25243002.

42. See, for example, E. Poole and R. Regoli, 'Violence in Juvenile Institutions: A Comparative Study', *Criminology*, vol. 21, issue 2, May 1983; D. Mears et al., 'The Code of the Street and Inmate Violence: Investigating the salience of imported belief systems', *Criminology*, vol. 51, issue 3, June 2013.

43. C. Briggs, J. Sundt and T. Castellano, 'The Effect of Supermaximum Security Prisons on Aggregate Levels of Institutional Violence', *Criminology*, vol. 41, issue 4, March 2006.

44. Ibid.

45. D. Mears and W. Bales, 'Supermax Incarceration and Recidivism', *Criminology*, vol. 47, issue 4, December 2009.

46. D. Nagin and G. Snodgrass, 'The Effect of Incarceration on Re-offending: Evidence from a Natural Experiment in Pennsylvania', *Journal of Quantitative Criminology*, vol. 29, issue 4, February 2013.

47. A good summary of the evidence on 'specific deterrence' is included in P. Nieuwbeerta, D. Nagin and A. Blokland, 'Assessing the Impact of First-Time Imprisonment on Offenders' Subsequent Criminal Career', *Journal of Quantitative Criminology*, vol. 25, issue 3, September 2009, pp. 227–57.

48. N. Pisa, 'Italian prisoners freed in amnesty go on the rampage', *Telegraph*, 6 August 2006: http://www.telegraph.co.uk/news/1525746/Italian-prisoners-freed-in-amnesty-go-on-the-rampage.html.

49. J. Hooper, 'Italy crime spree blamed on amnesty', *Guardian*, 3 November 2006: http://www.theguardian.com/world/2006/nov/03/italy.topstories3.

50. Pisa, 'Italian prisoners freed in amnesty go on the rampage'.

51. Hooper, 'Italy crime spree blamed on amnesty'.

52. All figures from – or calculated based on – Italian National Institute of Statistics (Istat), *Italy in Figures*, various years: http://www.istat.it/en/archive/30344.

53. See, for example, P. Buonanno and S. Raphael, 'Incarceration and Incapacitation: Evidence from the 2006 Italian Collective Pardon', *American Economic Review*, vol. 103, no. 6, October 2013, pp. 2437–65.

54. Stanford Law School Three Strikes Project, *Progress Report: Three Strikes Reform (Proposition 36)*, Stanford Law School Three Strikes Project and NAACP Legal Defense and Education Fund, 2013: http://www.law.stanford.edu/sites/default/files/child-page/441702/doc/slspublic/Three%20Strikes%20Reform%20Report.pdf.

55. Ibid.

56. W. Spelman, 'The Limited Importance of Prison Expansion', in A. Blumstein and J. Wallman (eds.), *The Crime Drop in America* (Cambridge University Press, 2006).

MYTH 10: LEOPARDS CAN'T CHANGE THEIR SPOTS

1. I. Compton-Burnett, *More Women Than Men* (Eyre & Spottiswoode (1933), 1951), p. 54.

2. O. Wilde, *The Soul of Man under Socialism*, in *The Complete Works of Oscar Wilde*, Kindle edition, 2010.

3. This description and the quotations are from an event at the London-based think tank Reform, 31 May 2013. Quotations are based

on hastily written notes but every effort was taken to ensure they were as accurate as possible.

4. My generalization is based on reconviction data for former inmates from the UK, where two-year reconviction rates are well over 50 per cent; the US, where two-year re-arrest rates have been over 60 per cent for some decades; and Australia, where over a third of prisoners will be back in prison within two years of release and many others subjected to other corrections sanctions. Confirmation of this data can be found in P. Langan and D. Levin, *Recidivism of Prisoners Released in 1994* (US Department of Justice, 2002), and J. Payne, *Recidivism in Australia: Findings and Future Research* (Australian Institute of Criminology, 2007). It is important to recognize that there are not yet reliable ways of comparing reoffending rates across different countries as they use a wide variety of measures for assessing reoffending and reconviction rates. See S. Fazel and A. Wolf, *A Systematic Review of Criminal Recidivism Rates Worldwide: Current Difficulties and Recommendations for Best Practice* (PLoS One, 2015).

5. In the UK, around 75 per cent of those sentenced to youth custody reoffend within a year: *Breaking the Cycle: Effective Punishment, Rehabilitation and Sentencing of Offenders* (Ministry of Justice, 2010).

6. C. Grayling, 'Speech by Lord Chancellor and Secretary of State for Justice Chris Grayling MP on the current state of crime and ways to improve rehabilitation', 20 November 2012: https://www.gov.uk/government/speeches/rehabilitation-revolution-the-next-steps.

7. R. Godwin, 'Meet me at the prison gates: how mentoring can give hope and help – and save the taxpayer billions', *Evening Standard*, 26 February 2013: http://www.standard.co.uk/lifestyle/london-life/meet-me-at-the-prison-gates-how-mentoring-can-give-hope-and-help-and-save-the-tax payer-billions-8511279.html.

8. Ibid.

9. Originally, the goal of payment by results was to attract private-sector investors – but few wanted to stump up the cash so the Big Lottery funded the bulk of the upfront investment: E. Disley and J. Rubin, *Phase 2 Report from the Payment by Results Social Impact Bond Pilot at HMP Peterborough* (Ministry of Justice, 2014), at https://www.gov.uk/government/uploads/system/uploads/attachment_data/file/325738/peterborough-phase-2-pilot-report.pdf.

10. 'Payment-by-results pilots on track for success' (Ministry of Justice, 7 August 2014): https://www.gov.uk/government/news/payment-by-results-pilots-on-track-for-success.

11. Ibid.

12. Ibid.

13. D. Barrett, 'Controversial scheme to cut reoffending misses key target: Government praises "promising" results but project fails to hit target to cut reoffending by 10 per cent', *Telegraph*, 7 August 2014: http://www.telegraph.co.uk/news/uknews/crime/11019027/Controversial-scheme-to-cut-reoffending-misses-key-target.html.

14. *Uncorrected Transcript of Oral Evidence: Policing Large-Scale Disorder*, 2011: http://www.publications.parliament.uk/pa/cm201012/cmselect/cmhaff/uc1456-i/uc145601.htm.

15. Full Fact, 'Boris Johnson corrected over youth reoffending figures', in *Full Fact*, 21 October 2011: https://fullfact.org/blog/boris_johnson_crime_youth_reoffending_justice-3055.

16. Probono Economics, *St. Giles through the Gate Analysis*, 2010: https://www.frontier-economics.com/documents/2009/12/st-giles-trust-through-the-gates-frontier-report.pdf.

17. N. Olah, 'Dylan Dufus vs Shabba', *Dazed and Confused Magazine*. The interview took place in 2013 but the precise date is not recorded.

18. C. Carlsson, 'Using Turning Points to Understand Desistance from Crime', *British Journal of Criminology*, vol. 52 (2012).

19. Ibid.

20. Ibid.

21. Ibid.

22. Ibid.

23. S. Maruna, 'Desistance and Development: The Psychosocial Process of "Going Straight"', in M. Brogan (ed.), *The British Criminology Conferences: Selected Proceedings*, vol. 2 (British Society of Criminology, 1999).

24. Author's notes from Reform event, 31 May 2013. Quotations are based on hastily written notes but every effort was taken to ensure they were as accurate as possible.

25. This effect is particularly clear from research on drug-addicted offenders: J. McIntosh, M. Bloor and M. Robertson, 'Drug Treatment and the Achievement of Paid Employment', *Addiction Research and Theory*, vol. 16, no. 1, 2007, pp. 27–45.

26. P. Stromberg, 'Ideological Language in the Transformation of Identity', *American Anthropologist*, 92, 1990, pp. 42–56.

27. S. Maruna, L. Wilson and K. Curran, 'Why God is Often Found behind Bars: Prison Conversions and the Crisis of Self-Narrative', in *Research in Human Development*, vol. 3 (Lawrence Erlbaum Associates Inc., 2006) , pp. 161–84.

28. Author's notes from Reform event, 31 May 2013. Quotations are based on hastily written notes but every effort was taken to ensure they were accurate as possible.

29. Carlsson, 'Using Turning Points to Understand Desistance from Crime'.

30. B. Bersani, J. Laub and P. Nieuwbeerta, 'Marriage and Desistance from Crime in the Netherlands: Do Gender and Socio-Historical Context Matter?', *Journal of Quantitative Criminology*, vol. 25, no. 3, 2009, pp. 3–24. See also R. Sampson, J. Laub and C. Wimer, 'Does Marriage Reduce Crime? A Counterfactual Approach to Within-Individual Causal Effects', *Criminology*, vol. 44, no. 3, 2006, pp. 465–508.

31. Author's recollection of visit to Willowdene Care Farm, Shropshire.

32. N. Pitney, 'Nothing stops a bullet like a job', *Huffington Post*, 24 September 2015: http://www.huffingtonpost.com/entry/greg-boyle-homeboy-industries-life-lessons_56030036e4b00310edf9c7a4.

33. P. Giordano et al., 'Gender, Crime, and Desistance: Toward a Theory of Cognitive Transformation', in J. Humphrey and P. Cordella (eds.), *Effective Interventions in the Lives of Criminal Offenders* (Springer, 2014).

34. M. Del Barco, 'Priest's Answer to Gang Life Faces Hard Times', 21 May 2010, *NPR*: http://www.npr.org/templates/story/story.php?storyId=127019188.

35. S. Farrall and A. Calverley, *Understanding Desistance from Crime*, Crime and Justice Series (Open University Press, 2006).

36. Giordano et al., 'Gender, Crime, and Desistance'.

37. Ibid.

38. Ibid.

39. Email correspondence with Professor Jorja Heap, UCLA, who is the lead investigator and author of a forthcoming book on the Homeboy Industries model.

40. Author's notes from Reform event, 31 May 2013. Quotations are based on hastily written notes but every effort was taken to ensure they were as accurate as possible.

41. http://www.wsipp.wa.gov/About

42. Washington State Institute of Public Policy, *Inventory of Evidence-Based and Research-Based Programs for Adult Corrections* (Washington State Institute of Public Policy, December 2013: http://www.wsipp.wa.gov/ReportFile/1542/Wsipp_Inventory-of-Evidence-Based-and-Research-Based-Programs-for-Adult-Corrections_Final-Report.pdf.

43. Ibid.

44. Ibid.

45. For example, those released from prison in the UK now receive priority access to the government's Work Programme Scheme, which aims to support the long-term unemployed.

46. J. Rutter, *What Works in Government – Lessons from the Other Washington*, 30 April 2012, Institute for Government: http://www.instituteforgovernment.org.uk/blog/4394/what-works-in-government-%E2%80%93-lessons-from-the-other-washington/.

47. Author's notes from Reform event, 31 May 2013. Quotations are based on hastily written notes but every effort was taken to ensure they were as accurate as possible.

MYTH 11: WE NEED RADICAL REFORMS TO REDUCE CRIME

1. Arthur Conan Doyle, 'A Scandal in Bohemia', in *The Adventures of Sherlock Holmes* (George Newnes, 1892).

2. Description based on C. Summers, 'Victims of "transferred malice"', BBC News online: http://news.bbc.co.uk/1/hi/england/west_midlands/4010485.stm#summers; and G. McLagen, *Guns and Gangs: The Inside Story of the War on Our Streets* (Allison & Busby, 2006).

3. D. Blunkett, cited in 'Blunkett targets gangster gun culture', BBC News online, 6 January 2003: http://news.bbc.co.uk/1/hi/uk_politics/2632343.stm.

4. T. May, cited in 'Press Release: Radical reforms for police announced', 26 July 2010: https://www.gov.uk/government/news/radical-reforms-for-police-announced.

5. Ibid.

6. An interesting analysis of *Daily Mail* readers' views of young offenders and how to deal with them can be found in G. Arnett, 'What do *Daily Mail* commenters think about young criminals?', *Guardian* datablog, 27 May 2013: http://www.theguardian.com/news/datablog/2013/may/27/daily-mail-comments-criminals-interactive.

7. M. Townsend and C. Davies, 'Mystery of the stolen Moore solved: bronze sculpture worth £3m was melted down and sold off as scrap for just £1,500, say police', *Guardian*, 17 May 2009: http://www.theguardian.com/artanddesign/2009/may/17/henry-moore-sculpture-theft-reclining-figure.

8. *Metal Theft, England and Wales, Financial Year Ending March 2013*, Home Office, 28 November 2013: https://www.gov.uk/government/statistics/metal-theft-england-and-wales-financial-year-ending-march-2013.

9. Data on US vehicle ownership can be found in the US Department of Energy *Transportation Energy Data Book*, Chapter 8, Table 8.5: http://www-cta.ornl.gov/data/chapter8.shtml.

10. According to arrest data from the FBI and population data from the US Bureau of the Census, cited in 'The Growth in Juvenile Motor Vehicle Theft Arrest Rates That Began in 1984 was Erased by 1999', *Juvenile Offenders and Victims, National Report Series,* December 2001: https://www.ncjrs.gov/html/ojjdp/nrs_bulletin/nrs_2001_12_1/page14.html.

11. Australian vehicle theft patterns for the 1980s are summarized effectively in *Exploring Motor Vehicle Theft in Australia: Trends and Issues in Criminal Justice*, no. 67, February 1997. British patterns can be found in *Crime in England and Wales* (Home Office, various years).

12. *Crime in England and Wales.*

13. Cited in M. Gladwell, 'Drinking Games: How Much People Drink May Matter Less Than How They Drink It', *The New Yorker*, 15 February 2010: http://www.newyorker.com/magazine/2010/02/15/drinking-games.

14. Ibid.

15. For one of the most thorough (and practical) studies of the reasons and remedies for alcohol-related violence see K. Graham and R. Homel, *Raising the Bar: Preventing Aggression in and around Bars, Pubs and Clubs* (Willan, 2012).

16. There are various studies providing general theories on the role and causes of violence in society which we have not fully examined. Common themes in broad explanations of violence include the importance of social roles (see, for example, L. Athens, 'Violent Encounters: Violent Engagements, Skirmishes, and Tiffs', *Journal of Contemporary Ethnography*, vol. 34, 2005) and the importance of the immediate environment (see, for example, T. Tedeschi, R. Felson and M. Wessells, *Violence, Aggression, and Coercive Actions* (American Psychological Association, 1994).

17. *Bouncers*, series 2, episode 1, shown on Channel 4, retrieved at: https://www.youtube.com/watch?v=rVbvyPrb7Hc.

18. Office for National Statistics, *Smoking and drinking among adults*, 2009, p. 61.

19. N. Prior, 'Award for drink-violence project', BBC News online, 18 November 2009: http://news.bbc.co.uk/1/hi/wales/8367316.stm.

20. J. Shepherd, *Effective NHS Contributions to Violence Prevention: The Cardiff Model* (Cardiff University, 2007), p. 10.

21. Ibid.

22. Ibid.

23. Author interview, London, 17 May 2014.

24. For a list of licensing restrictions, see *Scrap Metal Dealer Licence (England and Wales)*: https://www.gov.uk/scrap-metal-dealer-registration, last updated 27 June 2014.

25. SelectaDNA, 'Thames Valley Police Take the Shine off Metal Theft', January 2009: https://www.selectadna.co.uk/news/thames-valley-police-metal-theft.

26. E. Leedham, 'Scrap Metal Dealers Bill comes into effect', *Resource*, 1 October 2013: http://resource.co/materials/article/scrap-metal-dealers-bill-comes-effect.

27. Eau Claire Police Department, Detective Division, 'The Eau Claire, Wisconsin Metal Theft Initiative', 2008: http://www.popcenter.org/library/awards/goldstein/2009/09-01.pdf.

28. Author interview, London, 17 May 2014.

29. National Insurance Crime Bureau, 'Hot Wheels: America's 10 Most Stolen Vehicles', 18 August 2014. Further details can be retrieved at https://www.nicb.org/newsroom/nicb_campaigns/hot%E2%80%93 wheels/hot-wheels-2013#States.

30. Ibid.

31. Ibid.

32. See Honest John, 'Car Crime Census 2013: Top 10 Most Stolen Cars'. Honest John is a *Telegraph* newspaper columnist who now provides advice and other services, including insurance. The methodology the *Telegraph* uses to identify most stolen vehicles is one of the most robust available – based on individual requests to all police forces in England and Wales. See: http://www.honestjohn.co.uk/crime/top-10s/top-10-most-stolen-cars/?image=6 for details of most stolen cars and http://www.honestjohn.co.uk/crime/insight-and-analysis/car-crime-census-methodology/ for methodology.

33. Ibid.

34. The data on methods of theft is inevitably somewhat patchy but insurance companies such as Confused.com report this trend. See, for example, L. Avery, 'Avoid stolen car keys by securing your home', retrieved 25 August 2014: http://www.confused.com/car-insurance/archive/avoid-stolen-car-keys-by-securing-your-home.

35. A. Klein and J. White, 'Car theft tamed by technology, aggressive police work', *The Washington Post*, 23 July 2011: http://www.washingtonpost.com/

local/car-theft-tamed-by-technology-aggressive-police-work/2011/07/22/gIQAnCbrVI_story.html.

36. G. Laycock, 'The UK Car Theft Index: An Example of Government Leverage', *Crime Prevention Studies*, vol. 17, 2004, pp. 25–44. See http://www.docstoc.com/docs/120818681/Gloria-Laycock-THE-UK-CAR-THEFT-INDEX-AN-EXAMPLE-OF-GOVERNMENT.

37. Ibid.

38. D. Southall, P. Ekblom and G. Laycock, *Designing for Vehicle Security: Towards a Crime-free Car*, Home Office Crime Prevention Unit, 1985.

39. Laycock, 'The UK Car Theft Index'.

40. See an example of the Car Theft Index at Home Office Communication Directorate, *Car Theft Index 2004*, Home Office, December 2004: https://www.gov.uk/government/uploads/system/uploads/attachment_data/file/119342/Car_Theft_I_041.pdf.

41. Laycock, 'The UK Car Theft Index'.

42. Author interview, London, 17 May 2014.

43. N. Prior, 'Award for drink-violence project', BBC News online, 18 November 2009: http://news.bbc.co.uk/1/hi/wales/8367316.stm.

44. D. Gallagher, M. R. Brickley, R. V. Walker and J. P. Shepherd, 'Risk of Occupational Glass Injury in Bar Staff', *Injury*, vol. 25, issue 4, May 1994, pp. 219–20.

45. A good brief summary of findings can be found in J. Shepherd, 'Editorial: The Circumstances and Prevention of Bar-Glass Injury', *Addiction*, vol. 93, issue 1, 1998, pp. 5–7: http://www.ihra.net/files/2011/07/21/09.2_Shepherd_-_Circumstances_and_Prevention_of_Bar-Glass_Injury_.pdf.

46. J. Shepherd, R. Huggett and G. Kidner, 'Impact Resistance of Bar Glasses', *Journal of Trauma and Acute Care Surgery*, vol. 35, issue 6, December 1993, pp. 936–8.

47. Ibid.

48. Prior, 'Award for drink-violence project'.

49. Gallagher et al., 'Risk of Occupational Glass Injury in Bar Staff'.

50. Shepherd, *Effective NHS Contributions to Violence Prevention*.

51. Prior, 'Award for drink-violence project'.

52. Ibid.

53. B. Welsh and D. Farrington, *Effects of Closed Circuit Television Surveillance on Crime*, The Campbell Collaboration, December 2008. The balance of evidence says that CCTV is currently often poorly targeted and its cost-effectiveness could be increased if better use was made of evaluations to assess effectiveness of different placement strategies.

54. R. Homel, M. Hauritz, R. Wortley, G. McIlwain and R. Carvolth, *Preventing Alcohol-Related Crime through Community Action: The Surfers Paradise Safety Project*, 1997: http://www.popcenter.org/library/crimeprevention/volume_07/02_homel.pdf.

55. Ibid.

56. See, for example, Tedeschi, Felson and Wessells, *Violence, Aggression, and Coercive Actions*.

57. This scene was recorded in *Bouncers*, series 2, episode 1, shown on Channel 4, retrieved at: https://www.youtube.com/watch?v=rVbvyPrb7Hc.

58. Ibid.

59. Ibid.

60. Ibid.

61. See P. Routledge, 'Bouncer beats up MP', *Independent*, 17 November 1996; 'Jail for bouncer who headbutted MP', *Independent*, 15 March 1997; and P. Hetherington, 'Gangsters at the door', *Guardian*, 31 December 1998: http://www.theguardian.com/theguardian/1998/dec/31/features11.g24.

62. For details of the operation of the Security Industry Association see http://www.sia.homeoffice.gov.uk/Pages/about-us.aspx. It should be noted that the Security Industry Association is currently in the process of being dissolved or replaced with a body that is entirely independent of government.

63. Author interview, London, 17 May 2014.

64. J. Garland and M. Rowe, 'The "English Disease" – Cured or in Remission? An Analysis of Police Responses to Football Hooliganism in the 1990s', *Crime Prevention and Community Safety: An International Journal*, vol. 1, issue 4, 1999, pp. 35–47.

65. J. Benko, 'The radical humaneness of Norway's Halden Prison', *New York Times Magazine*, 26 March 2015: http://www.nytimes.com/2015/03/29/magazine/the-radical-humaneness-of-norways-halden-prison.html?_r=0.

CONCLUSION

1. Author interview, London, 17 May 2014.

2. Ibid.

3. B. Welsh and D. Farrington, *Effects of Closed Circuit Television Surveillance on Crime*, The Campbell Collaboration, December 2008.

4. Author interview, London, 17 May 2014.

 5. Author interview, London, November 2014.
 6. Author interview, London, 17 May 2014.
 7. Author interview, London, November 2014.
 8. Ibid.
 9. Author interview, London, 17 May 2014.
10. Ibid.

Index

Page references in *italic* indicate Figures.